CHINESE
LANGUAGE

Life

&

CULTURE

Kenneth Wilkinson

TEACH YOURSELF BOOKS

For UK order queries: please contact Bookpoint Ltd, 130 Milton Park, Abingdon, Oxon OX14 4SB. Telephone: (44) 01235 827720. Fax: (44) 01235 400454. Lines are open from 9.00–18.00, Monday to Saturday, with a 24-hour message answering service. Email address: orders@bookpoint.co.uk

For U.S.A. order queries: please contact McGraw-Hill Customer Services, P.O. Box 545, Blacklick, OH 43004–0545, U.S.A. Telephone: 1-800-722-4726. Fax: 1-614-755-5645.

For Canada order queries: please contact McGraw-Hill Ryerson Ltd., 300 Water St, Whitby, Ontario L1N 9B6, Canada. Telephone: 905 430 5000. Fax: 905 430 5020.

Long-renowned as the authoritative source for self-guided learning – with more than 30 million copies sold worldwide – the *Teach Yourself* series includes over 200 titles in the fields of languages, crafts, hobbies, sports, and other leisure activities.

British Library Cataloguing in Publication Data
A catalogue entry for this title is available from the British Library.

Library of Congress Catalog Card Number: on file

First published in UK in 2002 by Hodder Headline Plc, 338 Euston Road, London NW1 3BH.

First published in US 2002 by Contemporary Books, A Division of The McGraw-Hill Companies, 4255 West Touhy Avenue, Lincolnwood (Chicago), Illinois 60712–1975 U.S.A.

The 'Teach Yourself' name and logo are registered trade marks of Hodder & Stoughton Ltd.

Copyright © 2002 Kenneth Wilkinson

Typeset by Graphicraft Ltd, Hong Kong.
Printed in Great Britain by Cox & Wyman Ltd, Reading, Berkshire.

Impression number	10	9	8	7	6	5	4	3	2	1
Year	2007	2006	2005	2004	2003	2002				

ACKNOWLEDGEMENTS

This book could not have come into being without the kindness of the following people, all of whom deserve more than the thanks here. Suzanne Mordue (drawings), Gong Zengjia (drawings and expertise), Sun Lingsi (translation), Takako Ogi (computer) and Elaine Chan (stuff).

For the bulk of the artwork and for generally putting up with me: Yumi and Claude Masuda. Finally, this book is dedicated to the wonderfully beautiful city of Fukuoka where it was written, a place matched only by the warmth of its people's hearts. I will never forget any of you.

K.A.W.

CONTENTS

INTRODUCTION

This book is designed to give you as full a basic overview as possible in its 250 or so pages of the main aspects of China: the country, its languages, its people, their way of life and culture and what makes them tick.

You will find it a useful foundation if you are studying for examinations which require a knowledge of the background of China and its civilisation, or if you are learning the language, in, for example, an evening class, and want to know more about the country and how it works. If your job involves travel and business relations, it will provide valuable and practical information about the ways and customs of the people you are working with. Or maybe you simply have an interest in China for whatever reason, and wish to broaden your knowledge about the country and its inhabitants.

The book is divided into three sections:

■ **The making of China**
Chapters 1 to 2 deal with the forces – historical, geographical, geological, demographical, and linguistic – that have brought about the formation of the country we know as China, and the language and people we know as Chinese.

■ **Creative China**
Chapters 3 to 8 deal with the wealth of creative aspects of Chinese culture from the beginnings to the present day. These chapters take a look at the main areas of philosophy and religion, festivals and folklore, literature, entertainment, art and architecture, music, food, crafts and other facets of Chinese ingenuity, together with the people who have created and are still creating them.

■ **Living in China now**
Chapters 8 to 13 deal with aspects of contemporary Chinese society and the practicalities of living in present-day China:

education, health and Chinese medicine, the recent political history and present political structure of the country, work and leisure, Chinese attitude to the family and sex as well as certain characteristics perhaps peculiar to the Chinese. The final chapter takes a look at the country's future.

Taking it further

Each chapter ends with a section entitled 'Taking it further', where you will find useful addresses, websites, and things to see and do in order to develop your interest further and increase your knowledge.

The language

Within each chapter you will encounter a number of terms in Chinese, given in the corresponding Chinese characters, romanised 'pinyin' and with the meaning in English when they are first introduced. If you wish to put your language knowledge into practice, we have provided at the end of each chapter a glossary of useful words and phrases to enable you to talk or write about the subject in question.

We have been careful in researching and checking facts, but please be aware that sources sometimes offer differing information. Of course a book of this length cannot contain everything you may need to know on every aspect of China. That is why we have provided so many pointers to where you can find further information about any aspect that you may wish to pursue in further depth. We trust that you will enjoy this introductory book, and that it will provide leads to further profitable reading, listening and visiting.

Phil Turk
Series Editor

PRONOUNCING CHINESE WORDS

As we will see in Chapter 2, when pronouncing Chinese words, the sounds of letters correspond roughly to those used in English, the exceptions being the following:

Consonants	
Pinyin	**Pronounced as in –**
c	<u>ts</u>ar or ca<u>ts</u>
q	<u>ch</u>in
r	between French '<u>je</u>' and English '<u>r</u>'
x	between <u>s</u>ea and <u>sh</u>e
zh	<u>j</u>ump

Vowels	
ai	h<u>igh</u>
ao	c<u>ow</u>
e	h<u>er</u>
ei	h<u>ay</u>
i	like 'e' in 'th<u>e</u>' when after c, ch, r, s, sh, z and zh; otherwise as 'ee' in 'fl<u>ee</u>'
ian	y<u>en</u>
o	m<u>or</u>e
ou	d<u>ough</u>
u	y<u>ou</u> (when after j, q and x, as ü)
ua	q<u>ua</u>ck
uai	<u>wh</u>y
uo	<u>wa</u>r
ü	t<u>u</u> (the French word, said through rounded lips)

ACRONYMS

*Not all of these appear in the text, but China-related articles and documents often include a very large number of acronyms. The most common are given here.

CP – Communist Party

CCP – Chinese Communist Party

CPCC – Communist Party Central Committee

CPPCC – Chinese People's Political Consultative Conference

NPC – National People's Congress

SC – State Council

SEZ – Special Economic Zone

CAAC – Civil Aviation Administration of China

CITS – China International Travel Service

CITIC – China International Trust and Investment Company

MOFERT – Ministry of Foreign Economic Relations and Trade

JV – Joint [economic] Venture

RMB – *Renminbi* (literally: 'the people's currency')

PLA – People's Liberation Army

PSB – Public Security Bureau

PRC – People's Republic of China

ROC – Republic of China (Taiwan)

1 | THE MAKING OF CHINA

That China is a great country is seldom disputed. China began the last century as 'the sick man of Asia', bullied and exploited by colonial powers as they raced to carve out their slices of the world. China begins this century under very different conditions. Wielding massive economic power, she has reasserted herself as the anchor of east Asian stability. China is on the way to becoming a superpower, not just a one-dimensional, economic powerhouse like her neighbours, Japan and Korea, but as a military and political influence taking rank alongside the world's elite nations.

When people think of China, what comes to mind? Chinese food, a mysterious and complicated language, crowded cities and seas of bicycles? For some people the events in Tiananmen Square in 1989 are hard to forget. The hand-over of Hong Kong, human rights issues and the plight of Tibet have all turned the eyes of the world to China in recent years.

The western world often forms knee-jerk opinions on China as the result of news stories that fail to give consideration to the historical and cultural forces at work in the country. What follows is an attempt to present some facts through which it may be possible to see China in a new light.

China's culture is the complex result of the geography in which it took root and a long history of tradition and turmoil that has brought it to the present day.

The land and climate

China's cultural achievements are due, partly, to the size of the land it occupies. In Asia, it is surpassed only by Russia and easily dwarfs all other countries that it borders. Not surprisingly, its landscape and climate are highly varied.

The North

The **Běijīng** 北京 area of northern China is said to have only two long seasons: winter and summer. Winters are cold with temperatures getting down to as low as −10°C, while in summer it can be a bone-dry 40°C. Throughout the year there is very little rainfall, as a result the land is not as productive as the southern or central areas.

North (and west) of Beijing, the terrain becomes hilly and m The flatter parts of the northeast are covered wi wheat, corn and soybeans. The remote **Hēilóngjiāng** (bordering Russia) has an enormous amount of reclaim It is in this area that China's last major forests can

The desert areas of **Nèiménggǔ** 内蒙古 (Inne **Xīnjiāng** 新疆 are subject to cold weather Heilongjiang temperatures get as low as −40°C

The northwest stays dry all year. The Turp easily earns the title of China's hottest place of around 50°C. Northwestern wintertime r sometimes touching −30°C.

The South

A great deal of southern China lies w is high and the growing season is lo by hilly land, but the Delta Plain a is probably the most productive fa are brief and temperatures rarel temperatures can reach a swelte China suffers regular typhoon of the rainy season (July to S

Central areas

From a farmer's point of v are to be found in the central ar covers **Shànghǎi** 上海 and other majo Yangtze River basin that has earned the bowl of China'. The three cities of **Nánjīng** 南 **Chóngqìng** 重庆 have been dubbed the 'Three Fu of their long, boiling hot summers (the 'yellow plum' season

Features of the land

CHINESE LANGUAGE, LIFE & CULTURE

China's enormous populati demand for intense cultiva

surprisingly, vast areas of forest. consumed

4

Rivers

China has three mighty rivers, draining 50% of its land a most of its 1.3 billion citizens. The greatest and most f is the **Chángjiāng** 长江, known to foreigners as the Y simply means 'Long River', and is justifiably applie third longest. Its origin is in the far west. After crossing th Qinghai province in the far west. After crossing th Plain, it swerves into the East China Sea. Its 3,400 mile it spills into the East China Sea.

The **Huánghé** 黄河 (Yellow River) is hist Sorrow'. For much of its length, the riv the surrounding land. The result: fre massive loss of life. Its headwaters a colour is the product of sediment pic the loess plains of the north. Th terminate in Shandong where i

The **Zhūjiāng** 珠江 (Pearl R China. Its main tributary i mountains of Yunnan (so and East Rivers, the Zh Guangzhou (Canton) of southern China.

The people and their history

The Chinese take pride in the belief that their civilisation is traceable back to times of great antiquity. Chinese people rightly maintain that they have shared a longer culture and sense of unity than any other people or nation.

In 1963, a skull was discovered which is believed to be 600,000 years old. This made Peking Man (discovered near Beijing 40 years earlier) a mere youngster, dating back only 400,000 years!

The earliest Chinese settlements closely resembled those in other cradles of civilisation. These villages were found around the great bend area of the Yellow River in northern China, known to Chinese as the **Zhōngyuán** 中原 – *the original interior*. Findings show that these ancient people had been successful farmers, domesticating animals, using tools and building reed-roofed huts and pit houses. Such evidence can be reliably dated back to between 4000 and 3000 BC. At this time there was little that appears to be unique but by 3000 BC, pottery, silk, organised farms and wheels were in existence. Archaeology suggests Chinese civilisation began to take shape around 2000 BC but tradition dates it back to time immemorial. The span of Chinese history begins, fittingly, in legend.

The Yellow Emperor

Huángdì 皇帝 (the Yellow Emperor) was the legendary ruler of the Yellow River valley. He and **Yándì** 炎帝 (the Fiery Emperor) are said to have fathered civilisation by the invention of such things as the boat, cart, medicine, writing, paper and agricultural tools. To this day, Chinese sometimes refer to themselves as descendants of Yan and Huang.

Dynasties

Chinese history is divided into periods known as 'dynasties'. The system is similar to the European convention of naming periods after royal familes of the time (the Tudor Period, for example). A dynasty indicates the time in which the descendants of the founder ruled the country. A dynasty ended when power was taken from the royal family. Typically, this came through foreign invasions (such as the Mongols) and internal rebellions. The victorious leader would then become emperor – Son of Heaven (**Tiānzǐ** 天子). Defeat was evidence of the former emperor's loss of the divine right to rule (Heaven's mandate) and the righteousness of the victor's claim to power. In time the new dynasty would, if they abused their power, inevitably lose the mandate and be replaced by a new dynasty. Chinese history is characterised by the cycle of dynastic succession.

The Xià 夏 Dynasty (21st to 16th centuries BC)

Accounts of events in this period have a mythological flavour, but it is undeniably the starting point of the Chinese as a unified people, if only by tradition. The Xia began many centuries after the Yellow Emperor's time. The dynastic system is said to have begun when the popular and heroic leader, Yu, died and was succeeded by his son, Qi. The foundation of the dynastic system marked the point where a primitive society turned into a civilisation: a society based on the family unit and the right to ownership.

The Shāng 商 Dynasty (16th to 12th centuries BC)

Skilfully wrought artifacts suggest that this was China's bronze age. Shang people were superstitious. Many oracle bones have been unearthed and their inscriptions indicate that over 3,000 characters were in use even at this early time. However, literacy was confined to fortune tellers and noblemen. Shang rulers ran a slave society. The dynasty controlled northern China and skirmishes with other tribes allowed the Shang to enslave captives. Slaves were put to work in a master's house or tilled the land. In the worst cases they were sacrificed to the household ancestors. The records state that the last Shang emperor was a hated tyrant who was swiftly conquered by King Wu, bringing the dynasty to an end.

The Zhōu 周 Dynasty (1122 to 256 BC)

The Zhou emperors divided the country into many states, each controlled by a relative of the royal family. The rule of law prevailed: severe and cruel punishments were meted out and strict codes of ritual were maintained among the ruling classes.

The Zhou ruled for nine centuries, making many advances. The first half of the dynasty (1122 to 771 BC) is known as the Western Zhou and the second half (771 to 221 BC) is the Eastern Zhou.

The Great Wall

In the latter part of the Eastern Zhou, widespread use of iron and a rapidly growing population led to bitter warfare between the states. This period is aptly called the Warring States period. The prolonged fighting had a number of consequences: a major one was the emergence of wandering scholars, the most famous being **Confucius** (see Chapter 3). The humanitarian code of ethics he advocated replaced the harsh rule of legalism and has dominated Chinese society ever since. This and the introduction of iron and a middle class mark the Zhou Dynasty as the blooming period of ancient Chinese civilisation.

The Qín 秦 Dynasty (221 to 206 BC)

The short-lived Qin Dynasty was the father of China's **Great Wall** – **Chángchéng** 长城. Built to keep out marauding tribes from the north, they were originally a series of smaller walls that were later extended to cross the entire span of the country. The first Qin emperor was the mighty **Qín Shǐhuáng** 秦始皇, who overturned Confucius' ideals and indulged in book burning and the execution of scholars. He was buried outside the then capital city of **Xī'ān** 西安 along with a (now famous) terracotta army to protect him in the afterlife.

The Qin dynasty is remembered for unifying and expanding the Chinese empire, but perhaps more importantly, as the source of the name 'China'.

The Chinese name for the country **Zhōngguó** 中国 – Central Country or more romantically Middle Kingdom – was the name of the group of states clustered around the Zhongyuan, before the Qin conquest. Zhongguo is the name of China today, but it is more frequently translated as 'Middle Kingdom'.

The Hàn 汉 Dynasty (206 BC to 220 AD)

A peasant rebel was the first Han emperor. The empire was built on a backbone of Confucianism, beefed-up with superstitions and borrowings from other philosophies. Overall, the system was far better than that of the brutal Qin. Written examinations on Confucian lore became the means of selecting officials. An imperial university was established and a class of bureaucrats was born. The Han reached its zenith under the reign of **Wǔdì** 武帝, the 'Martial Emperor' who waged many successful campaigns in the west, suppressing barbarian hordes and capturing horses. The majority of Chinese today belong to the **Hanzu** family, named after this dynasty. Chinese characters are also known as **hanzi**, after the same name.

The period saw many advances: in agriculture, paper, textiles and warfare. The country fragmented again following the collapse of the Han in 220 AD. The Period of Division lasted four centuries, coming to an end in 581 AD, when the country was brought together by the forces of the new **Suí** 隋 Dynasty which was itself overturned in 618 by the most powerful ruling house, the Tang.

The Táng 唐 Dynasty (618 to 907)

This was the golden age of civil and artistic development. All the arts flourished, especially poetry, painting and pottery. China became cosmopolitan, trading heavily in foreign goods via the Silk Road and its maritime ports.

China also became the centre of world **Buddhism** (see Chapter 3). Although it had entered China during the first century AD, the Tang rulers decided to award it official sanction. The monk Tripitaka (**Xuán Zàng** 玄奘), accompanied by the Monkey King (**Sūn Wùkōng**

孙悟空), went to India to collect sacred scriptures. Their adventures are recorded in the 16th-century novel *Journey to the West* often known as *The Monkey King*.

The Sòng 宋 Dynasty (960 to 1279)

Song society was prosperous and secular. Commerce thrived and great cities grew. Merchants and tradesmen were wealthy, despite being lowly in the Confucian order. Scholars extended Confucian principles to become the basis of a system of national government. Examinations to fill the ranks of the bureaucracy continued. Calligraphy was revived and progress was made in the areas of printing and porcelain. Civilian values were supreme. Perhaps this is why China lost millions of men in failed attempts to stop the Mongols. When the Mongols reached Beijing (northern capital), the Song had uprooted and moved its capital southward, to **Hángzhōu** 杭州. Marco Polo would later remark that the new capital was 'without doubt, the finest and most splendid city in the world'. This period from 1126 to 1279 is known as the Southern Song. Despite losing their northern base, merchants began the revolutionary practice of taking to the seas in huge vessels (junks) with the aid of compasses. The paper money economy continued to maintain the growth.

The Song is famous for its historical record writing (**Sīmǎ Qiān** 司马迁 who lived in this period is the most famous author of Chinese history), landscape painting (influenced by **Daoism** and Buddhism; see Chapter 3) and ships which could carry up to 1,000 people and were the biggest in the world at the time.

The Yuán 元 Dynasty (1279 to 1368)

The tribal descendants of the great **Genghis Khan (Chéngjísī Hàn** 成吉思汗) were the founders of the Yuan Dynasty. Beijing became a Mongol outpost. Despite their military prowess, the Mongols were inefficient static rulers, finding their nomadic traditions incompatible with the urban systems they now controlled. Consequently, they adopted the Chinese model of rule. Yuan emperors designed the palaces that still dominate the centre of Beijing. The Mongols were hated and numerous secret societies aimed to undermine them. After Kublai Khan's death in 1294, his inept successors provoked a series of rebellions that finally cost them their dynasty.

The Míng 明 Dynasty (1368 to 1644)

Ming emperors reigned with far more power than their predecessors. The size and influence of the scholar–bureaucracy that supported them increased accordingly. The commercial classes that had arisen in the earlier Song Dynasty were becoming more powerful also. Cities began to grow as never before. Ming porcelain with its characteristic white and blue colouring saturated international markets and earned a reputation for which it is still famed today.

Culturally, the Ming achieved less than the brilliant Han, but succeeded in restoring the country after a century of foreign occupation. The Ming period is exemplary of the archetypal dynastic cycle: economic rehabilitation following upheaval, restoration of political stability, an enduring period of relative peace, gradual decline and, finally, collapse.

Some of the Ming's most significant achievements were the maritime successes of the Muslim eunuch **Zhèng Hé** (Cheng Ho) 郑和 in the early 15th century. These gave learned Chinese a much broader world perception after the return of expeditions to the Indian Ocean, the Red Sea and the Persian Gulf.

The **Imperial Palace/Gùgōng** 故宫 (Forbidden City) was built in this period and the whole country was brought under the control of the central government.

The Qing 清 Dynasty (1644 to 1911)

The Qing was another foreign dynasty. This time they came from Manchuria, in the northeast of the country. Formerly they had been known as the Juchen people: barbarians who had periodically mauled the northern portion of the Chinese empire. Qing emperors reigned through the last age of China as a great empire. They saw humiliation at the hands of foreign powers who exploited their technological backwardness. To make things worse, the Qing faced numerous internal rebellions too, one of the more serious being the quasi-Christian cult **Tàipíng Tiānguó** 太平天国 (Taiping Rebellion, literally Heavenly Kingdom of Great Peace). These were put down, but not easily. Two crushing defeats against Britain (the **Opium Wars, Yāpiàn Zhànzhēng** 鸦片战争 of the 1840s) brought home the fact that they had a lot of catching up to do. Further defeats followed, the most insulting being by China's diminutive neighbour, Japan, in the 1890s.

The Qing tried desperately to strengthen themselves through the purchase of foreign technology and the use of Chinese know-how, but try as they might, they could not restore the Confucian order that had governed China for the last two millennia. At the same time, they squandered wealth on western fancies. Probably the most outrageous being a marble replica of an American steamboat, built with money that was supposed to be going to the navy.

The last great revolt of the era was the notorious **Boxer Rebellion** – **Yìhé Quán** 义和拳 (literally Righteous Fists). On the orders of the Empress Dowager **Cí Xǐ** 慈禧, they attacked foreigners and ran riot in Beijing, burning churches and the houses of westerners. Allied foreign power overcame them and forced the Peace of Peking treaty on China. This was the last in a series of failed attempts to remove foreign influence over China. The failure of the Boxers and the imperial family's inability to negotiate successfully, led to growing support for nationalist movements.

The Republican Period: Mínguó 民国 (1911 to 1949)

Nationalist forces lead by **Dr Sun Yatsen (Sūn Zhōngshān** 孙中山) took control of the government and brought an end to over 2,000 years of monarchic rule, removing the child emperor **Pǔ Yí** 溥仪. Sun Yatsen was swiftly replaced in 1912, by **Yuán Shìkǎi** 袁世凯. The period began idealistically: a constitution was drafted and elections scheduled for 1913. The **Guómíndǎng** 国民党 (the People's National Party, known widely as the Kuomintang) was formed in preparation. Yuan schemed to assassinate political rivals and establish himself as the new emperor. By 1914, he had made himself president for life. After his death in 1916, some of his underlings scrambled for power in Beijing, others became warlords of outlying areas. Sun Yatsen returned to power and became generalissimo of a new order in 1923. He relied heavily on the newly formed Soviet Union. He appointed **Jiǎng Jièshí** 蒋介石 (Chiang Kaishek) as his successor before his death in 1925.

The period between 1928 and 1937 is sometimes called the **Nationalist Era**. It too began in hope, but Japanese aggression and Soviet interference made political progress and peace impossible.

Political ideologies had been flooding in, among them Communism, which had gained popularity following the revolution in Russia. Chiang, in his effort to assert control, drove Communists out of the cities. They were, however, well received in the countryside and their power base grew. Chiang decided that they were a bigger danger than the Japanese and undertook several campaigns to destroy them. The Communist Red Army under the leadership of **Máo Zédōng** 毛泽东 was finally fenced in in 1934. Their escape from their idyllic **Jiāngxī** 江西 Soviet base and subsequent 6,000-mile (9,654 km) trek became known as the legendary **Long March – Cháng Zhēng** 长征.

In 1936, Chiang united his forces with those of the Communists in an attempt to rout the invading Japanese.

For China, World War II began in 1937 after a minor battle with Chinese forces provided the excuse for Japanese soldiers to occupy Beijing. By 1939, Japanese forces had overrun the greater portion of the east coast and by 1940 had installed their own puppet rulers in the great cities of Shanghai, Nanjing, Guangzhou and, of course, Beijing. The Japanese military inflicted a number of atrocities on the mostly civilian Chinese they conquered, the most infamous being the Nanjing Massacre of 1937. It is estimated that around 20 million Chinese died at the hands of Japanese troops.

Naturally, anti-Japanese feeling was very high. The Communist–Nationalist united front fought hard but was undermined by feuds between Nationalist generals and was not able to capitalise on the massive military donations given by the United States. When Japan's defeat came, the Communists were better poised to take control since the Nationalist forces were too far to the rear. Civil war resumed. US airlifts helped Nationalist troops retake the cities, but the countryside remained firmly with the Communists.

Communist forces, despite gross inferiority in terms of weaponry and funding, had one crucial asset: popular support. Nationalist armies had lost half a million men by 1948, two-thirds of which was through defection. When Nanjing and Shanghai fell in 1949, Nationalist resistance disintegrated. By autumn, Communist forces controlled the mainland, except Tibet. Chiang Kaishek and his cronies had fled to Taiwan.

The People's Republic of China (1949–present)

The official name for this period is also the full name of the country: 中华人民共和国 **Zhōnghuá Rénmín Gònghéguó**.

Mao period (1949 to 1976)

On 1 October 1949 Mao Zedong proclaimed the People's Republic of China established. The Communist Party claimed its takeover to be a victory of the people; the Chinese people had finally 'stood up'. Foreign aggression, imperial enslavement and the rule of the oppressive Guomindang were in the past. The country was liberated. The Red Army became the **PLA** (People's Liberation Army) **Rénmín Jiěfàngjūn** 人民解放军, Chinese intellectuals returned from abroad and the majority of local officials remained in power.

The Communist Party inherited a country in ruins, ravaged by a century of fighting and turmoil. Nonetheless, the revolution was a popular one and **'the masses'** (**qúnzhòng** 群众, as Mao liked to call them) were enthusiastic about a new order under the leadership of Mao. Characteristically, the era began optimistically: the Communists lived up to their Socialist ideals and gave land to the peasants, nationalising factories and industry and bringing experts and technology from Soviet Russia. Thought Reform campaigns began, the purpose of which was to prepare the populace for the Socialist state that was soon to come.

By the mid-1950s Mao felt the need to recruit the opinions of China's intellectuals. The Hundred Flowers Movement was begun in the hope of encouraging constructive comment. However, those whose criticisms were too severe found themselves persecuted and imprisoned in the subsequent Anti-Rightist Campaign.

Mao, distrustful of intellectuals and out of favour with the post-Stalin USSR, turned to his beloved peasant masses to deliver Socialist utopia. The result was **The Great Leap Forward** – **Dà Yuè Jìn** 大跃进 – of 1958. Using revolutionary fervour as its primary fuel, the idea was to propel the country into a state of Socialist prosperity. The population was mobilised and great projects in building and agriculture were initiated. The fields were overplanted with seed and village collectives turned good metalware into scrap in backyard furnaces that were supposed to increase steel production. The result was inevitable mass hardship, the failure of the crops and the withdrawal of Soviet assistance bringing about widespread famine.

The 1960s brought greater problems. The disastrous Great Leap left the party ideologically compromised and divided on plans for a future course. 'Pragmatists' pushed for a relaxation of economic laws to allow private enterprise. As they appeared to be gaining ground, Mao retaliated with the unleashing of the **Cultural Revolution** in 1966. Mao probably felt that this was the perfect antidote to the reforms being pushed by the pragmatists which challenged his vision of Socialist China. It would also serve nicely as a means of punishing those who were attacking his leadership.

The Hot Period is the name given to the violent beginnings of the movement. Mass campaigns ravaged the country, usually involving assaulting things or individuals which stood in opposition to Mao's thoughts which were bound, scripture-like, in the famous *Little Red Book* (**Zuìgāo Zhǐshì** 最高指示 – *'The Highest Principles'*). The foot soldiers of the revolution were the infamous Red Guards, the most passionate and youthful followers of the Mao cult. The period is remembered for violence, vandalism and waste. Millions of innocent people suffered, were sent away for 're-education', publicly humilated or worse. Approximately 15 million people died in the purges. The Cultural Revolution finished with Mao's death in 1976.

Waiting in the wings were the pragmatists, among them a Long March veteran and victim of the Cultural Revolution, **Dèng Xiǎopíng** 邓小平. The events of the last decade were quickly denounced as a disaster and, suddenly, the country was facing a new revolution.

The Reform era (1976 to present)

Deng promoted Socialism with Chinese characteristics. Entrepreneurial capitalism was encouraged, agricultural collectives were disbanded and peasant families were given the land, to do with as they pleased. Deng's Four Modernizations – **Sìgè Xiàndàihuà** 四个现代化 (agriculture, science, defence and industry) – were the keys to transformation. The experts returned to run things. Academic success and technical knowledge once again took precedence over ideological commitment. Economic relations with developed countries were permitted and China, with its enormous population and low labour costs, quickly became the workshop of the world.

In the early 1980s, special economic zones were established to persuade foreign companies to invest in China. There has been a distinct shift away from Stalinist heavy industry towards light industry and a massive reduction in the number and importance of state-owned enterprises. The *iron rice-bowl*, **tiě fànwǎn** 铁饭碗, system whereby all workers were guaranteed a basic income is increasingly rare. Nowadays, peasant households have an income based on crops directly under their control.

Deng's reforms were not implemented without criticism. In keeping with tradition, Deng employed the policy of slacking off at one end while tightening up at the other, to appease his critics. Ideological work was encouraged and officials were instructed to crack down on economic crimes. At the same time, entrepreneurs were granted more and more freedom to operate inside the rapidly opening economy.

Throughout the 1980s, artists, writers and even the press benefited from the reforms: enjoying increasing amounts of liberty in expression and even criticism.

However, the bubble seemed to burst in the summer of 1989. Deng ordered the PLA to fire on unarmed pro-democracy marchers in Tiananmen Square; the iron fist had slammed down once again.

Deng died in February 1997. In his place stands Jiang Zemin, the former Mayor of Shanghai.

The China he has inherited is still a troubled one, despite phenomenal economic successes (China has sustained the world's highest output growth rate since reforms began in 1979). China has a 'floating population' of some 100 million unemployed peasants. Organised crime is far beyond the point of control and the figures for petty crime are also soaring. Environmental issues such as deforestation and air pollution are becoming increasingly serious. The collapse of the one child policy has accelerated population growth. The disparity between rich and poor is increasing: while many are better off, others are now poorer than they were before the reforms. State-owned enterprises continue to drain government funds as never before. Human rights questions remain unresolved and Chinese law is still largely ineffective in protecting the rights of citizens.

For all its flashy skyscrapers and mobile phones, it is evident that the country is still lacking in fundamental areas, not the least of which is a sound ideology. The Orwellian doublespeak of the current regime makes this very apparent.

The four most important political figures of the 20th century

Dr Sun Yatsen/Sūn Zhōngshān 孙中山 (1866 to 1925)

He was born in Guandong Province and received schooling in various places, including Hawaii. He graduated in medicine from a college in Hong Kong in 1892 whereupon he promptly abandoned academia in favour of politics. After a failed uprising in Canton in 1895, he fled the country. In his 16 years of exile, he travelled widely: Europe, the United States and Japan, all the while gathering support and raising funds for his cause. A successful rebellion in Wuhan brought Sun back to China in 1911. This inspired revolts in other provinces and, as leader of the Guomindang (Nationalists), Sun was quickly elected to be the provisional president of the new republic. He was hastily forced to resign in 1912 and was replaced by the devious Yuan Shikai. His grievances with policy prompted him to raise a new army and attempt a second revolution. After this failed, Sun left for Japan. Returning in 1917, he attempted to construct a new government finally gaining control of the country in 1923.

Sun Yatsen's political philosophy can be summarised in his **Three Principles of the People/Sān mínzhǔyì** 三民主义: Nationalism, democracy and livelihood. The Soviet Union was Sun's crutch. He modelled his party on that of the USSR and his government became increasingly dependent on Russian aid. He established the Whampoa Military Academy and appointed Chiang Kaishek to be its president. He died of cancer in 1925. His tomb in Nanjing is a national shrine and his portrait is still displayed periodically in Tiananmen Square.

Máo Zédōng 毛泽东 (1893 to 1976)

Mao is China's and perhaps the world's greatest revolutionary. In recent years his achievements when measured against his mistakes seem small. He was a poor statesman and never managed to mature far beyond the role of peasant rebel. A native of Hunan province and the son of a relatively wealthy grain-dealing peasant father, his schooling was erratic but he graduated from the First Provincial Normal School of Changsha in 1918.

While in Beijing, Mao became involved in the **Wǔsì Yùndòng** 五四 运动 – **May Fourth Movement** which erupted in demonstrations on 4 May 1919. This movement came principally from popular dissatisfaction with the Treaty of Versailles, in which China (who had supported the Allies in World War I) was forced to accept the handover of former German concessions to Japan. Feeling betrayed and disgruntled with the west, Chinese students appealed for alternative ideologies. The protests were an attack on the traditional Chinese order (Confucianism). They demanded the introduction of a vernacular written language (hitherto, written language had been an inaccessible relic of the imperial age) and a promotion of science.

The success of the Russian Bolsheviks turned many intellectuals towards Communism. The Moscow-sponsored Comintern organisation (Communist International) was, by 1920, distributing Communist literature throughout the country and helping to start groups dedicated to Socialist revolution. At the head of one such group was the young Mao Zedong. In 1921, Mao helped establish the Chinese Communist Party (CCP) **Gòngchǎn Dǎng** 共产党. He left his job as a school principal in Hunan to become a full-time revolutionary. At this time Mao devised his great plan for the liberation of the country: take the countryside and surround the cities. He planned to mobilise the untapped potential of the peasant masses to bring power to the Communists.

After the disintegration of Nationalist forces in 1949, Mao became the ruler of China, presiding over the victorious Communist Party as the chairman. Mao's relationship with the USSR was always unsteady (Stalin along with the USA had backed the Nationalists). Stalin, ever paranoid, was intimidated by such a massive competing Communist power on Soviet borders. Mao came to regard the USSR as traitors to the cause of global Socialism.

For the first five years of his leadership, Mao rarely appeared in public, he had been relegated to the status of a ceremonial figure. Mao was at odds with many of the policies being initiated by his comrades. Believing that his revolution was being undermined, Mao's Great Leap Forward was begun in 1955. The country narrowly avoided complete collapse; town and countryside alike suffered the consequences of putting ideology ahead of reality.

Similar events followed in the 1960s. Mao's influence continued to grow. Before long, his popularity had evolved into a dangerously powerful cult. The Great Proletarian Cultural Revolution (full title) inflicted unprecedented amounts of destruction on individuals, property and society at large. **Zhōu Enlái** 周恩来 (his second-in-command) was a moderating influence on Mao, but his radical wife, **Jiāng Qīng** 江青 urged him to press the masses for greater ideological zealotry. The results were a decimated economy, a shattered education system and an impotent bureaucracy. Mao died on 9 September 1976 and a power struggle began almost immediately.

Dèng Xiǎopíng 邓小平 (1904 to 1997)

The year 1976 marked a watershed in China's history. Many of the CCP's ageing leaders remained in power, but their influence was waning rapidly. Deng was the son of a wealthy Sichuan family. He studied in Paris where he met Zhou Enlai. After his return to China in 1924, he joined the CCP. He began his revolutionary career as an underground agitator and endured the Long March of 1934 to 1935. In the Cultural Revolution, his moderate ideals earned him the label of 'bourgeois freak' and he was dragged through the streets of Beijing wearing a dunce's cap. Throughout his political career, Deng resisted the rigid party line and his early efforts to push economic developments through 'capitalist methods of production' made him fall foul of the **Gang of Four** – **Sìrén Bāng** 四人帮 (a group of hardcore Mao fanatics led by Jiang Qing). After Mao's death and the fall of the Gang of Four, Deng emerged as supreme leader.

The economic reforms of the 1980s clearly illustrate Deng's priorities. Western observers initially praised Deng for the economic reforms he had begun, but held him responsible for the incidents in Tiananmen Square, pointing to his dismissal of the politicians who had favoured democracy, leniency toward dissidents and concessions to the protesters.

Jiāng Zémín 江泽民 (1926–)

When the CCP was purged of its moderates in June 1989, Jiang was appointed General Secretary and chosen to be heir apparent to Deng. Information about Jiang's early days is scarce. He joined the CCP as a student in Shanghai. In the 1950s he was sent to Moscow for training in engineering and subsequently worked his way to the highest position at a car plant in northeastern China. He is a relative newcomer to government, not holding a post until 1980.

He lacks the credentials of Mao and Deng (he has no revolutionary record and no long-standing political allies) but his institutional standing is still impressive: in 1992 he became Secretary General of the Party, President of China and Chairman of the Military Affairs Commission. Many believe that his rapid climb to power was partly the result of his strong ideological stance and firm hand when dealing with student demonstrations during his time as Mayor of Shanghai. Policies under Jiang Zemin continue to follow trends set by Deng Xiaoping, so much so that the skylines of most major Chinese cities are completely unlike those of 20 years ago.

The pattern of Chinese history

Few cultures are shaped more by history than that of the Chinese. Present-day Chinese life is similar to a play being acted out, the background scenery is like the past, inanimate but constantly in the picture.

To the ancient Chinese, their civilisation stood at the centre of the world, indeed was the world. They called their country **Zhongguo** (Middle Kingdom) to reflect this. Emperors were the Sons of Heaven, recipients of Heaven's Mandate (the divine right to rule). They believed that they were the elect beneficiaries of qualities required of a ruler by heaven. When their power ended, it was because the gods had taken away the mandate and the emperor no longer had the right to rule. The new emperor would promptly set about rewriting history according to his own design. Each ruler demanded historians to illustrate the failings of their predecessors while celebrating their own virtues and successes. This form of historical rewriting is not unique to the Chinese, but Chinese historical revision was so frequent and thorough that it became institutionalised. The Chinese Communist Party, despite attempts to separate itself from China's imperial legacy, has proved itself more than expert as historical revisionist, regularly referring to altered versions of recent and distant past events to support or attack present-day policies.

The Chinese have a wary respect for history. On the one hand, they believe their unity and identity as a people is encoded in the events of their ancestors, on the other hand: in recent years, many have seen history used to justify irrational politics, discredit and shame innocent people and too often wielded as a weapon of propaganda.

GLOSSARY

五星红旗 **Wǔxīng Hóngqí** five-starred red flag of China
国 **guó** country
民族 **mínzú** people, ethnic group
土地 **tǔdì** land
山 **shān** mountain
河 **hé** river
海 **hǎi** sea
海岸 **hǎi àn** coast, shore
高原 **gāoyuán** plateau, highland
植物 **zhíwù** flora, plants
花 **huā** flower
竹 **zhú** bamboo
动物 **dòngwù** animals
野生动物 **yěshēng dòngwù** wildlife

沙漠 **shāmò** desert
历史 **lìshǐ** history
地理学 **dìlǐxué** geography
入侵 **rùqīn** invade
文明 **wénmíng** civilisation
皇帝 **huángdì** emperor
代 **dài** dynasty
战争 **zhànzhēng** war
革命 **gémìng** revolution
古代 **gǔdài** ancient times
我对 _____ 有兴趣。 **Wǒ duì _____ yǒu xìngqù.** I'm interested in _____.
我想去 _____ 。 **Wǒ xiǎng qù _____.** I want to go to _____.

Taking it further

Books

General history

China. A History, Arthur Cottrell, Random House, 1990. An excellent general introduction.

Ancient / traditional

A History of Chinese Civilization, Jacques Gernet, Cambridge University Press, 1991. The only book you will ever need about traditional China.

Modern

The Search For Modern China, Jonathan Spence, W.W. Norton and Co., 2000. Heavyweight but very thorough.

Mao / Communism

Red Star Over China, Edgar Snow, Grove Press, 1973 (revised edition). A classic account of turmoil and politics in pre-1949 China.

The New Emperors: Mao and Deng, a Dual Biography, Harrison E. Salisbury, HarperCollins, 1992.

Travelogues

Riding The Iron Rooster: By Train Through China, Paul Theroux, Ivy Books, 1990.

Behind The Wall: A Journey Through China, Colin Thubron, Penguin any edition.

Guidebooks

China, Lonely Planet. In every way easily the best guidebook.

Websites

A library of pictures and documents related to the last 500 years of Chinese history: http://www.cnd.org/fairbank/

Everything connected to travel and tourism, attractions and sightseeing. In English and Chinese: http://207.152.99.199/Lifestyle/Travel.html

THE LANGUAGES OF CHINA

Early Chinese

Few languages say more about their speakers than Chinese. To the Chinese, culture is synonymous with literacy and stands at the very centre of their concept of civilisation. Not surprisingly, the Chinese language is very old (legend cites the creator as being the Yellow Emperor, some 4,500 years ago). Archaeological research has uncovered inscriptions that are possibly 8,000 years old and it is very likely that these are the forerunners of Chinese characters.

We have little idea how the language may have sounded, but we know that 3,500 years ago, ancient Chinese were using characters that are still in use today. Of the written languages in use at that time, only the Chinese system has survived.

The evolution of characters

The earliest known characters are found on Shang Dynasty oracle bones. Bones and shells were etched with inscriptions for the purpose of divination. They were heated in fires and the cracks were said to indicate the outcome of the problem etched into the bone. These etchings were stick-like because they were basically scratches. With the coming of bronze, more variety in style emerged. Around 200 BC, the introduction of simple ink pens produced fundamental changes in writing. Characters became more rounded in appearance and Chinese still use this style of character on their name chops (ink stamps which are used in place of signatures).

Soon after, ink brushes changed characters again. Lines became straighter and more angled, taking on a more organised and logical appearance. Many subsequent styles emerged: some highly elaborate, but modern characters more or less stem from this style of ink brush writing. The 20th century has seen many changes in the Chinese language, among which is the simplification of thousands of characters.

Are characters important to understanding modern China?

As we saw in Chapter 1, Chinese culture is the unique product of many factors, not the least of which is a language that has remained relatively consistent and, therefore, comprehensible despite the enormous periods of time involved. Linguists like to debate the relationship between language and culture (do words determine thought or vice versa?). This alone makes Chinese characters enlightening, especially if we note the following as one of many possible examples.

Early characters (pictographs and ideographs; explained in the next section) were classified as **wén** 文. It is interesting that the word for culture, **wénhuà** 文化, uses this character. To some extent, this indicates the ancient respect for the written language. An understanding of characters provides many such insights into the formation of early Chinese society (and arguably modern China too), its perceptions of the world and the values it attached to them.

All languages provide information about the people who use them and Chinese is no exception to this, but Chinese culture holds literacy (and by extension, education) in such esteem that it is difficult to go to higher levels of understanding without at least some knowledge of the written form and spoken language.

An understanding of Chinese characters is highly important to an appreciation of traditional and modern culture. Since it can be read by all Chinese, regardless of what dialect they speak, the written language is a great symbol of cultural unity and uniqueness as well as evidence of Chinese influence over other cultures (Vietnam, Korea and Japan).

What exactly are Chinese characters?

This is a simple question with a complex answer. To the uninitiated, they are intricate little drawings and this is far from incorrect. Around 100 AD, six definite types of character were identified.

The earliest characters were **pictographs**, stylised pictures of objects and phenomena such as animals, the moon, mountains and so on. In this respect, early Chinese differed very little from other early languages.

Modern Chinese retains some of these purely pictographical characters (though the number is small). The characters for sun 日, moon 月, man 人 and tree 木 are said to belong to this category of character, although in the case of many characters, the connection is speculative, not definite.

The second category of character is the **ideograph**. There are a small number of these that are easily interpreted. For example: 一 represents the number one, 二 is two and 三 is three. All the remaining thousands of characters are combinations of pictographs and simple ideographs.

To convey more sophisticated concepts, characters were formed thus: 日 + 月 = 明 (the characters for sun and moon are put together into a single character to give the meaning 'bright'). Similarly: 女 + 子 = 好 (woman and child = 'good'). This kind of character is sometimes referred to as a **logical aggregate**.

Phonetic elements were added to later characters. These combine the meaning of one character with the sound of another. The word for 'think' (**xiǎng**) consists of 心 + 相 = 想. In this case, the word **xiǎng** was assigned a character of the same sound, but to convey meaning, an ideographic element (心 meaning 'heart') was added. Such an element is known as a **radical**. These characters could be termed technically as **phonetic complexes**.

The remaining two types of character are associative transformations and borrowings. Despite the technical sounding name, **associative transformations** are simply characters which have had their meanings extended to incorporate related concepts. **Borrowings** consist simply of words that originally lacked their own character but had the same (or similar) pronunciation as that of another and so use that character.

A famous early dictionary claims that only 4% are true pictographs, 1% are simple ideographs, 13% are logical aggregates and an overwhelming 82% are phonetic complexes (although this figure probably incorporates a high number of logical aggregates too). In short, this breakdown suggests that only a very small number of characters are really pictographs, so it is inaccurate to describe them as such. But as the essential building blocks of all characters, pictographs are still important to an understanding of the written language.

Chinese radicals?

Chinese dictionaries arrange characters according to radicals, 部首 **bùshǒu**. To find a character, the radical must be determined. There will be a section in the dictionary that lists characters with that radical. (Radical is better and more literally defined as *section heading*.) The list will be broken into sections containing characters with the same number of strokes. For example, if we want to find 星 (*star*):

1 Identify the radical. In this case it is 日 (*sun*).
2 Locate 日 in the dictionary's radical table.
3 Count the number of strokes in the remaining part of the character: 生 requires five strokes, so we go to the five-stroke subsection.
4 The dictionary will then give a pronunciation and/or a page number.

Identifying the character can be difficult in the early stages of learning Chinese because complex characters contain a number of elements which could be the radical: 日 and 生 are both radicals so it is often a matter of trial and error before the conventions of classification become familiar.

The theory of classification centres on the understanding that every character has at least one semantic component: 日 in the case of 星. This means that readers should be able to make a guess which radical the character is listed under. In practice, however, it is not so easy; the system places many characters under radicals to which they have no relation. Also, many radicals indicate a phonetic, not a semantic property and this complicates things further.

Spoken Chinese

There are hundreds of different languages and dialects spoken by the Chinese. Most of these, however, are used by relatively small numbers of people. China has eight major languages (more about these later). These differ in both pronunciation and grammar so much that they are sometimes said to be as different as languages within the Germanic or Romance language families. A famous study concluded that the major dialects differed mostly in pronunciation (80%), vocabulary (40%) and grammar (20%).

However, the reliance on characters means that differences in vocabulary can be overcome just by knowing what characters make up the word. The differences in pronunciation are overstated too. A speaker of one dialect has no need to memorise the pronunciation of every word of another. The many thousands of words in a dialect are composed of only a few thousand characters. Once these have been learnt, it is relatively easy to cross from one dialect to another.

All Chinese languages are tonal, that is words are said on tones that determine the meaning of the word. **Mandarin** (the standard dialect of the mainland) has relatively simple tonal patterns. For Chinese speakers to learn another Chinese dialect is undeniably easier than for a non-Chinese language speaker. The main reasons are: similarity in grammatical structure (differing only 20% at most), familiarity with use of tones and comprehension of underlying cultural concepts.

The Sino–Tibetan language family

Chinese languages and their many dialects are said to belong to this particular language family. The membership and classification of languages under this category is however, rather complicated. 'Sino' refers to the many Chinese languages and 'Tibetan' indicates those languages found mainly around Tibet and Burma.

The evolution of standard Chinese

Throughout history, the mutual unintelligibility of Chinese dialects added to the difficulty of governing the country. Characters and complex written forms also complicated things. The first attempt at language reform was made under **Qín Shǐhuáng** (the first emperor of China) who wanted to simplify characters and increase the phonetic (sound) and semantic (meaning) content to ease the learning process.

Subsequent changes to the language were resisted. The bureaucratic classes of the imperial era championed tradition over change since the writing of complex characters was the mark of the scholarly classes. Educated people used language as a symbol of prestige and a means of distinguishing themselves from less fortunate people. The imperial examination system – **kējǔ** 科举 – deepened the problem by requiring the use of highly elaborate written forms (characters, handwriting and grammar were assessed).

The history of Chinese languages is slightly paradoxical when we consider that, throughout the vast span of Chinese history, Chinese characters were considered to be a unifying force, connecting millions of people who could never have understood each other verbally. Yet the majority of people were mostly illiterate and the written system itself was completely unlike the spoken form of popular language. As we saw earlier, writing has been traditionally associated with supernatural forces and it was believed by scholars throughout the ages that the populace was generally unworthy of written knowledge. Consequently, writing was reserved for a minority who used it primarily for the use of Confucius-approved activities such as commentary on the classics (see Chapter 5), history writing and poetry. This classical language was known as **Wénxué Yǔyán** 文学语言.

It was perhaps because of such tight control over mass learning that the Chinese found themselves technologically inferior to the foreigners who arrived in force in the 19th century. The Qing Dynasty suffered many embarrassments as they tried to pit traditional Chinese learning against foreign powers backed by industrial revolutions and an increasingly scientific knowledge of the world, warfare and commerce.

The May Fourth Movement of 1919

In the early part of the 20th century, disgruntled intellectuals and students campaigned heavily for the revision of Chinese values, which they saw as holding China in stagnation, philosophically and scientifically.

This period marked the beginning of the Chinese linguistic revolution. Writers pushed for the introduction of a simpler, vernacular written form that would be closer to everyday speech. Although such a language had been in existence since the Song Dynasty, it had remained largely unused. In 1922 **Báihuà** 白话 (common language) was recognised as the new national language. This would later become known as **Pǔtōnghuà**.

Pǔtōnghuà 普通话

This language is known to English speakers as **Mandarin** and sometimes as **Standard Chinese**. Mandarin is based on the northern dialects with its pronunciation based on the dialect of the Beijing area (北方话 **Běifānghuà**). The term 'Mandarin' comes from **Guānhuà** 官话, the language of officialdom in the Ming and Qing Dynasties.

When the Nationalists replaced the Qing government in 1911, attempts began to formulate a new language. After failed efforts to mix dialects, it was decided that Mandarin should be promoted, this would be known as **Guóyǔ** 国语 (national language). Communist reformers relabelled this as **Pǔtōnghuà** 普通话 (general language) in the 1950s.

Today, the language spoken by two-thirds of Chinese is **Pǔtōnghuà**. In Taiwan, it is still known as **Guóyǔ** and differs slightly, since the Nationalists who set up government in Taiwan in 1949 were based formerly in Nanjing (south of Beijing) and the regional influence is reflected in pronunciation differences.

To most Chinese, the common language is called **Hànyǔ** – 汉语, after the **Hàn** 汉 people who make up the largest ethnic group in China (91.59%).

Simplified characters

In 1956 the Chinese Communist Party undertook a scheme to radically alter aspects of the language. At first, they considered replacing characters with an alphabetic system, similar to that used in Vietnam (before the French came, they too had written in Chinese characters), but the idea was scrapped in favour of retaining characters, albeit in simplified versions.

In 1956, the first list of modifications removed 29 characters and altered 428. Later, in 1964, a revised list of 2,238 was presented.

Simplification was done with the intention to promote mass literacy. It took many forms but in all cases emphasis was on reducing the number of strokes required to write a character. Older characters are sometimes known as full-form characters (**fántǐzì** 繁体字) and simplified versions as short-form characters (**jiǎnhuà zì** 简化字).

Nonetheless, since no revision of the phonetic or semantic properties occurred, it is unlikely that simplified characters are significantly easier to learn than the slightly more complicated original versions.

Recently, the number of radicals in use in mainland China has been reduced to 178. Radicals with only a few characters listed under them were removed and many had become obsolete anyway.

The number of characters is also decreasing quickly. An early Qing Dynasty dictionary listed 50,000 characters. Nowadays, an educated person could probably recognise around 6,000 characters. In China, knowledge of around 3,000 characters is necessary for general life (in Taiwan, it is about 4,000). Literacy for peasants was defined as only 1,500 characters and for workers as 2,000.

Pīnyīn 拼音

The word literally means 'phonetic spelling'. A system of writing the sounds of characters was introduced in 1958. It uses letters of the Roman alphabet (along with marks over vowels to indicate tones) and was designed to facilitate character learning. It is now the standard system of spelling Chinese words with Roman letters. It has replaced earlier, more complicated systems and its comprehensibility has made it invaluable to foreigners who study Chinese or travel in China.

The main Chinese languages

For many centuries there has been only a single method of writing Chinese and the long common literary and cultural history contained within this and the recent push toward standard Chinese has left many languages relegated to the position of dialects. In fact, they are sometimes as different from one another as French is from Italian. The languages of the southeast are particularly distant from Mandarin. To complicate things even more, there are varieties within the languages, some diverse enough to be referred to as languages in themselves. It is therefore difficult to get accurate figures on the numbers of people speaking any Chinese language. These are the eight major Chinese languages in order of popularity.

Pǔtōnghuà 普通话 (Mandarin/Guóyǔ/Hànyǔ)

Since 1949 the official language of the People's Republic of China (PRC). Virtually all Chinese have been educated in this language and consequently speak it at least a little. It is the language which foreigners should learn. Its popularity is expected to grow as the Chinese sphere of influence continues to expand. It is currently the world's most spoken language: almost a quarter of the world's population are speakers and the number of people learning the language outside China continues to grow (particularly among speakers of other dialects resident abroad).

Others

Wú 吴 is spoken by almost 10% of the population of China. Despite this enormous number of speakers, it is relatively unheard outside its native areas of Shanghai, Anhui, Zhejiang and Jiangsu.

Yuè 粤 is popularly known outside China as Cantonese. Only 5% of the population speaks this language, but it is the one that is most frequently encountered by foreigners. For historical reasons, most Chinese immigrants (especially in the USA) are Cantonese speakers and therefore it is the language of most Chinatowns in western countries. This language is common in the south of China, particularly Guangdong and Hong Kong. Until very recently, almost all Chinese films available outside China were made in Hong Kong and used the Cantonese language. Elsewhere in China, Cantonese is becoming popular as mainlanders try to set up business with the wealthy former colony. Cantonese has nine tones (compared to the four of Mandarin) which makes it perhaps more difficult to master.

Xiāng 湘 is strongest in the south central areas around Hunan.

Mǐn 闽 is divided into two:

> **Mǐnběi** 闽北 Northern Min. Spoken in northwestern parts of Fujian.

> **Mǐnnán** 闽南 Southern Min. The southeastern parts of the country such as Zhejiang, Fujian, Hainan Island and Taiwan.

Kèjiā/Hakka 客家 is also commonly heard in Chinatowns (particularly in the UK). Traditionally, Hakka is the name of a nomadic people who were once widespread in China, but settled mainly in southern areas. The language is most concentrated between Fujian and Guangxi. In Mandarin **Hakka** is pronounced **kèjiā** and the characters mean 'guest people'. Deng Xiaoping is a famous Hakka person. The pronunciation of many Hakka words is very close to their Mandarin equivalents.

Gàn 赣 is spoken in the Jiangxi area of China and southeastern Hubei.

Varieties of Pǔtōnghuà

A comfortable level of Mandarin is spoken by a reliable 70 to 80% (minimum) of the population. Pǔtōnghuà outside Beijing is influenced by regional accents and local expressions that do not exist in the standard language. The three main strands of Mandarin are Northern, Eastern and Southwestern Mandarin.

Beijing people have an attitude similar to residents of southern England who like to claim they have no accent. Beijingers are, however, much crueler and delight in poking fun at regional differences in the national language. Impersonation of other accents is the stock material of many comedians. One famous example is 'da' which to Beijingers means 'hit', but in Shanghainese means 'wash'. Consequently, barbershop stories provide hours of fun for snooty northerners.

Varieties of written language

Officially, there is only one system of written language and, to most native Mandarin speakers, it is the written form of their spoken language. Before Mandarin, literate people could read classical texts and communicate with each other in the classical language, regardless of their native dialects. The aggressive promotion of **Báihuà** (based on northern vernacular language) and, later, Putonghua prevented vernacular written forms of dialects from developing. Speakers of dialects such as Cantonese were left with no written language despite their rich cultural heritage. Paradoxically, many southern dialects are much closer to earlier Chinese than Mandarin is. This is evident from old poetry which does not rhyme in the modern language, but sounds much better in various other dialects.

Recent advances and the future of modern Chinese

Some people still believe that ultimately, Pīnyīn will replace character writing, while others point to the now widespread practice of using long-form characters to give an air of sophistication to names of mainland hotels, nightclubs and merchandise. New codes of spelling have been devised for diverse uses such as telegraphy, flag signalling, signing for the deaf and Braille. Putonghua continues to grow inside and outside China. The once Cantonese-dominated Hong Kong has signed up for Mandarin lessons following the hand-over and mainlanders show off their entrepreneurial successes with a fashionable smattering of Cantonese.

Computers are also improving communication in Chinese. Advanced software now enables spoken input and soon the use of touch pads will allow characters to be entered into computers by the user writing on them. The future growth of Mandarin will depend very much on how the authorities apply their interpretations of 'standardisation'. Language adoption encroaches on ethnically sensitive areas, especially in regions where the people consider themselves as very different from the majority of Han Chinese.

The influence of Chinese

The use of characters extends well beyond the boundaries of modern China and countries such as Taiwan and Singapore. These days Chinese is found all over the world. All the great European, American and Asian cities have Chinatowns and it is not uncommon to see street signs in Chinese.

Historically, the greatest importers of Chinese were her neighbouring countries, particularly Japan and Korea. Characters are an inherent part of the modern Japanese language, known as **kanji**. Although supplemented by two syllable-based alphabet systems, kanji remains elemental to written Japanese. Much older written Japanese was only slightly different from Chinese. For this reason, Japanese school children can still study classical Chinese.

Before the 15th century, Korean was written entirely in Chinese characters (known to Koreans as **hancha**). Their own system, **hangul**, has eliminated the need to write or read most Chinese characters. Most Korean academics have a good knowledge of Chinese characters since they are essential for studying Korean history or culture. Despite this, the use of characters among young Koreans is in decline.

Non-Chinese languages

Officially, there are 55 recognised minority groups in China (8.41% of the population or 95 million people). Considering this high number, it is not surprising, that non-Chinese languages are fairly common in modern China. These languages are highly diverse and the bulk of the speakers are concentrated mostly in northwestern parts of the country. In descending order, the four most common non-Chinese languages are: **Uyghur**, **Mongol**, **Korean** and **Tibetan**. In southerly parts of China there are many exotic languages connected closely to the Tibeto–Burman part of the Sino–Tibetan language family. As such they are far closer to languages spoken in South East Asian countries (Vietnamese, for example) than to Mandarin.

Language and ethnic issues

Some experts contend that minority languages are dying as a result of Chinese attempts to unify the country. This seems to be true in the case of Tibetans whose national minority constitutes around 4 million people, yet figures for speakers of the main three Tibetan dialects reflect only about a quarter of this number.

Presently there are groups in Xinjiang, Tibet and Inner Mongolia (the biggest minority areas) who are pushing for the restoration of their language as a symbol of cultural identity.

English 英语 Yīngyǔ

All Chinese people who attend university must study English as part of their courses. Nowadays, colleges, secondary schools and even primary schools that do not teach English are rare. Consequently, there are millions of Chinese who have at the very least, a basic knowledge of English. In the early 1980s 'English Fever' began and this has been revitalised by the recent fad for 'Charismatic English' (which basically involves shouting phrases) and appeals greatly to the Chinese passion for noise. The demand for English continues to grow as China opens up and more and more Chinese move to foreign countries. Unfortunately, many Chinese speak English on the pattern of their mother tongue. As a result, they often sound very rude and direct to foreign ears.

A closer look at Chinese

The prospect of learning Chinese is daunting to many foreigners. The written system appears tremendously complicated and the sound seems very alien too. Speakers of European languages assume that the grammar will be equally challenging. With a little investigation however, several myths about Chinese can be debunked:

1 An understanding of the basics of the written form are all that is required to begin reading and writing the language. Knowledge of about 1,500 characters equates to a vocabulary of many thousands of words.

2 Usually, our contact with spoken Chinese comes via speakers of Cantonese which has a more complex tonal system than Mandarin.

3 The grammar is not nearly as difficult as that of European languages.

Written Chinese looks difficult!

As we have seen, Chinese has no alphabet and is often criticised for being overcomplicated as a result. When compared to an alphabetic system (such as that used in English), Chinese has some advantage for the learner because characters give information on meaning, whereas alphabetic systems only indicate pronunciation.

Chinese has an enormous vocabulary, but it is composed of a much smaller number of building blocks. If the simpler characters can be recognised, the meaning of complex words can be guessed:

海 (sea) + 盗 (thief) = 海盗 (pirate)
电 (electric) + 话 (words) = 电话 (telephone)

This show us how Chinese words are created. Some interesting words have been coined to define new technology:

激 (sharp) + 光 (light) = 激光 (laser)
激光 (laser) + 唱 (sing) + 盘 (plate) = 激光唱盘 (compact disc)

Chinese contains many words which have the same sound but different meanings (**homophones**), for example, the characters 供, 工, 功 are all pronounced '**gōng**' but have different meanings:

供 means supply or provide
工 means work as in 工人 worker
功 occurs in 功夫 (**gōng fū**/kung fu)

Which way do you read it?

Chinese books are conventionally bound on the opposite side from books written in European languages. This is because Chinese can be written in a variety of ways, the traditional way being vertically, in columns from top right to bottom left. Among overseas Chinese this is probably still the preferred method, but in mainland China, most writing is done horizontally (left to right) as in English. One reason for this is that modern Chinese writing often includes English words which have to be rotated 90 degrees and written sideways to fit into the traditional pattern! The traditional way also causes problems when writing scientific papers because equations could become very confusing! Everywhere in the Chinese world scientific material is always written in the format of English.

In normal Chinese texts, there are no spaces between characters, so beginners face the problem of not knowing whether they are looking at a single-character word or a longer multiple-character word. As vocabulary increases this problem fades; the brain learns to guess what is what.

First steps in writing Chinese

As with any language, learning Chinese begins simply. Textbooks present vocabulary logically, giving the most essential words first and, in as much as is possible, the characters chosen will contain a small number of strokes, this makes them easier to write. Characters can contain between 1 and 7 strokes:

一　人　大　木　立　老　足

With simple characters, stroke order is easily learned. All the lines (strokes) of every character are written methodically (usually starting at top left, for example). Simpler characters like those we have just seen, are likely to be radicals (see the earlier section). Also, when put together, they can make up more complex characters:

人 + 立 = 位 (person + standing = place)

Simple characters can also form (two or more character) words:

大 + 人 = 大人 (big + person = adult)

At early stages, textbooks will contain characters, pīnyīn for pronunciation and English translations:

Pronunciation (pinyin)	wǒ	nǐ	shì	péngyǒu
Characters	我	你	是	朋友
Definitions (English)	me/my	you	is/are	friend

Then we are ready to attempt some grammar:

> **nǐ   shì wǒ péngyǒu**
> 你　是　我　朋友
> Definition   you are my friend

First steps in speaking Chinese

It may be this aspect of the language which offers foreign learners the greatest challenge (although Arabic is supposed to be more difficult for English speakers). As we have already discovered, all Chinese languages are tonally based and since Mandarin contains only four tones, it is relatively easy.

The tones of Mandarin

All the tones (声 **shēng**) of Mandarin are common to the English language. However, in English tones convey attitude or emotion; in Chinese they are directly related to the meaning of the word. To native speakers, tonally separated homophones are as different to the ear as 'big', 'bag', 'beg' and 'bog' are to English speakers.

The first tone: 阴平 **yīnpíng**

This could be described as a high, level tone. It is not too unlike holding a note when singing. It is indicated as a ⁻ over the vowel of a pinyin word, for example, 发 (send out) has the pronunciation of **fā** which sounds like 'far' in English only with the vowel sound held twice as long and the pitch a little higher.

The second tone: 阳平 **yángpíng**

This is a rising tone, the vowel sound is raised. The sound is similar to the questioning tone in English, as in 'It is?' (I don't believe you). It is shown by a ´ mark over the vowel of a pinyin word, for example, 罚 (punish) is pronounced **fá** which rhymes with 'car' ('What, a *car*?').

The third tone: 上声 **shǎngshēng**

Commonly known as the falling-rising tone. This is the one that usually causes learners most problems. Its starts as a mid-low tone, falls then rises. The tone is common to several British dialects

(Geordie, in particular) and sounds like a mixture of astonishment and exclamation. It is indicated by a little ˇ over the pinyin, for example, 法 (law) is said as **fǎ** ('It's very *far*!?'). It helps to remember that this sound rises at the end, suggesting disbelief.

The fourth tone: 去声 qùshēng

This has the sound of finality, it is a sharply falling tone. It sounds a little like a mother telling a naughty child 'no!' and is easy to mimic. Words with a ˋ mark over the vowel have this tone, for example, 珐 (as in 珐琅 **fàláng** enamel) is said on the fourth tone **fà** ('It is too *far*!').

The fifth tone: 轻声 qīngshēng

This tone is not usually included in descriptions of Mandarin. There are a few words where no marks appear to indicate a tone. In these cases, the word is unstressed, i.e. it is a neutral tone, for example, 呢 (ne) as in 你呢 (nǐ ne)? ('What about you?').

Pronunciation

For the foreigner, pinyin provides a great deal of information about the peculiarities of pronouncing Chinese and for the Chinese themselves, it permits the writing of their words in Roman letters.

Even if you want to learn only a few phrases for travelling in China, you would be well advised to study the conventions of pinyin. If you are more serious about learning Chinese, there is no alternative. The table at the beginning of this book (p. xiii) will help you grasp the basics.

Grammar

Many Chinese and teachers of Chinese say that Mandarin has no real grammar. Of course, this is a slight exaggeration (all languages have some kind of grammar). However, when compared to European languages, the grammar of Chinese is indeed far simpler (no gender, plurals or 'the' to complicate things!).

Tenses

In Chinese, tenses are far simpler than in English (where -ed is put on the end of a verb to indicate past tense, walked, for example). English is full of irregularities to confuse foreign learners (go becomes went, not goed!) but in Chinese there are no such problems because time words (today, last week, etc.) provide tense:

Wǒ jīntiān qù Xiānggǎng
我 今天 去 香港
I today go Hong Kong = Today I'm going to Hong Kong

Wǒ zuótiān qù Xiānggǎng
我 昨天 去 香港
I yesterday go Hong Kong = Yesterday I went to Hong Kong

Wǒ míngtiān qù Xiānggǎng
我 明天 去 香港
I tomorrow go Hong Kong = Tomorrow I'll go to Hong Kong

Classifiers

An interesting feature of many Asian languages, classifiers describe things being counted, similar to saying 'three *bottles* of milk' in English. They are sometimes called counters or measure words, in Chinese 量词 **liàngcí**:

sān pǐ mǎ
三 匹 马
three [classifier for animals] horses

liǎng běn shū
两 本 书
two [classifier for books] books

sān shí jǐ gè rén
三 十 几 个 人
30 several [classifier for people] people = more than 30 people

Vocabulary

Traditional grammarians divide vocabulary into two broad categories: meaningful words and empty words which have a grammatical function only. Words in this latter category are called particles 助词 **zhùcí**. Maybe the reason for such a wide criterion for categorisation is that even in modern Chinese, there are virtually no words that can be described exclusively as a noun, verb, adjective etc.:

Wǒ kàn huà

我 看 画

I look at pictures [In this example 画 (**huà**) is a noun, i.e. *picture*]

Wǒ huà huà

我 画 画

I draw pictures [Here, 画 is both the verb *draw* and the noun *picture*]

Particles

These words alter the sense of a sentence, but have little or no meaning in themselves. Most particles have no tone:

Nǐ shì zhōngguórén

你 是 中国人

You are Chinese [If we add the particle 吗 (**ma**), we get a question form]

Nǐ shì zhōngguórén ma?

你 是 中国人　吗?

Are you Chinese? [Note: no change in word order, unlike English]

The particle 了 (**le**, no tone) causes a few problems for beginners of Chinese. It indicates a recent change of state:

Wǒ chī bǎo le

我 吃 饱 了!

I'm stuffed! / I've eaten enough!

Structure

It may come as some relief to discover that Mandarin basically follows a word order not unlike English, i.e. it displays the subject–verb–object order:

Wǒ chī ròu

我 吃 肉

I eat meat

Simple sentences such as this correspond directly to their English equivalents. Some linguists propose that basic word order is better described as topic–comment, since it is common to hear sentences such as: 'As for the Chans, they've just moved house.'

Given that grammar is rarely taught to Chinese children and that the language is uninflected (verb forms do not change) there is an argument for saying there is no grammar. However, it is more correct to say that the structure of Chinese is highly word-order dependent rather than based on rules per se.

Some tips for learning Chinese

Without a doubt, Chinese is a difficult language to learn, especially in the early stages. Character learning is probably the most challenging aspect, but after a few hundred characters, the brain learns to remember them more efficiently. There is no getting around it, a certain amount of rote learning is necessary to get those first characters lodged in!

In the beginning it is best to listen to as much Chinese as possible (preferably in a language laboratory) and exposure to the natural speech of native speakers works well. Mimicry is often the best way to pick up a feel for a new language (try imitating your Chinese friends!) and it sometimes helps to exaggerate the sounds, particularly the tones.

Most people who dedicate themselves to private learning achieve good results with tape and book programmes. Chinese requires only patience, not exceptional linguistic ability as is commonly assumed. As with any other language, the more you devote yourself to studying it, the better you will become.

GLOSSARY

言语　**yányǔ**　language
外语　**wàiyǔ**　foreign language
方言　**fāngyán**　dialect
发音　**fāyīn**　pronunciation
口音　**kǒuyīn**　accent
字　**zì**　word, character
语法　**yǔfǎ**　grammar
写　**xiě**　write
听　**tīng**　listen
说　**shuō**　speak, talk

看　**kàn**　read
生词　**shēngcí**　new vocabulary
词汇　**cíhuì**　words and phrases
动词　**dòngcí**　verb
名词　**míngcí**　noun
形容词　**xíngróngcí**　adjective
说两种语言的　**shuō liǎngzhǒng yǔyán de**　bilingual
我(不)会说汉语　**Wǒ (bù) huì shuō Hànyǔ**。　I (don't) speak Chinese.

Taking it further

Books

General

Chinese, Jerry Norman, Cambridge University Press, 1988. About the language, not a textbook for learning it.

Characters

Cracking the Chinese Puzzles, T.K. Ann, Stockflows Co. Ltd, 1987. The last word on Chinese characters, their history and meanings.

Mandarin

Teach Yourself Chinese: A Complete Course For Beginners, Liz Scurfield, Hodder & Stoughton, 1993.
Teach Yourself Beginner's Chinese Script, Liz Scurfield and Lianyi Song, Hodder & Stoughton, 2000.

Cantonese

Teach Yourself Cantonese: A Complete Course For Beginners, Hugh Baker and P.K. Ho, Hodder & Stoughton, 1996.

Learning

Chinese language courses are not easy to find. The Chinese communities of large cities usually offer lessons but these are typically geared towards Chinese children. Short of joining a full-time university course, asking around in a local Chinatown is probably the best bet.

Many local radio stations broadcast programmes in Chinese (usually Cantonese) and listening to these is a good way to familiarise yourself with the language.

Websites

Dedicated to helping people learn Chinese on the net, a number of interesting features including 1,000 online Chinese character flashcards: http://www.mandarintools.com

3 | CHINESE RELIGION AND PHILOSOPHY

Beliefs of the Chinese

China is sometimes referred to as the land of **three teachings** (三教 **Sān Jiào**): meaning Confucianism, Daoism and Buddhism. But, as you might expect, there are a far greater number of religions represented in China than three!

In the Chinese world, religion and philosophy constantly overlap. Furthermore there are no distinct divisions between the secular and spiritual aspects of life the way there are in many western traditions.

Broadly speaking, there are few belief systems in China that correspond closely to those of the revealed teachings, such as Christianity, Islam and Judaism. Therefore, most Chinese are relatively unconcerned with questions about the afterlife, heaven and divine retribution. Contrariwise, when they fall on hard times, they sometimes (perhaps jokingly) ask themselves what they did in a former life to justify the hardship.

China is changing rapidly. Science and knowledge of the world have expanded minds just as in other countries, also the Mao era attacked every form of traditional practice, including religion (it was regarded as mere 'superstition') but more than 2,000 years of traditional beliefs and practices could not be wiped out completely. The customs and practices of Chinese people all over the world have roots in practices which originate largely from the three teachings.

The Chinese populace is well aware that the government is offering little in terms of an ideology to replace religion and spiritual practices, consequently there has been a revival of religious and spiritual activity among mainland Chinese.

To gain some understanding of the principles that prop up modern Chinese society we must begin with a look at the three great philosophies that have had centuries of influence over Chinese society. On top of these we will consider the beliefs of the general people who, throughout history, have scaled down the loftier teachings to fit with local customs. Such practices are often labelled 'traditional' religions and continue to be widely practised today.

Confucianism (儒学 Rúxué)

This is probably the most 'Chinese' of the three teachings. The other two have similarities with traditions outside China, but Confucianism was the product of Chinese thought and has determined Chinese culture with more consistency than Buddhism or Daoism.

Confucius was a political theorist, philosopher and teacher. His ideas have influenced not only China, but a number of countries within the Chinese sphere of influence (especially Korea). Confucianism has nothing to do with 'confusion' (although some people think there is some connection!). The name comes from its founder, Confucius, who lived about 2,500 years ago (551 to 479 BC). His real name was **Kǒngfūzǐ** 孔夫子 (Master Kong) and 'Confucius' is the result of the Latinisation of this name.

Background

Confucius lived when China was enduring one of its most chaotic periods, the Warring States period 战国 **Zhàn Guó** (475 to 221 BC). Over 12 states were fighting each other for control. The great disorder and the suffering that came from this probably influenced Confucius' thinking immensely. Confucius was from an aristocratic lineage but suffered poverty in the early years of his life. That he rose from poverty to the rank of minor official through hard studying is an example that millions of Chinese try to mirror. At the age of 30 or so, he began running private schools. Through these schools, his teachings matured and grew in influence. His techniques were said to be good, but, more importantly, the content of his teachings had much relevance to the problems of the day. His fame grew and he is said to have had around 6,000 students.

One of his greatest teaching innovations was the use of elicitation (student contribution), which went contrary to the common use of spoon-feeding knowledge to students. He is said to have promoted

Confucius

the notion of equality between student and teacher and encouraged students to speculate, using their own opinions. Paradoxically, these constitute the very opposite to the classroom traditions which subsequently developed in Confucian countries, although his idea of teaching according to a student's aptitude is still given lip service in modern China.

His political theories took shape and he undertook a series of journeys to visit the rulers of various states to offer them his advice. He was repeatedly rebuffed. He returned to his home in the state of Lu and at the age of 68 he set about amassing more students, this time from all sorts of backgrounds. Confucius retained sympathy for the poor (since he had been lowly once too) and his teachings had a distinctly compassionate character. He collected ancient manuscripts and sought to utilise the knowledge to bring about a second golden age.

Confucian philosophy

Confucius did not claim to be a prophet or have any supernatural powers. His power lay only in his ability to persuade rulers that his core concept of benevolence, if applied correctly, would make them loved by the people, instead of feared. But what, according to Confucius, was 'benevolence'? His own quote in answer to this was: 'Benevolence is love to all men'. Confucius advocated that all men occupy a position in the hierarchy of society. They were expected to reciprocate the respect that came from their position and, in turn, observe their own responsibilities to those in other parts of the social order. In short, Confucius maintained that a code of ethics should be inculcated into the very fabric of society. That code would ensure morality and mutual respect. The code would rest on a tightly structured, philosophically based hierarchy, that would, in theory at least, extend from the emperor at the top down to the lowliest surf at the bottom:

The Emperor
↓
Scholar / officials
↓
Peasants
↓
Merchants
↓
Craftsmen
↓
Soldiers
↓
Slaves
↓
Underclass (prostitutes, beggars, entertainers)

In practice, the model was seldom realised; it was difficult to say for sure who was more despicable: soldiers, craftsmen or slaves!

Merchants wielded far more influence than the model suggests, as did high-ranking soldiers, so it was more of a *theoretical* basis for society. Despite this, Confucius' model gave civilians and officials preference over the potentially destabilising influence of merchants and military men. Confucius feared that any political system would be weakened if it were subject to the unpredictable forces of economics or military control.

The model illustrates another fundamental Confucian precept, namely stability over chaos. Confucius believed that stability (even a state of naivety) was preferable to disruption. The maintenance of peace and well-being between people was the principle objective of his teachings.

Confucius promoted the ideal of education. Through correct (i.e. Confucian) education he argued that a man could be cultivated towards altruism, which was the true nature of men anyway.

His primary interest was etiquette and conduct between people. Properly defined social relations would lead to proper conduct, which would in turn foster social harmony. Confucius believed that there were five 'cardinal' relationships:

1 Ruler (emperor) and ruled.
2 Husband and wife.
3 Parents and children.
4 Older and younger brothers.
5 Friend to friend.

If the parties in these relationships knew their places in respect to each other, and acted appropriately, society would function well.

He maintained that people should look to the past to learn the lessons of history. Only by 'continuing the past' was it possible to 'open up the future'. Thus he claimed that history, being of unparalleled importance, should command the most attention of any subject.

Confucius insisted that caution precede any decision and that, generally, it was better to follow than initiate.

Religious/spiritual Confucianism

Underlying all Confucius' teachings was the concept of 'filial piety'. This is an elaborate expression for 'obedience to parents'. Confucius stressed that filial piety was the bond that would hold society

together. To Confucius, society was a big family with the emperor as
the father. The family model was of immense importance since this
was the basic social unit and the place where filial piety would be learnt.
Confucius stressed that the elders in the family should command the
most respect (particularly the men) and that a family's ancestors
should be venerated also. Confucian teaching reinforced the already
existing practice of ancestral appeasement. Sometimes this is called
'ancestor worship' but it is really only remembrance, similar to placing
flowers on graves. Confucius is also said to have feared heaven,
particularly the 'Mandate of Heaven' which allows a ruler to rule. He
is supposed to have said: 'He who offends Heaven has none to whom
he can pray'. It is very likely that Confucius talked about such things,
not out of personal belief, but because he saw them as yet another
means of reinforcing filial piety. Personally, he did not believe in
spirits or ghosts, but it would have been heretical to discredit them.
Nonetheless, over the centuries Confucian temples sprouted up all
over the land and the emperor himself was required to acknowledge
Confucius' spirit on special occasions.

Works of Confucius (经传 Jīngzhuàn)

Confucius spent his last years busily editing and adding to some of
the old books he had collected during his lifetime. These became known
as *The Five Classics* (五经 **Wǔ Jīng**):

>*The Book of Songs*　诗经　**Shī Jīng**
>
>*The Classic of History*　书经　**Shū Jīng**
>
>*The Spring and Autumn Annals*　春秋　**Chūn Qiū**
>
>*The Record of Rites*　礼经　**Lǐ Jīng**
>
>*I Ching* / *The Book of Changes*　易经　**Yì Jīng**

Long after his death, his sayings were collected and formed his most
famous work, ***The Analects*** (论语 **Lùn Yǔ**). This book is the nucleus
of the Confucian canon (a number of books concerning Confucian
philosophy) that was compulsory reading material for generations of
scholars and indirectly affected the course of Chinese history for more
than 2,000 years.

Confucian practice

His teachings affected Chinese society at every level. So much so that
the preceding description of Confucian philosophy just about sums

up the nature of Chinese society, past and present. All Chinese are highly status conscious since 'filial piety' depends on an acknowledgement of that status. Every relationship a person makes is conducted along Confucian lines of reciprocal respect and give and take. For this reason Chinese still take a very dim view of issues that challenge someone's status (e.g. disobedience to parents).

Did Confucius really live?

Sinologists (China specialists) have recently been concerned with this question. The small number of works that are traditionally claimed to be from Confucius' own pen appear to be written by other people. Some claim that 'Confucius' was a name invented by early Jesuit priests. The theory is that they invented the story of an ancient scholar to identify him as the author of various strands of traditional philosophy. Whatever is true, one thing is certain, 'Confucius' represents, without doubt, the single most important school of thought in Chinese history.

Daoism (道教 Dàojiào)

Otherwise known as 'Taoism'. This could be called the 'ineffable philosophy', the first line of the book of Daoism sums it up completely: 'The dao that can be spoken of is not the true Dao.' Any attempt to describe Daoism betrays only the speaker's misunderstanding; in other words, the Dao is indescribable.

Lǎo Zǐ 老子

The semi-mythical figure of **Lao Zi** (Lao Tzu or Laocius) is credited as the founder of this philosophy. Like Confucius, he lived around 500 BC. His name means 'Old Boy' because the legend has it that he was carried inside his pregnant mother for 80 years and was born with white hair! Some traditions have it that he met Confucius, but this is very uncertain. Precious little is known about Laocius' life but if he were a real person, it is likely that he worked for some time in the mystical arts, presumably as an astrologer in the royal court of the Zhou Dynasty (see Chapter 1). The earliest accounts of his life were written at least 400 years after his supposed passing. Scholars today believe that Laocius is more of a representative figure, an embodiment of a type of scholar or wise man, than a real individual. He is traditionally accredited with the writing of the ***Dao-De Jing***, which

Lǎo Zǐ

contains the essence of his philosophy. The sayings it contains suggest it is the product of more than one author, crossing a span of centuries, not a single person. Nonetheless, Daoism became a highly influential philosophy and Lao Zi himself was considered an imperial ancestor during the Tang Dynasty.

The *Dào Dé Jīng* 道德经

The title could be defined as *The Classic of the Way and its Power*. It is the elemental scripture of the Daoist religion. **Dao** or ('Tao') means *way* or *path* and points to a way of life, a manner of living or thinking. The book is fairly lightweight, containing only a small number of terse and slightly perplexing sayings (epigrams). Lao Zi is said to have written the book while on a journey westward, from which he never returned.

Daoist philosophy

The central principle is the existence of a subtle, yet mighty force that runs through everything, giving form and life to all things. It is similar to the Muslim idea of Allah, in that it is essentially unknowable, but it is the unifying force behind the whole of creation. The goal of the Daoist is to align himself with the flow of the Dao. Daoism has no concept of sin like Christianity or Judaism, instead it claims that human wrongdoing is a result of losing sight of the Dao. Daoism stresses that everything is actually a unified whole, but most people see things only from a very self-centred viewpoint. In other words, ignorance stems from attitude (like looking out of a small window and believing you can see the entire world) whereas the Daoist is aware he cannot see the entire world and knows he constitutes but a small part of it.

Daoists believe that everything is in a constant state of change, the only permanent thing being the Dao itself. To a Daoist, a long, healthy life was directly dependent on how much an individual had complied with the flow of the Dao. This may be the root of the traditional Chinese obsession with long life. Daoists maintained that it was possible to become fully immortal through the Dao.

Since the Daoist's goal was to develop a mystical connection with the Dao, most of his life would be spent as a reclusive, meditating. To western minds, Daoism is often associated with pacifism and this is not completely incorrect. However, Daoism became highly influential (both inside and outside China) in the development of many martial arts and combat strategies.

The true Daoist wholeheartedly rejects assertiveness, competition and ambition. He/she has contempt for things such as social status, material wealth, rank, academia and luxury. All of these distract from the true purpose of life (seeking the Dao and living according to it) and are the product of ignorance and egotism, hence they become the cause of conflict which is the very antithesis of Daoist ideals.

Daoist practice

The intricacies of Daoist philosophy provided much intellectual stimulation for the lettered members of Chinese society. For the common people, the ideals of philosophical Daoism had less appeal and a watered-down Daoism prevailed among the populace. Daoism became inextricably associated with all manner of mystical mumbo jumbo. Some 'Daoists' made a good business from selling immortality pills, reading fortunes or performing exorcisms. Some followers of the Dao became hermits, wandering the countryside and supporting themselves on the sale of charms and potions.

Daoism began with no gods, but quickly acquired a whole range! The most famous were the popularly worshipped **Eight Immortals** 八仙 **Bā Xiān** (eight people who were supposed to have achieved immortality).

Various mountains acquired spiritual significance as the homes of gods and immortal beings. Daoism had great appeal to the millions of superstitious people in traditional China. Among its most famous patrons was the emperor Qin Shi Huang Di. He dispatched an expedition to the eastern sea to find an island of immortals where the Daoists said the herb of immortality grew. Daoism quickly degenerated into something of a longevity cult. Many rulers patronised alchemy in search of the elusive Elixir of Life.

The practice of Daoism took on a highly ritualistic colouring. Formalised Daoism developed an institution similar to a priesthood. Daoist priests (道士 **Dàoshì**) shaved the sides of their heads and lived inside the grounds of temples with their families. Mystical rites became very elaborate. One Song Dynasty emperor built an enormous Daoist temple for the practice of Daoist ceremonies. For centuries, Daoism was favoured by Chinese rulers, but when the Mongols came, the religion was replaced by Lamaism (a form of Tibetan Buddhism) but this also acquired the flavour of popular Daoism before too long.

From the 14th century, Daoism split into two major sects: one was concerned with self-cultivation as a means of attaining immortality; the other focused on magic spells, charms and spiritualism. Of the two, the former was probably closer to the original Daoist ideals.

Zhuāng Zǐ 庄子

In the 4th Century BC, another philosopher, Zhuang Zi, expanded on Daoist philosophy. His interpretation was slightly different; he taught that wise people ride the flow of life without attempting to steer it. His notion of enlightenment centred on freeing oneself from habits and desires which stand between the individual and the universal Dao. His philosophy is contained in *The Zhuang Zi*, named after himself.

Higher Daoism

Throughout history, the higher, more original Daoist teachings were preserved by the scholar gentry. Since there was no requirement for an individual to be exclusive to any single school, it was common to see the lettered classes perform Confucian rites on weekdays and be practising Daoists outside work hours.

Whereas mass Daoism had incorporated traditional gods and local superstitions, Daoism for the educated was concerned much more with theory than practice.

Daoist themes of immortality, portals to paradise and mountains of longevity heavily influenced literature and, more particularly, art. In Chinese art, it is common to see paintings that depict blissful rustic scenes of lakes, trees and mountains. In the pictures it is common to find wandering deities or other Daoist symbols such as cranes.

Daoism and Confucianism

It might appear that in many ways, Daoism contradicts Confucianism. Confucianism is based on control (albeit, ideally self-control) where Daoism is concerned with spontaneity. Confucianism also requires people to conform to hierarchy and responsibility, where Daoism strongly advocates that first and foremost an individual should be at one with himself/herself. Despite these differences, the two have sat comfortably side by side for thousands of years. In the Chinese tradition, the differences complement rather than contrast, appealing to different sides of human nature. The concepts of non-interference and acceptance over challenge are basic to both, consequently neither attempted to revise or supplant the other.

Changes in Daoism

It began as an abstract system of thought, practised by small numbers of people. After a few centuries it had grown into a communal religion, still later it emerged as a popular folk religion combined with a multitude of other beliefs and practices. Before the Communists took power in 1949, there were 20,000 open temples throughout China. In all its forms, Daoism has been a consistent feature of and major influence over traditional Chinese society.

Buddhism (佛教 Fójiào)

This is China's greatest religious import. It came from India where it began as an offshoot of Hinduism. Its creation occurred around the same time as (or perhaps a little earlier than) Confucianism and Daoism. Buddhism is not a product of Han Chinese civilisation like Daoism, but nevertheless it flourished alongside the other two teachings, at times gaining even more importance and influence over Chinese society.

The Buddha (佛 Fó)

Around 2,500 years ago, India was a collection of small states, each with its own languages and traditions. In one northern state (in present-day Nepal), a boy was born into the royal family who would later become known as the Buddha. His name was Siddhartha Gautama and he was prince of the Sakya Kingdom. For this reason, he is sometimes referred to as **Sakyamuni** (释迦牟尼 **Shìjiāmóuní**) Buddha.

His early years were spent within the confines of the royal palace. His father carefully prevented him from seeing beyond the palace walls, fearing that knowledge of death and sickness would distress the boy. As a young man he happened to stray outside one day and was quickly confronted by the suffering his father had sought to protect him from. Thereafter he left the royal household and set about a quest to find a means of putting an end to the inevitable suffering of sickness and death that faces all living things.

A Chinese-style Buddha

At that time in India there were many people on the same path and the young prince soon became acquainted with others who had forsaken worldly life for higher understanding. For many years he lived among ascetics, men who put themselves through all manner of physical and mental hardships to acquire deeper understanding of the mysteries of existence.

Sakyamuni came to realise that fasting, painful postures or beating oneself only amounted to punishing the body. At the time, there were a variety of schools of yoga and meditation being practiced all over India, most connected to one strain of Hinduism or another. The Buddha started to meditate, but without the guidance of a teacher from any existing discipline. He wanted to attain a pure form of spiritual realisation, uncoloured by the religions of the day. Finally, at the age of 35, after many years of meditating, he reached realisation and became 'enlightened'. Thereafter he became known as the 'Buddha' which means 'enlightened/awakened one'.

Enlightenment (悟 Wù)

This is a difficult concept to describe; indeed it took the Buddha the remaining years of his life to do so. At the moment of enlightenment, he is said to have seen the true nature of all things. He became aware of all his past lives and acquired a thorough knowledge of the laws of karma and the consequences of human action. Enlightenment brought knowledge of the true self (sometimes this is called revealing the 'Buddha face' and some statues depict this as a man peeling off an outer face to uncover his real face beneath). He realised the mechanics of the cosmos and the place of all things in the great mechanism of life, he also perceived the interrelatedness of every living thing down to the smallest creature. He gained insights into the composition of matter and described it in terms very similar to those used by modern-day physicists.

Buddhist philosophy

The basics of Buddhist philosophy (dharma 佛法 **Fófǎ**) can be found in Hinduism. The underlying concept of both is karma. This is the force that determines the nature of rebirth (reincarnation) and the consequences of all actions. All living things are locked into a karmic cycle (the wheel of life 法轮 **Fǎlún**) whereby they are subjected to facing the results of their deeds and bound to repeated incarnations until they attain liberation. Between incarnations in physical worlds (such as our own) there are various hells and heavens which souls may go through to clear a karmic debt or reap some reward. But even these are experienced temporarily (even though your spell in paradise might last a million years) and the individual soul must sooner or later be thrown back into a new body to begin the suffering of the living once again.

That all life is suffering is a key Buddhist precept. Old age and sickness face every living thing and are unavoidable. To be free of rebirth is to be free of suffering. Only enlightenment brings true liberation and therefore life should be spent in pursuit of this. Worshipping gods does not bring enlightenment neither do good deeds (although these may bring good karma), only meditation can do this. Correct meditation practice leads to nirvana (涅磐 **Nièpán**). This is not really a heaven but a state of absolute serenity where the soul is free of all desires and is united with the forces of eternal harmony. Only in nirvana does all pain and suffering cease.

The Buddha made few comments about gods and the creation of the world, he said instead that creation had always existed and that such questions merely distracted people from meditation.

Buddhist philosophy does not attribute human wrongdoing to sin, but to ignorance, consequently it is very compassionate. To Buddhists, the cause of suffering and ignorance lies in desire and meditation is the best method of rising above this state.

Buddhism comes to China

Around 526 AD, a Buddhist missionary arrived in China. He is traditionally known as Boddhidharma (达摩 **Dá Mó**), the 'Blue-eyed Brahmin'. In Chinese art he is depicted as an ugly but humorous character with a hairy face and a big nose to accentuate his foreignness. Although Buddhism had arrived in China at a much earlier date (67 AD), Boddhidharma is credited with the establishment of a system of meditation which was to characterise Chinese Buddhism thereafter.

The Chinese learned a great deal from Buddhism, the vocabulary of the language was expanded to accommodate new concepts for which no words previously existed. In translating *sutras* (Buddhist scriptures) from Sanskrit (the dead language of ancient India) they also discovered the tonal nature of their own language. Buddhism introduced a whole new world of ideas, symbols and icons into the Chinese world and took on a very Chinese character as it adapted to accommodate existing gods and similar teachings.

Boddhidharma found much fertile ground for his teachings as Daoism had familiarised many people with concepts similar to those in Buddhist dharma. The conservative and modest nature of the religion appealed to Chinese rulers. China became the stronghold of Buddhism following persecution of Buddhists in India as a result of a revival of Hinduism. Thousands of temples were built, among them the various **Shaolin Temples** 少林寺 **Shǎolín Sì** (they were a fusion of Daoist and Buddhist schools) which became reputed as the birthplace of **Gōngfu** 功夫 literally 'moral effort' (kung fu), the Chinese martial art.

Buddhism practice

Buddhist temples were powerful social institutions. They had many practical social functions (crèche facilities, orphanages, schools, money lending and jumble sales) and were popular with the people. At times they became so wealthy and powerful, they were attacked by paranoid governments. Buddhism survived because the literate classes were intrigued by its philosophical novelties which complemented Daoism nicely and the common people could readily identify Buddhist deities with traditionally worshipped figures. Boddhisattva (菩萨 **Pú Sà**) worship was particularly popular among the people. (Boddhisattvas are compassionate beings who postpone their own entry into nirvana in order to assist the faithful on earth.) The Chinese goddess **Guan Yin** (who is a little bit like a Virgin Mary figure – see later) quickly acquired boddhisattva status.

Buddhism pleased the eyes as well as the hearts of everyday people. A vast array of deities adorned temples and the sculptures were made with great artistry. Ceremonies for the dead, mantra recitation, incense burning and simple ideas of salvation gave Buddhism sufficient mass appeal to help it survive two millennia.

Zen (禅宗 Chán Zōng)

This is the Japanese name for the most famous school of meditation that developed in China. The Chinese name is **Chán**. Its influence can be seen in the literature and painting of the Tang and Song Dynasties. This school is supposed to be directly traceable to Boddhidharma/Da Mo (the Japanese call him **Daruma**) and it blends many Daoist ideas of universal oneness with austere meditation to lead to an experience of this oneness.

Buddhism versus Daoism

Even though these two schools never overtly competed to convert people to their practices, there was a small amount of rivalry in very early times. The first Buddhists came to China as envoys of a well-funded missionary religion. By contrast, Daoism was much more reclusive and passive. Consequently, it was quickly overshadowed by the glitzy paraphernalia of the new religion. Daoists established a kind of pope to compete with Buddhism for political influence, but could not raise their doctrine to the lofty heights of Buddhist philosophy. Over the centuries, there were times when the rivalry escalated into violence, vandalism and book burning. Various governments made Daoists convert or face death. In retaliation, Daoists wrote texts claiming Buddha was merely a reincarnation of Lao Zi and so on. To survive, Daoism had to censor itself and remove anything that was likely to offend Buddhist morals. Consequently, the Daoists lost some of their most advanced knowledge: practically everything connected with sex as a spiritual practice and the many mysterious consciousness-altering drugs that they had developed over the centuries.

Buddhism, Daoism and Confucianism

The generally passive nature of Buddhism and the approved form of Daoism were compatible enough to allow Chinese rulers to let them coexist within a society that was essentially Confucian. Confucianism was tolerant of religion as long as it did not encroach on political concerns. Only Buddhism was purged by late Tang Dynasty rulers, but it did not lose its importance as an influence over Chinese society. All three philosophies allowed and actually reinforced long-standing local superstitions and belief systems further embedding them into Chinese culture as the centuries went on. Consequently, they all became intertwined, overlapping elements of a greater whole and, to the average person, defining a custom as Confucian, Buddhist or Daoist was not important.

The three teachings today

Chinese society today retains a good deal of the legacy of these three schools. Confucianism is particularly healthy in all its forms, not surprisingly, especially in family life. Respect for parents is as important as it ever was and Chinese still subscribe en masse to the notion of 'family first'. The preference for boy children seems to grow stronger with each new generation (Confucius considered girls to be a nuisance at best) and if present birth trends continue, men will outnumber women by 14 to one by 2015!

Chinese people still try not to exhibit emotion publicly or talk about personal matters (Confucius had no place for such things). To many westerners, Chinese still appear reluctant to 'rock the boat', be creative (Confucius said copying was better) or exercise initiative.

Popular Daoism seems to have come back too. Chinese medicine (but not all) is once again being dished out on the basis of a mish-mash of pseudo-science and Daoist terminology. Elderly Chinese are as fascinated as ever with life-preserving potions and healing concoctions, reminiscent of the old Daoist obsession with longevity.

The indifference and passivity of the Chinese attitude on global issues such as the environment or human rights could be interpreted as similar to the fatalist tendencies promoted by both the Buddhist and Daoist schools.

Traditional beliefs

Long before Daoism became an 'ism' the ancient Chinese believed in a non-personal creative energy that brought the universe into existence. Before this, only chaos existed. Order and creation was created by harmonising two complementary forces: **yīn** 阴 and **yáng** 阳, this simple but profound concept is expressed by this image:

The correct name for this symbol is the 太极 **Tàijí** (Great Eternal). The light side represents the male aspect of the cosmic Dao. It is the symbol of light, assertion, creation and all things positive. The darker side is the female aspect, signifying yielding, night and negative phenomena. The symbol represents the continuous flux of these energies: just as one reaches its apex, it begins to recede and the other develops. Each half contains a minor portion of the other (the dots) indicating that the two are really one, forever locked in a state of dynamic balance. Should the balance be broken, all creation would return to chaos.

The ancient Chinese believed that harmony and order was the natural way of things, seeing that disorder only had bad effects. Thus they sought to implement the simple philosophy of balancing opposites in as many aspects of their lives as possible (sweet and sour dishes could be classed as evidence of this!). Exclusivity to any single philosophy, religion or otherwise would have bad consequences. In practice, this helped Chinese society develop the characteristics of tolerance, modesty and moderation.

Religion was far from organised and universal. It centred on communal village practices and superstitions. There would be public shrines containing idols of gods, local heroes or respected elders that had died. Not much was written about folk customs so it is hard to know for sure how seriously they were taken (the literate minority of the day thought it far too trivial to record) but worship probably centred around remembrance and incense burning.

The Chinese believed (and many still do) that the souls of their ancestors were present and could bring them good or bad fortune depending on how they were respected by those who survived them. Consequently, ancestor appeasement was popular among Chinese even in antiquity. Worship would involve bowing to small shrines, leaving token offerings of food and burning incense.

Daoism and Buddhism brought many new gods and people made or bought statues to keep in their homes. The God of Wealth (**Cái Shén** 财神) was probably the most universally worshipped (after all, the majority of Chinese were poor peasants) with the Kitchen God (灶 神 **Zào Shén**) in second place (he was also the God of the Family).

People would give gifts in the form of incense or fake money to earn their favour. There were (and still are) a very large number of gods and over them all sat the Mighty God (上帝 **Shàngdì**) but he was rarely worshipped directly by common folk.

Guān Yīn 观音

Most Chinese families have a figure of this goddess somewhere in the home. She has been widely worshipped for hundreds of years. She has many names, but her main Chinese name Guan Yin means 'Hearer of Cries'. She is popularly recognised as a compassionate being who hears the cries of people who have fallen on hard times. She is also associated with fertility and commonly invoked as a guardian of children. Although temples to her could at one time be found all over China, she was particularly popular among women in the south of the country. Like the Virgin Mary, there are many stories of her appearing to people and working miracles.

Guan Yin – Goddess of Compassion

Adopted belief systems

Being so vast it is natural and correct to assume that China's many neighbours have contributed to Chinese culture. Buddhism is the most famous example, but China has received other philosophies and religions which have, at least in recent years, had significant impact on the Chinese world.

Christianity (基督教 Jīdūjiào)

The earliest Christian group in China was the Nestorians (originally a Syrian sect). Jesuit priests brought a more recognisably European Christianity in the 16th century. The famous Jesuit priest Matteo Ricci charmed the Ming court with a display of foreign technology. Early Catholics permitted converts to continue with or combine their own traditions with Christianity. In the 18th and 19th centuries missionaries from Europe flooded into China, partly out of religious duty and partly as a precursor to the military presence that would soon after land on Chinese shores. They were mainly protestant and far less tolerant of native customs.

In 1949 the Communist Party that officially disapproved of religion offered the many Christian bodies in China an ultimatum: combine into one church or be collectively kicked out. The result was a blend of the various denominations into one, far more eclectic and simplified doctrine. Paradoxically, it seems as if Christianity in China is growing rapidly. In recent years there have been many evangelical Christian groups active in China (they are typically based in Singapore or other nearby countries) and these have a strong following among young Chinese. Today, nearly 15 million Chinese profess to be practising Christians.

Islam (伊斯兰教 Yīsīlánjiào)

Although linked much more closely to Chinese history than Christianity, Islam is traditionally regarded with some suspicion. Islam is represented by very large numbers of Chinese (among them many Han Chinese: the **Hui** minority, for example) but it is strongest in the far west of the country. The Silk Road brought Islam into the heart of China, via Muslim traders. As the empire expanded westward it acquired huge areas of Turkic Central Asia and its large Muslim (Uyghur) population.

There is a long tradition of Muslim Chinese modifying Chinese culture to meet their needs and living happily alongside Buddhists and Daoists. Despite this, since the extreme western boundaries of the Chinese empire were considered anarchic places and were the seat of many revolts, Chinese rulers typically associated Islam with instability.

Like all religions, it was attacked during the Cultural Revolution but seems to be gaining some momentum once again. Mosques are reopening and the state is (on the face of it) far less concerned about the practice of Friday prayers among the faithful. In some Chinese cities, the Call to Prayer can be clearly heard and women wearing head coverings walk freely in the streets.

Islam, as it is practised in China, is unlike that of nearby countries such as Pakistan or Afghanistan. Generally, it is much more informal and it is common to see Uyghur men publicly drinking beer and women dressed like non-Muslims. There are approximately 20 million Muslims living in China today.

Socialism (社会主义 Shèhuì Zhǔyì)

The single most influential philosophy of the last century was, for China, Socialism. Everyone in China who lived through the Mao era was directly affected by this school of thought. War, famine, economic disasters and social upheaval all came from the efforts of Mao and the Communist Party to catapult China into a Socialist paradise. Soon after their failures, Chinese rulers knew changes would have to be made. Following Mao's death, enormous reform measures began.

Subsequently, the vast majority of Chinese today live their lives in accordance with the ideals of 'Socialism with Chinese Characteristics', although to most this equates to clothing entrepreneurial capitalism in Socialist jargon. The general populace seems aware that there is no real Socialism in China (even if the government in power claim to be Communists) and the way to get ahead is through profit. This duality of attitude presents no problem to most Chinese, since the practice of marrying contrasting philosophies to meet pragmatic ends has a long tradition in China (yin and yang?).

The Chinese revolution like all revolutions began optimistically and was ideologically sound. However, no amount of socialist zeal or propaganda could bring China up to the level of competitive economies. After the fall of the Soviet Union and the dictatorships of Eastern Europe, the Chinese government, then ideologically destitute, pushed capitalism with renewed passion, all the while trying to relabel it as Socialism with a few borrowings from capitalism. It seems the Chinese people had never forgotten how to make money, despite the revolution, and adapted to this new philosophy almost overnight.

GLOSSARY

神 **shén** gods, deities
宗教 **zōngjiào** religion
哲学 **zhéxué** philosophy
神秘主义 **shénmì zhǔyì** mysticism
灵魂 **línghún** soul, spirit
教主 **jiàozhǔ** founder
教义 **jiàoyì** religious doctrine
教条 **jiàotiáo** religious beliefs
孔庙 **Kǒngmiào** Confucian temple

刹 **chà** Buddhist temple
居士 **Jūshì** lay Buddhist
佛经 **fójīng** sutra (Buddhist scripture)
教堂 **jiàotáng** church
圣经 **Shèngjīng** the Bible
基督教徒 **Jīdūjiào tú** Christian (person)
清真寺 **qīngzhēn sì** mosque
古兰经 **Gǔlánjīng** the Quran
伊斯兰教信徒 **Yīsīlánjiào xìntú** Muslim (person)

Taking it further

Books

Christianity

The Liberating Gospel in China: The Christian Faith among China's Minority Peoples, Ralph R. Covell, Baker Book House, 1995. A detailed history of Christian missions in China.

Confucianism

The Analects, Confucius, Penguin Classics, 1976.
Mencius, Penguin Classics, 1976.
Manufacturing Confucianism: Chinese Traditions and Universal Civilization, Lionel M. Jensen, Duke University Press, 1997. A modern assessment of the myths and traditions built around Confucius.

Buddhism

A Buddhist Bible, Dwight Goddard, Beacon Press, 1999. First published in 1932, it includes translations of Buddhist scriptures from many sources. Interestingly the Chinese section contains the *Dao De Jing*, so you get good value for money!

A Short History of Buddhism, Edward Conze, One World Publications Ltd, 1993. The author is one of the great authorities on Buddhism. This book is the history of Buddhism in a straightforward, rich but readable format.

Daoism

The Tao of Pooh, *The Te of Piglet*, Benjamin Hoff, Penguin, 1994. Two books that give the essence of Daoism exactly as Lao Zi would have liked: simply and with humour. Make these your first choice!

The Elements of Taoism ('Elements of' series), Martin Palmer, Thorson, 1991. By far the best introduction to Daoism. It is dense with facts but is well ordered and easy to read.

The Tao of Physics, Fritjof Capra, Flamingo, 1991. A good introduction to a number of East Asian philosophies and a (slightly technical) discussion of their similarities to modern physics. A fantastic book!

Websites

Hundreds of links covering every imaginable aspect of Buddhism: http://www.dharmaring.org

Music, articles and texts: http://taoism.net

Confucian texts in both Chinese and English: http://www.confucius.org

4 | FESTIVALS AND FOLKLORE

Chinese traditions and festivals are closely related to complex, mystical concepts of time, similar to those found in western astrology. The traditional, lunar calendar makes setting dates difficult, so in modern China there are two calendars in use today.

The solar calendar (阳历 Yánglì)

This is the same calendar as used in western countries. Chinese months are not known as January, February, March etc. but as Month 1, Month 2, Month 3 and so on. This is the official calendar and all holidays and festivals that began in modern times are celebrated on days of this calendar. The public holidays of modern China are:

New Year's Day	1 January
International Women's Day	8 March (only women get this day off)
Labour Day	1 May
National Day	1 October

By far the biggest day in the modern Chinese calendar is National Day 国庆节 **Guóqìng Jié**, which commemorates the founding of the People's Republic in 1949 and is the start of a two-day public holiday.

There are a small number of other days that have political importance. While not national holidays they still remind Chinese of key events in their recent history:

Youth Day	4 May (anniversary of the May Fourth Movement, see Chapter 1)
Founding of the Party Day	1 July (celebrating the origin of the Chinese Communist Party)
Founding of the PLA Day	1 August (celebrating the origin of the Red Army)

Chinese calendars contain dates in both the modern (Gregorian) system and the older, traditional system, which is based on the lunar cycle.

Festivals and the traditional Chinese year

This is the calendar that the Chinese have used throughout most of their history. Its antiquity is reflected in its name: **Xià** 夏, which refers to the mythical dynasty of the same name (see Chapter 1) when it was supposed to have been created. It is also known as the Farmer's Calendar **Nónglì** 农历.

Months in the traditional Chinese Year are known as **moons yuè** 月 and have either 29 or 30 days. The calendar is arranged so that the first day of each month coincides with a new moon and the 15th day corresponds to a full moon. However, the 12 lunar months do not equate to a real (solar) year, so an extra, intercalary month **rùnyuè** 闰月 is added every third year. This 13th month is inserted anywhere between the second and 11th month.

Combining the two calendars presents a few problems, so the Chinese use almanacs to determine the Gregorian dates of lucky or unlucky days.

Chinese people like to refer to such almanacs when setting dates for marriages, opening businesses or having children. Traditionally, the calendar was critical to the timing of events, both on a personal and social level. All the great Chinese festivals occur at special times in the traditional calendar.

The Spring Festival (春节 Chūn Jié)

This is the Chinese equivalent of Christmas and New Year rolled into one. It celebrates the beginning of the New Year according to the Farmer's Calendar. To avoid confusion with the 1 January New Year, it is now called Spring Festival in mainland China.

It falls between 21 January and 20 February and provides the biggest celebration of the Chinese year. It is a time when families like to be together and often travel great distances to do so. The official holiday is three days long, but generosity is customarily given to those who have more travelling to do.

The last days of the old year are spent thoroughly cleaning the house and preparing the New Year feast. Chinese people like to eat fish at this time because the word for fish is pronounced the same way as the word for abundance, so a request for fish invokes a plentiful new year. Sticky cakes are eaten too.

In the home, people give offerings of food to their ancestors or the gods of the land and home. Families like to hang New Year pictures in their homes. These might feature fish, harvests or children, all healthy and plentiful. Red is synonymous with wealth so parents give lucky money to their children in little red envelopes and strips of red paper bearing auspicious messages are hung on either side of the entrance to the house to bring good fortune into the home.

There are many public celebrations too. Lion dances 狮子舞 **Shīzi wǔ** are performed (and at other times of the year too, but the New Year dance is always the biggest). These involve many people carrying a costume animal through the streets, the main troupe member at the head. Traditionally members of rival kung fu schools competed with each other to display their group's prestige and physical skills, but nowadays all manner of people participate to the sound of pounding drums and deafening firecrackers to scare away evil spirits.

Lantern Festival (灯节 Dēnghuì)

This festival concludes the New Year Celebrations. It is held on the first full moon of the year, 15 days into the first month. Many shapes and colours of silk and paper lanterns are hung outside homes. This festival is associated with glutinous rice dumplings stuffed with various sweet fillings. These are known to Beijingers as 元宵 **yuánxiāo**, which is another name for the festival.

Grave Festival (清明节 Qīngmíng Jié)

The Chinese name for this festival means 'clear and bright' and refers to the cleaning of the family graves which takes place on this date. The cleaning is a gesture of respect for the departed. Graves are often decorated in their recognition. Nowadays, grave cleaning is rarely performed by urban Chinese since it is law to cremate dead bodies. However, most modern Chinese honour their dead on this day through some form of commemoration. Unusually, this festival is determined by the solar / Gregorian calendar and falls on either 4 or 5 April.

Dragon Boat Festival (龙舟节 Lóngzhōu Jié)

This is probably the most energetic Chinese festival. It takes place on the fifth day of the fifth lunar month and involves frantic boat races up and down rivers in rural China. For a long time it was banned due to its feudal associations, but its popularity is once again growing inside and outside China. The boats are dressed up as dragons and raced, the purpose being to tame the dragons who were believed to be alive in the rivers and responsible for causing floods. The date commemorates the suicide of the minister Qu Yuan who, after being expelled by the king, drowned himself. Fishermen raced to save him

Dragon Boat Festival

but failed. To protect his soul, they beat drums and slapped the water with their oars. The boats are the biggest flat water racing canoes in the world. They are between 40 and 90 feet (12 and 27m) in length and were made of teak. Nowadays they are made of fibreglass and accommodate a crew of up to 22 paddlers sitting two abreast, a steersman at the back and a drummer at the front.

The food of this festival is a glutinous rice ball stuffed with savoury or sweet fillings and wrapped in a bamboo leaf.

Mid-Autumn Festival (中秋节 Zhōngqiū Jié)

This festival coincides with the autumn equinox, when the moon is at its fullest and brightest, on the 15th day of the eighth month. It is also called the Moon Festival and is associated with the image of a rabbit since in Chinese legend a rabbit is said to occupy the moon, eternally pounding the drums of immortality. Traditionally, it was common for people to meet and philosophise while gazing at the moon. The food of this festival is the delicious but heavy, round moon cake 月饼 **Yuèbǐng**.

The Chinese zodiac (黄道 Huáng Dào)

Cycles of time are important elements of Chinese culture. Perhaps the most famous cycle is the 12-year zodiac, each year of which is named after a special animal. A person born during that year is said to have the characteristic of that animal. To many Chinese, the year of a person's birth is highly significant, since it not only determines the character of that person but also the physical and psychological makeup of the individual. The animal sign is seen as a key factor in a person's successes, failures and overall happiness.

Furthermore, the hour of a person's birth is significant because each animal is said to govern specific hours (one 12th) of the day. The Chinese animal zodiac directly reflects the theory of yin and yang (see Chapter 3) and can only really be understood with knowledge of this principle in relation to time.

The zodiac yin-yang

The Chinese have a cyclic concept of time: just as night follows day, so would the energies of yin and yang alter in a predictable manner on a yearly basis. One year, yang would be weak and yin strong and an animal was chosen to represent this state. Furthermore, the day being a microcosm of the year, is also divided into 12ths. Each two-hour division of the day is named after a zodiac animal who is believed to embody the state of the balance of yin and yang at that moment.

The year you were born in determines what animal you are and the hour of your birth influences what kind of ox, monkey, rat etc. you will be. Remember, the Chinese New Year begins around February, so if you were born in January, you belong to the year before. Use the following to discover your Chinese zodiac animal and then compare yourself with the description of the animal. You may be surprised!

Rat (鼠 Shǔ)

1900, 1912, 1924, 1936, 1948, 1960, 1972, 1984, 1996, 2008

This animal epitomises the energy of yin. Rat people born at night will be brave and successful since this is when they are at most at home. If born during daylight hours, their lives will be miserable and marked by a tendency toward cowardice. A rat's life can be divided into three periods: the first provides wealth and good luck but the second will be far less fortunate. The last third of the rat person's life will be modest but comfortable.

Rat people are most compatible with partners who are born in the ox, monkey or dragon years. They are most likely to come into conflict with people who are born in the year of the horse.

The rat is at its strongest in the yin (darkness) hours; its energy peaks between 11pm and 1am.

Ox (牛 Niú)

1901, 1913, 1925, 1937, 1949, 1961, 1973, 1985, 1997, 2009

If born at night, ox people will have easy lives where all their needs are met and their lives may even be considered sheltered. If born during the day, they will have to toil their entire lives to make ends meet. Ox people tend to be calm, quietly confident and relaxed. On the downside, they can be stubborn and lack passion. They can also display a little cruelty on occasion and are not the most patient people. An ox's life typically begins in happiness, but the second part brings misfortune through emotional difficulties. In the last third of his life there is much tranquillity to look forward to.

The ox's time is from 1am to 3am. Oxen are best paired in marriage with rats, snakes and cocks. Dogs, horses and sheep should be avoided.

Tiger (虎 Hǔ)

1902, 1914, 1926, 1938, 1950, 1962, 1974, 1986, 1998, 2010

A powerful animal that was once common in China, the animal is associated with a number of mystical powers. Its ferocity comes from the growing power of the yang as day breaks; the tiger's time is between 3am and 5am. Tiger people who are born at night will be particularly fierce. Like all cats, the tiger is a very powerful nocturnal creature. Tiger people can have fiery spirits and be easily offended. While they are often bright and quick-thinking they can be selfish and over hesitant too. They make good protectors, keeping away the traditional three enemies: evil spirits, fire and thieves.

A tiger's life will be charmed in the beginning, but the second part will be troubled. Growing wisdom will allow the tiger a peaceful life in later years.

In marriage tigers are best suited to horses, dragons and dogs. Snakes and monkeys bring trouble for the tiger.

Rabbit (兔 Tù)

1903, 1915, 1927, 1939, 1951, 1963, 1975, 1987, 1999, 2011

People born in this year are very likeable. They are not given to any extreme behaviour and are moderate in all their attitudes. They are liked because they tread carefully and are reluctant to take sides or make enemies. They are placid but not passive. They choose their moments carefully and have sound intuition. Even their negative traits are mild, conceit being their only real failing. There lives are continually peaceful.

In marriage, they are best suited to sheep, pig and dog people. They are likely to have difficulties with people born in the dragon years, but bigger problems will come via rats and cocks.

The rabbit's hours are from 5am to 7am.

Dragon (龙 Lóng)

1904, 1916, 1928, 1940, 1952, 1964, 1976, 1988, 2000, 2012

Among many other things, the dragon is the symbol of change. His time is between 7am and 9am, when yang is in the ascendancy. This is when night becomes true day and the dragon is the master over this dramatic time. Traditionally, dragons are venerated in Chinese culture as agents of transformation. They are associated with harmony, wealth, power and long life.

Dragon people are believed to possess a great sense of honour and courage. They are intelligent and energetic. Their negative traits are stubbornness and inconsistency but they are generally compassionate and unlikely to indulge in idle chitchat.

Dragon people will succeed in relationships with snakes, monkeys and rats. They should be cautious of oxen, other dragons and rabbits. Dogs should be avoided as much as possible!

Snake (蛇 Shé)

1905, 1917, 1929, 1941, 1953, 1965, 1977, 1989, 2001, 2013

From 9am to 11am the power of yang continues to increase; this is the period of the snake, a slippery creature, capable of much twisting and turning. Snake people are thought to be deceitful and inconsiderate. Their ambitiousness borders on ruthlessness and they often lose their friends on the way to their goals. They can be stingy with money too.

Snake people are not completely bad: they are often intelligent, materially rich and attractive to the opposite sex. The first two-thirds of a snake's life are always good, but the last phase can feature much sadness.

Snake people make good marriage partners for ox and cock people. Monkeys bring catastrophe into snake lives and pigs or tigers make the worst spouse.

Horse (马 Mǎ)

1906, 1918, 1930, 1942, 1954, 1966, 1978, 1990, 2002, 2014

The time for this animal is the apex of the yang (11am to 1pm). A horse person who is born in the daytime will be full of good spirit. Their lives will be busy and very productive. If born at night, horse people will experience contentment and comfort.

Horse people need freedom and often prefer the open air. Being highly articulate they are sociable and charming. Overall, their lives are happy, they are popular and well liked.

Horse women tend to be weak and are often exploited in relationships. On rare occasions, they exercise their tempers and this often creates further problems. Generally they are not easily rattled and their horse qualities of intelligence and humour serve them well.

The first two-thirds of a horse person's life may be a little turbulent, but the tranquility of the final phase will more than make up for this.

Horse people make good spouses for tigers, dogs and sheep. Rats must be avoided at all costs!

Sheep (羊 Yáng)

1907, 1919, 1931, 1943, 1955, 1967, 1979, 1991, 2003, 2015

People born in sheep years make the best wives and husbands! Their time of day is between 1pm and 3pm, a time of tranquillity that suits the character of the animal well. Yin energy is growing at this time and the female nature of this energy is expressed in the mothering nature of the sheep.

Sheep people are famous for their honesty, calm and compassion. Their negative traits are gullibility and slight cynicism. Sheep prefer to follow, not lead, but they are always dependable.

A sheep person's life will begin well but the second phase will be a period of emotion-related problems. Good fortune awaits them in the last third of their lives.

Sheep are best matched in marriage to horses, pigs or rabbits; the rat must be kept away! Dog and ox people will bring trouble to sheep people.

Monkey (猴 Hóu)

1908, 1920, 1932, 1944, 1956, 1968, 1980, 1992, 2004, 2016

The time of the monkey is from 3pm to 5pm, when the power of yin is growing ever stronger. Monkeys embody many negative female traits such as vanity and irritability. By the same token, they possess many qualities traditionally associated with female energies: creativity, innovativeness and adaptability.

Monkeys are at their best when matched with dragon and rat partners. Snakes, pigs and dogs do not get along with monkeys and tigers should be treated with great caution.

Cockerel (鸡 Jī)

1909, 1921, 1933, 1945, 1957, 1969, 1981, 1993, 2005, 2017

The cock takes over when the moon begins to be visible. Cock people born at night will be introverts in life, sensitive and may even attract bullies. Their qualities are humility and modesty. If born in the day, cock people are arrogant, highly independent and prone to bad decision making.

Generally, cock people are outspoken and very sure of themselves ('cocky'), they tend to be intelligent too.

The cock's time is between 5pm and 7pm. They are best in marriages with ox, snakes and dragons. Dogs, rats and other cocks bring problems. Rabbits should be avoided.

Dog (狗 Gǒu)

1910, 1922, 1934, 1946, 1958, 1970, 1982, 1994, 2006, 2018

This animal guards the yin in the vulnerable hours of 7pm to 9pm. If born during the day, dog people will lead a good life. If born at night they will literally 'work like a dog' their entire life.

Dog people are generally likeable. They are loyal, trustworthy and responsible. They will wrestle with tasks until they are complete 'like a dog with a bone'. They like to stay away from crowds as they do not tolerate everyone they meet. They are sometimes prone to out-of-character erratic behaviour.

The best marriage partners for dog people are rabbits, horses and tigers. Oxen and cocks make the worst spouse. Dragons and sheep spell disaster.

Pig (猪 Zhū)

1911, 1923, 1935, 1947, 1959, 1971, 1983, 1995, 2007, 2019

As the yin power reaches its zenith between 9pm and 11pm, tranquillity is found. The nature of the pig exemplifies the fine line between calmness and laziness. Pigs are said to be lazy and slightly dull!

They are gentle but temperamental animals and seldom complete tasks in an efficient manner. Their positive attributes are courtesy, reliability and a little shyness.

Pigs are best married to the tamer animals, especially sheep and rabbits. Other pigs are not compatible. Monkeys and (particularly) snakes must be kept away.

Symbols in Chinese culture

An understanding of the symbolic language of Chinese culture provides a deep insight into the fundamental ideas that have influenced its development over the centuries. Chinese philosophy is embedded in a small number of key mystical ideas. Once these have been decoded, the complexity of the culture is no longer the obstacle it may once have been.

The *I-Ching* (易经 Yì Jīng)

This is possibly the world's oldest book. It will be discussed in more detail in Chapter 5, but here it is important to remember that it is an elaborate book of divination. The name means 'changes' in Chinese and so in western countries it is often known as *The Book of Changes.*

According to the book, the universe and every event within it unfolds in accordance to a grand mystical sequence. Likewise, human destiny is predictable once the grand order of things has been shown and this is what the *I-Ching* does.

The book contains 64 images. The images (*Thunder over the Lake* for example) are attached to numbers. To find the answer to a question, the reader selects a number through some random process such as flipping a coin and matches the outcome with one of the images. An interpretation of this image provides the answer to his question.

The Eight Trigrams (Bā Guà 八卦)

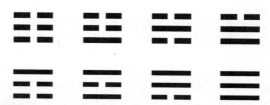

The eight *gua*

The eight trigrams

This refers to the eight *gua*, sometimes referred to as trigrams because they consist of three lines. Each line represents a different level of reality. The outer line (top) expresses the superficial/physical aspect. The middle refers to substance or the thinking level. The bottom/inner line is closer to the essence of the Dao and symbolises the spiritual dimension. To illustrate this, the above diagram is helpful.

These symbols represent the forces of yin and yang. The broken lines ▬ ▬ represent yin, the female energy and the solid lines ▬▬▬ are yang, the male energy. The eight trigrams can be combined in sequences to express every manifestation of the yin–yang principle. They embody and express the most fundamental forces of the universe. It is no coincidence that the Chinese consider eight to be the luckiest number or that *The Book of Changes* consists of 64 (8 × 8) images. The **ba gua** and its many variations are considered to be very powerful tools for divination (in use with the *I-Ching*), charms, spiritual protection and feng shui.

Fēng shuǐ 风水

Recently, this has become very popular outside China as something of a New Age fad. The name literally means *wind* [and] *water*. It is the practice of aligning objects in such a way as to allow the most efficient flow of energy through and around them. Traditionally, the Chinese believe that a subtle energy permeates everything and that interference with this produces disharmony, which in turn has bad effects. Feng shui principles govern the planning of buildings and the arrangement of rooms and furniture inside them to utilise this energy for the well-being of the occupants. Feng shui is really the advice of the *I-Ching* in practice

The Five Elements (五行 Wǔ Xíng)

The ancient Chinese believed that everything was constructed from five essential elements: metal, wood, water, fire, and earth. All things, organs of the body, food, time, compass directions and even colours, can be understood in terms of these elements. The important thing is to ensure that the elements are balanced as much as possible; if they are not, bad effects will occur. In the case of the body, illness will result (more about this in Chapter 9) and traditional medicine will reduce or increase the power of a particular element to bring about a cure.

The character of the zodiac animals can be interpreted through the five elements and feng shui is heavily dependent on this principle too.

Twelve Earthly Branches (十二地支 Shíèr Dìzhī) and Ten Heavenly Stems (十天干 Shí Tiāngān)

Ancient mystics used this metaphor to describe the nature of the mysterious forces of the universe. The Twelve Earthly Branches are basically the same as the 12 animals of the Chinese zodiac and the Ten Heavenly Stems describe the five elements in more detail (one element is divided into two stems).

The Cycle of Sixty (花甲子 Huājiǎzǐ)

Traditionally, time is divided into cycles; macrocycles (many hundreds or thousands of years) and microcycles (hours and minutes). The Cycle of Sixty is one such cycle. After the 12-year zodiac cycle is completed five times (each cycle corresponding to one of the five elements) the cycle begins again.

Lucky charms and talismans

Chinese people are, by tradition, superstitious. There has never been a single religion or philosophy that has required the wholesale abandonment of traditional practices or customs regarding fortune telling or other popular forms of spiritual practices. Thus, such customs are still prevalent today and worth a closer look.

Jade (玉 Yù)

This is the favourite precious stone of Chinese people. It is associated with many positive powers, including the ability to keep away malign influences. For this reason, it is often given to children. Jade occurs frequently in Chinese culture, despite there being no jade mines in China. Daoists ground it into powders to make longevity potions and whole suits of jade were made to preserve the bodies of emperors.

Jade comes in many beautiful shades of green and is favoured by Chinese women not only for its cosmetic value but because it is commonly believed that it can attract wealth and health to the wearer. Chinese often give gifts of jade before long journeys are undertaken since it is believed to protect travellers, similar to Saint Christopher.

Chinese say that if jade pales, the wearer will become poor; conversely, if it darkens, he or she will become wealthy.

Pa Kua/Ba Gua mirrors

These are usually octagonal and decorated with the marks of the eight trigrams (**ba gua**). The mirror is circular and hung over a door to scare evil spirits away by reflecting their own faces, thereby preventing them from entering the house.

Talismans (护身符 Hùshēn Fú)

Like the mirror, these are used to ward off evil spirits. Typically, they consist of small mantras (magical sequences of words) or prayers written on small pieces of paper or cloth. Buddhist talismans are written on yellow cloth and contain extracts from sacred texts and have a small picture of the Buddha on them. Taoist talismans are also written on yellow cloth but feature extracts from the *I-Ching*.

Talismans can be bought at temples and are worn or carried on the body or hung on doors. Children were often given talismans because they were believed to be vulnerable to evil spirits.

Fortune telling (算命 Suànmìng)

In many western societies, going to a fortune teller is often seen as an act of desperation. It is generally at odds with organised religion and interpreted as something of a crutch for those who have little else in their lives. To Chinese, it is the act of a person who wishes to make the most of their fortune. Chinese approach fortune tellers for pragmatic reasons. They often want to know when the best time will be to start a business, get married or who to get married to. They usually go with specific questions in mind. Western fortune-telling practices are often associated with occult or anti-religious sentiment, but to the Chinese they are merely a part of ordinary life and have few negative connotations.

Despite inheriting many philosophies which are based on predictable cycles of events and times, the Chinese are not (generally speaking) fatalistic people; the future is perceived to be unfolding along broad but not unbendable lines. Therefore, fortune telling is seen as another way of aligning oneself with higher forces to bring about harmony and the benefits that will result from doing so.

Palmistry (手相学 Shǒuxiāng Xué)

The belief that lines on the palm of the hand can describe a person's fate is strong in Chinese culture. They are also believed to reveal character, attitudes, health and luck in marriage. The art of palm reading can be reliably traced back to the Zhou Dynasty, when a famous book on the subject was written.

Chinese palmistry has two disciplines: chirognomy (based on the fingers) and chiromancy (focusing on the palm).

Chinese palmists classify seven types of palm which indicate the general character of the individual:

> psychic – the idealist
>
> natural – base or animalistic person
>
> squarish – the practical sort
>
> mixed – mediocrity, no outstanding qualities or inabilities
>
> spatulate – anxious and rash
>
> philosophical – unsure and easily confused
>
> conical – the artist.

In Chinese palmistry, the finger joints, bones, wrists, nails and elbows are scrutinised.

Face reading (相面 Xiāngliǎn Fǎ)

The belief that the face can reveal a person's fortune also goes back to the Zhou Dynasty. To this day, many Chinese believe that the features of the face can be interpreted in terms of yin and yang. This is read from the relative proportions and shapes of the facial features. There are ten distinct types of face, each type indicating the qualities and negative traits of the person as well as providing information on his/her fate. People with small earlobes are considered to be unlucky in money matters. Face readers may also ask for your date and time of birth to give a better reading. They can be found in the streets, around the market areas of most Chinese cities.

Casting lots (抽签 Chōuqiān)

This is possibly the world's oldest method of fortune telling. Fortune sticks are the most common method. Seventy-eight sticks are contained in a bamboo case. Each stick has a number and shaking the case causes a stick to fall out. The number on the stick is matched against a prophetic or philosophical extract from a book of divination (the *I-Ching*, for example) to provide a prediction or insight into a sitution. The books of divination are not standardised and are sometimes unique to the temples where the sticks are found.

The answer does not suggest an absolute outcome; rather it indicates one of many courses the future may take. The object of fortune sticks and other Chinese divination methods is not to obtain a clear picture of the future but to gain some philosophical understanding of the present and choose the best time to undertake important projects or make life-changing decisions.

Almanacs (年鉴 Niánjiàn)

Many Chinese families prefer to bypass the fortune tellers and discover their fates through the use of almanacs. These contain readings based on the Chinese zodiac and identify the good and bad aspects of every day of the year. These books describe detailed methods of self-divination techniques. Today, there are many computer programs available to help get enquirers straight to the reading.

Blood type (血型 Xuèxíng)

It is hard to tell how serious Chinese today take the belief that individuals of certain blood types share common characteristics. It is certainly widely held and is a popular conversation topic for Chinese, Japanese and Koreans.

The characteristics associated with the blood types vary massively and almost everybody seems to have their own definitions.

The overwhelming majority of Chinese have 'B' type blood and this (according to Chinese) is generally good. 'B' blood people are believed to be modest, hardworking and so on. (Japanese, however, say they are lazy and untidy!) 'A' blood people are said to be arrogant, aggressive and preoccupied with efficiency. If you fold your napkin neatly, your fellow diners may conclude that your blood type is 'A'. The Chinese often claim that the 'A' group-dominant countries such as Germany and Japan support the stereotype!

'AB' is a mixture of both and definitions of these people seem to be dependent on nothing more than opinion and a combination of the 'A' and 'B'.

Europeans and Africans have high numbers of 'O' group people. According to some, 'O' people like leadership and tend to be trustworthy, loyal types.

GLOSSARY

节日 **jiājié** festival
传说 **chuánshuō** legend
传统 **chuántǒng** tradition
神话 **shénhuà** mythology
圣诞节 **Shèngdàn Jié** Christmas
齋月 **Zhāi Yuè** Ramadan
晚会 **wǎnhuì** party
历法 **lìfǎ** calendar
符号 **fúhào** symbolism

占梦 **zhànmèng** dream divination
占星 **zhànxīng** astrology
迷信 **míxìn** superstition
民俗 **mínsú** folklore, customs
我(不)相信 ＿＿＿。 **Wǒ (bù) xiāngxìn** ＿＿＿. I (don't) believe [in] ＿＿＿.
幸运 **xìngyùn** lucky
晦气 **huìqì** unlucky

Drums and dragons make a Chinese festival

Taking it further

Books

A Dictionary of Chinese Symbols: Hidden Symbols in Chinese Life and Thought, Wolfram Eberhardt, Routledge, 1986. The key to reading Chinese culture is an understanding of its symbols. This book is well illustrated and its simple definitions make it very accessible to novice and expert.

The Chinese Pakua: An Exposé, Ong Hean Tah, Pelanduk Publications, 1991. An in-depth examination of one of the most central (and complicated) components of Chinese mysticism.

Websites

Links to thousands of sites covering every aspect of Chinese mysticism. Probably the best site on the web: http://www.zhouyi.com

Feng shui, articles, supplies and links. A good site if you are serious about feng shui: http://www.hawkfeather.com/fs.html

Includes history, background and *I Ching*:
http://www.chinese.astrology.com

Designed to attract tourists but contains some good information and photographs of the major festivals:
http://www.peacock.tnjc.edu.tw/ADD/TOUR/keep.html

More festival information and pictures (from the Taiwanese government): http://www.gio.gov.tw/info/culture/cultur16.html

5 | LITERATURE

Background

As we saw in Chapter 2, China is the only country in the world that uses the same written language as it did more than 3,000 years ago. The reason for this is the use of characters, not letters. Many characters represent ideas (ideographs) and so need not be sounded to convey meaning. The continuity of the written language has affected the development of Chinese literature profoundly in that style and content remained very consistent despite the span of centuries.

Throughout the history of traditional Chinese society, writing had to have graphical appeal so characters in handwriting or in print were chosen for aesthetic as well as semantic reasons. Consequently, the art of calligraphy enjoyed great prestige and for at least 16 centuries it was regarded as a fine art, comparable to painting in European culture.

Books and Chinese culture

Learned Chinese were true bibliophiles, their love of knowledge necessitated a deep respect for books. The earliest books were

Books wrapped in traditional manner

written on tablets of flattened bamboo and proved quite robust. After the invention of paper, books became much easier to handle and quicker and cheaper to produce. The invention of this new medium (paper) was critical to the intellectual development of the country. It led not only to increased literacy, but also to a more widespread distribution of books. This may be another reason why Chinese civilisation was in many ways far ahead of others in the ancient world.

During the Sui Dynasty (581 to 618 AD) block-type printing was invented. This worked by carving negative images of the characters into a page-sized wooden block. When this was inked, it acted like a rubber stamp. Before 745 AD, books were bound in leaves, thereafter they were kept wound in rolls. In the Middle Ages, books became similar to those found in China today. They were held together by stitches and the volumes were stacked to make a box effect that was covered with cloth and tied for protection. Movable type came into use in the 11th century, but mechanical printing was not invented by the Chinese, as is often thought. The Chinese did, however, make the world's first encyclopaedia. It appeared almost a century before its European rival and was four times the size of the *Encyclopaedia Britannica*.

Subject matter

China has a very deep literary past. The oldest writings consisted of philosophical and religious pieces and Chinese characters have been associated with mysticism ever since oracle bones were used in divination. It was believed that reciting passages from the *I-Ching* (see Chapter 4) or *The Great Learning* (大学 **Dà Xué**) could ward off evil spirits. So strong was the belief in the sacred nature of writing that people often slept with copies of such books under their pillows. The correct way of disposing of a book was said to be through fire, an idea the first emperor of China would take a little too far!

The works of Confucius are the heart of Chinese literature and these were based on early essays on the organisation of society, laws and politics. Literature was, for the greater part of Chinese history, largely reserved for the writing of such serious material. Confucius advocated that history, philosophy, poetry and calligraphy should be the material of writing. Anything else simply debased the art.

Despite this, novels and dramas dealing with all manner of subjects emerged and even thrived in later dynasties.

History writing

This was the primary function of the written language and the core of Chinese literature. Confucius taught that the lessons of history should be remembered when assessing the present or planning the future. Consequently history writing (and rewriting) became an obsession with leaders and scholars alike. After the fall of every dynasty (and sometimes after the fall of emperors within dynasties) history was rewritten. A 'grand history' of the former dynasty was commissioned and scholars made sure that the contents did not offend their masters.

In 213 BC, the first emperor of China, Qin Shihuang (see Chapter 1), ordered the burning of all books which appeared to threaten him – 焚书坑儒 **Fénshū Kēngrú**. This was the most significant event in early Chinese literature. Most of the books written before this time were either destroyed or had to be pieced together at a later date.

The most famous author of Chinese history is **Sīmǎ Qiān** 司马迁 who could be likened to a Chinese Herodotus (i.e. the 'father of history'). His book *Records of the Historian* 史记 **Shǐjì** is the most famous account of early Chinese history and is an invaluable insight into life in those early times. It was finished in about 85 BC and took 18 years to write. Much of it is apocryphal (part-myth) as it contains accounts of events that occurred in the previous 2,000 years. It is still highly important not only as a record, but as a model which provided the format for history writing up until the 20th century.

Ironically, much of Chinese history is poorly documented, largely because scholars chose what to record on the basis of compatibility with Confucian standards. Hence, the lives of ordinary people and the day-to-day running of society were neglected as subject matter. The diaries of foreigners (typically Jesuit priests, traders and monks from nearby countries) provide the best source of this kind of information. Similar to churches in Europe, temples also kept records, but few have survived.

Philosophy

Given that the connection between the written word and supernatural forces was so important to the early Chinese, it is not surprising that many of the greatest pieces of literature were philosophical. Despite many thousands of surviving texts on such subjects, a single book stands at the centre of all Chinese philosophy.

The *I-Ching*/*Book of Changes* (易经 Yì Jīng)

We looked at this briefly in Chapter 3, but since it is the cornerstone of the bulk of Chinese mysticism and the most original piece of Chinese literature, it is worth another mention.

Because of the many hexagrams (pairs of trigrams) and their attached definitions, it was thought at one time that this book was actually some kind of elaborate dictionary, defining a long-dead language. This was partly correct since it does attempt to describe a language, albeit not a human one, but the mysterious language of the forces that govern the universe. Its subject is the intricate workings of the cosmos (the 'Dao' if you like) and its definitions are appropriately abstract.

In an effort to explain its complex images, Confucius spent much of his life adding commentaries to the book (it was in existence long before he was born) and scholars have added to it continuously over the centuries. To the Chinese mind, it occupies a place similar to the Old Testament in western cultures (one reason being it took a similar length of time to write).

The starting point of the book was a collection of 64 pairs of trigrams (hexagrams). These are based on the yin and yang: yin is a broken line and yang a solid line. There are 64 symbols because this number represents all possible combinations of the system and reflects all the various manifestations of the Dao/cosmos.

To each hexagram is attached a title, a judgement, an image and an interpretation. The judgement shows the course of action appropriate to the hexagrams. The interpretation gives a few poetic lines to clarify the judgement, which is often obscure. The image interprets the hexagram, again in language that is difficult to understand.

Together, the three texts give answers to questions concerning the present, past and future. To arrive at the answer, the diviner had to perform an elaborate ritual involving the use of 50 fortune sticks. The way these fell would reveal a reading which supposedly had relevance to the questioner's situation.

The following hexagram is the first of the 64, all the lines are unbroken and so it represents the ultimate symbol of yang energy. The many commentaries that were tagged on after the judgement and the image helped the enquirer interpret an answer to his question:

Qian: The Creative

The Judgement
The Creative works sublime success.
Furthering through perseverance.

The Image
The movement of heaven is full of power.
Thus the superior man makes himself strong and untiring.

Nowadays, there are simpler methods of accessing the *I-Ching*, such as computer programs, but the readings are still basically the same.

The book was used by every influential Chinese thinker, including **Lao Zi** (the founder of Daoism, see Chapter 3) who drew some of his more profound conclusions from this source. The book is still used all over the Asian world, where it continues to influence business and politics. Some very powerful Japanese financial and political figures are known to consult the *I-Ching* before every important decision.

Recently, many good books have come out which claim to make the *I-Ching* accessible to the lay person and I recommend some of these in the bibliography since the *I-Ching* is not an easy read, having baffled even the greatest Chinese minds for centuries!

The *Dào Dé Jīng* 道德经

This is the original text of Daoist philosophy, supposedly penned by the mysterious figure of Lao Zi (see Chapter 3). The book contains only a small number of verses, each one illustrating the magnificent complexity of the Dao and the humble simplicity required to be at one with it.

It is also a very beautiful (if a little perplexing) poem with a mystical atmosphere that can be appreciated as much in English, as in the original Chinese:

The Way

The Way that can be spoken of is not the true Way;
The world that can be constructed is not true.
The Way manifests all that happens and may happen;
The world represents all that exists and may exist.
To experience without intention is to sense the world;
To experience with intention is to anticipate the world.
These two experiences are indistinguishable;
Their construction differs but their effect is the same.

Beyond the gate of experience flows the Way,
Which is ever greater and more subtle than the world.

Sun Zi's *Art of War* (孙子兵法 **Sūn Zǐ Bīngfǎ**)

In recent years, diluted interpretations of this book have made their way to the bookshelves of millions of yuppies and middle managers. Despite the New Age hype, it is still a book on military strategy and the philosophy it is often famed for amounts to little more than tactics and common sense (occupy the high ground, outnumber your enemy for example). Its 'oriental' flavour brought it a cult following among certain businessmen and influential people, but really it does not attempt to tackle anything deeper than warfare. People with an interest in history and military technique will find this book very insightful.

Poetry (诗 Shī)

The history of Chinese poetry is very long. The classics of Confucius contain a book of poetry, *The Book of Songs* 诗经 **Shī Jīng**, but this was compiled centuries before Confucius' time. Confucius gave poetry to his students to study because he saw the poems and songs as very illustrative of the sentiments of ordinary people. It is said that this was the very reason the book was put together: leaders wanted to know the feelings of common folk and so sent agents to record their songs.

Confucius' recommendation of poetry as a valid art form ensured that for the following two millennia the greatest minds in China would try their hands.

Early poetry

The Book of Songs consists of 305 poems describing the lives of ordinary people, their jobs, joys, sorrows, toil and duties in war. During the Warring States period, romantic poetry emerged. This dealt with patriotic themes as well as mystical images of paradises in the afterlife. In the Han Dynasty, a style of poetry using five-character lines developed. While both these periods were healthy in terms of famous poets and good poetry, they are not comparable to the Tang Dynasty.

The Tang Dynasty (618 to 907 AD)

This is the uncontested golden age of Chinese poetry. The greatest anthology of Tang poetry contains almost 50,000 poems. In only 300 years, Tang poets had produced more than all the poets in the 2,000 years before them. Not only is the period great for its number of poems but also for its forms, imagery and range of themes.

This age brought a blossoming in many aspects of Chinese civilisation, not only poetry. Some people rightly wonder why any particular age should be so much more fruitful than preceding or subsequent periods. In the case of the Tang Dynasty, there are a few important reasons behind the golden age.

Sui Dynasty emperors had begun the imperial examination system (科举 **kējǔ**) to select officials from among scholars. In the Tang Dynasty, the children of many rich families studied poetry to sit these tests.

The coexistence of the three teachings gave space for freedom of thought. Hence, there was much material and imagery at the poet's disposal.

A unified country meant that scholars could travel far and wide, learning from different styles on the way.

Thanks to the Silk Road (丝调之路 **Sīchóuzīlú**), influence from western and Central Asia did much to enrich Chinese culture in this period.

Most poets liked to write about the conditions of the country and the lives of normal people. The treasury of Tang poetry is inexhaustible, but there are two poets who are particularly well known to most Chinese people. They are **Li Bai** and **Du Fu**.

Lǐ Bái 李白 (701 to 762 AD) was born not in China but in Central Asia, since his ancestors had been sent there for disobedience to Sui Dynasty rulers. He moved to **Sìchuān** 四川 with his merchant father and began to study the Confucian classics as well as other texts. As a young man he travelled widely but never took the civil service examinations. Nonetheless, at the age of 42 he was given a minor posting in the capital **Cháng'ān** 长安, but found the experience disappointing. He was jailed briefly during a rebellion but survived and died much later at the age of 62. He wrote around 900 poems describing people's lives, natural scenery and his own wishes and sorrows. He is without doubt the favourite poet of the Chinese people:

Drinking Alone With the Moon
From a pot of wine among the flowers
I drank alone. There was no one with me –
Till, raising my cup, I asked the bright moon
To bring me my shadow and make us three.
Alas, the moon was unable to drink
And my shadow tagged me vacantly;
But still for a while I had these friends
To cheer me through the end of spring.

I sang. The moon encouraged me.
I danced. My shadow tumbled after.
As long as I knew, we were boon companions.
And then I was drunk, and we lost one another.

Shall goodwill ever be secure?
I watch the long road of the River of Stars.

Dù Fǔ 杜甫 (712 to 770 AD) was born in **Hénán** 河南 and from childhood was a fanatical reader. He too travelled the length and breadth of the country. At the age of 35 he settled in **Cháng'ān** 长安 and tried to get a government post. His many attempts were unsuccessful and his disappointment led him to sympathise with the poor and downtrodden members of society. He wrote poetry about the hardships faced by ordinary people, frequently contrasting these with the excesses of the rich. His poems are sometimes referred to as 'poetic history' since they are not only similar to a chronicle of everyday life, but also describe a number of political and military situations of the period. His trademark was realism and he pushed this to new heights:

A View Of The Wilderness

Snow is white on the westward mountains and on three fortified towns,
And waters in this southern lake flash on a long bridge.
But wind and dust from sea to sea bar me from my brothers;
And I cannot help crying, I am so far away.
I have nothing to expect now but the ills of old age.
I am of less use to my country than a grain of dust.
I ride out to the edge of town. I watch on the horizon,
Day after day, the chaos of the world.

Calligraphy (书法 Shūfǎ)

This is the last of the four literary arts that formed the standard curriculum for scholars in the imperial era. To the Chinese, calligraphy means much more than elegant, stylised writing, the way it is in most western cultures. Calligraphy reflects something much deeper than skill with a brush. It was believed that calligraphy had a spiritual dimension since the scholar was bound to conform to the defined nature of language, but free through calligraphy to express both himself and the essence of the message being communicated.

To become skilful, scholars had to practise every character and every stroke within it, over and over again. Just as in **qi gong** or other forms of meditation, dedicated practice allowed people to be free of worldly worries. Through calligraphy, it is said that people can achieve higher levels of patience and concentration, ultimately these bring expanded states of spiritual awareness or a feeling of oneness with the Dao.

Calligraphy today is still considered to be a semi-spiritual discipline. It is thought that it is possible to keep fit and relax through regular practice. In both China and Japan, expert calligraphers were renowned for their long lives. Non-Chinese can appreciate calligraphy too: the ability to read the meaning of the characters is not important, as much writing is so stylised, even Chinese have difficulty reading it. Calligraphy is essentially an abstract art and so it is unnecessary to ask 'what does this mean?' as the form alone can be enjoyed and that is actually the whole point of the art.

Novels (小说 Xiǎoshuō)

The Chinese word for this kind of writing means 'small talk' and it reflects the attitude of most scholars (orthodox Confucianists by definition) toward fiction. Despite never gaining respectability on a par with the four Confucian disciplines, Chinese fiction flourished and many of the great books remain entertaining even by modern standards.

Towards the end of the Yuan (Mongol) Dynasty, one of China's greatest epics was written, *The Romance of the Three Kingdoms* 三国演义 **Sānguó Yǎnyì**. Up until this point, fiction, although healthy, had not reached such a level of sophistication. The same author, **Luó Guànzhōng** 罗贯中 (1330 to 1400?), is also said to have written another highly important book, *The Water Margin* 水浒传 **Shuǐ Hǔ Zhuàn** (sometimes called *All Men are Brothers*). This book fared well in post-1949 China when many others were banned or censored. The reason being that the semi-historical story is about a band of outlaws and their opposition to the old political system (presumably the authorities likened the bandits to themselves and the tyrant rulers to the former Nationalist government!).

Fiction made its greatest advances in the Ming Dynasty (1368 to 1644). The period is full of outstanding vernacular literature (stories written in everyday language). Perhaps the most famous example is *The Monkey King*, the tale of the Monkey God, **Sūn Wùkōng** 孙悟空 who, after causing trouble in heaven, has to protect the monk Tripitaka (**Xuán Zàng** 玄奘) who is going to India to bring back some sacred scriptures. Along the way they are joined by Pigsy, who is half-man half-pig, and Sandy, a river god. Together they overcome many difficult situations and enemies. The story is more accurately called *Journey to the West* 西游记 **Xī Yóu Jì** and was written by **Wú Chéng'ēn** 吴承恩. Perhaps because of the action and strange mythology involved, it is still very popular today, in translation, comic book and TV series form.

The Ming Dynasty also produced China's most erotic and romantic masterpieces. *The Golden Lotus* 金瓶梅 **Jīn Píng Méi** is the most well known example of such writing and was considered extremely risqué until very recently.

The Qing Dynasty (1644 to 1911) was far less productive. Stories about the supernatural were popular, but the most famous novel is without doubt *The Dream of the Red Chamber* **Hóng Lóu Mèng** 红楼梦 by **Cáo Xuěqín** 曹雪芹 (1715 to 63?). It concerns the doomed love of two young people against the backdrop of a powerful family in steady decline. Although written in an easy to read vernacular, it is still a very lengthy piece and far too detailed to make light reading for most modern readers.

Modern literature

The May Fourth Movement of 1919 marked a watershed in Chinese literature. Disgruntled intellectuals campaigned for the introduction of a readable written language to make literature accessible to everyday people. This, they claimed, was the first step towards shaking off the immense baggage of history that was depriving China of the kind of enlightenment that had catapulted western countries so far ahead.

Magazines were the vanguard of the uprising. *New Youth* 新青年 **Xīn Qīngnián** was particularly avant-garde and published some of the very first major pieces of writing in the new vernacular language, **Bái Huà** 白话.

1919: literary renaissance

Several great writers gave tremendous momentum to the changes. One of the most famous writers who emerged to put their weight behind the cause was **Lǔ Xùn** 鲁迅. His story *Diary of a Mad Man* (狂人日记 **Kuángrén Rìjì**) published in *New Youth*, was a masterpiece of satire, a witty attack on the traditional system that was believed to be holding China back. His later book *The Story of Ah Q* (阿Q正传 **Ah Q Zhèngzhuàn**) delivered a similar message, this time attacking the conservative tendencies of the political elite of the time.

Early writing such as this was the foundation of the realist style which was to characterise the beginnings of the new literature in China. For this reason, Lu Xun came to be known as the father of modern Chinese literature.

Newspapers were the platform for more and more groundbreaking literature and were hastily consumed by the masses of optimistic Chinese youth and intellectuals. Very soon a split occurred dividing writers and their periodicals into two separate camps: *Creationist Society*

(创造社 **Chuàngzào Shè**) /romantic school, versus the art-for-life's-sake *Literary Research Society* (文学研究会 **Wénxué Yánjiū Huì**).

Before long, such periodicals became the vehicles of competing ideologies that had flooded into the country to fill the vacuum left by the collapse of the Qing Dynasty. When leading figures of the bigger Literary Research Society began converting to Socialism, many of the nation's intellectuals became sympathetic to the cause of the Communists.

Despite the split, none of the writers' efforts went to waste. Both schools contributed to the virtually overnight development of a new literary style and succeeded in decisively burying the antiquated literary style of imperial China.

1920s and 1930s

This was a turbulent time in Chinese history. Conflicting ideologies clashed continually both in the streets and on paper. Even anarchism had a foothold, but the majority of China's intellectuals had more moderate liberal leanings and Socialism won their support. Literature in general took on a heavily politicised character. More and more students returned from study overseas and brought with them ideas from the many countries they had experienced, such as the USA, Britain and Japan.

The Japanese invasion of Manchuria (northeast China) brought forth an explosion of patriotic literature, as many young novelists were forced south. Poetry also changed dramatically, influenced heavily by the political tensions of the day.

Despite politics, or perhaps because of it, fiction reigned supreme in the 1930s. The art of the short story and the modern novel had been established by the May Fourth pioneers but continued to mature, bearing the most fruit less than two decades later. Social issues were the favourite subject matter of the greatest writers of the period including **Máo Dùn** 茅盾, author of the most famous novel of the time, *The Family* (家 **Jiā**), an autobiographical piece which attacked the traditional family system.

The war years

During the war against the Japanese, most writers retreated far inland to escape the fighting. Most of the countryside was firmly under

Communist control and many writers were employed to produc patriotic Socialist literature and fill magazines and newspapers with plays, poems and news from the various fronts.

Many famous authors such as Mao Dun, **Bā Jīn** 巴金 (a forme anarchist) and the female writer **Dīng Líng** 丁玲 continued to produc good work throughout the war years. Ding Ling became China's firs influential Socialist/realist novelist. Her books have been the materia of many researchers interested in the situation of women during thi period.

The Mao era

Many Chinese writers saw it as their duty to help the new Communis government. Mao called for a new patriotic literature and, following the example of the Soviet Union, proclaimed that literature should serve the people (the 'broad masses'). The role of writers would be to capitalise on the increasing popularity of literature to deliver politica messages. It was suggested that writing should come from and go to people from all walks of ordinary life (soldiers, workers and peasants). In keeping with the Soviet model, society would be carefully described in terms of what it should be, rather than how it was.

This ideological filter produced **Socialist Realism** (社会主义现实主义 **Shèhuìzhǔyì Xiànshízhǔyì**), which was really just another form o propaganda. Few of the May Fourth writers who had lasted the cours were prepared for this new realism and were quickly carted off fo re-education during the Cultural Revolution. If literature ran counte to the proletariat ideal of the day, even famous writers like Ding Lin quickly found themselves in trouble.

The reform era

Following the death of Mao, many writers who had suffered bu survived the Cultural Revolution were brought back and 'rehabilitated' The censorship of the Mao era was slowly eased. The first sign o liberalisation came in the form of *Scar Literature*, which describe the hardships and suffering of people (real and invented) during the mayhem of the previous decades. Translated literature began to floo in as it had done at the beginning of the century and, before long writers were sensing a new literary revolution in the pipeline.

Today's Chinese literature

In the Socialist scheme of things, the arts and media are the voice of the party and alternative, nagging, critical or independent writing is by default subversive. As we have already seen, the rate of change in China has been and continues to be tremendous. Despite a brief lapse during the Cultural Revolution, overall change in most aspects of Chinese life has been rapid and dramatic. Today's Chinese writing shows the victory of supply and demand over censorship as well as a reflection of current trends in popular taste.

State control

To be granted publication, a book must first pass the official organ of censorship, the State General Press and Publications Administration (SGPPA), which sits directly beneath the Propaganda Department of the Party Central Committee. While there are many hundreds of publishers in the country, all are controlled by the SGPPA, which has a department in every province in China. The state-run **Xīnhuá** 新华 book company controls most of the bookshops in China and the government is therefore (in theory) able to regulate the production and sale of everything in print.

Not only is material carefully examined for 'spiritual pollution' and 'incorrect' information, but writers themselves are screened too. Once admitted to the Chinese Writers' Association, they are salaried, housed, insured and pensioned. Therefore, to write anything even slightly controversial is a very big gamble that few writers are willing to take.

All manuscripts must have SGPPA approval to obtain a **shūhào** 书号 book number. This is a registration number, which in 1987 became China's own ISBN system. Without such a number, no book may be printed legally. This creates a very effective form of information control and, until recently, made it virtually impossible for writers to make a living outside the system. This system of book production is known as the 'red route'. Throughout the 1980s and 1990s however, state control over book publishing and consequently censorship weakened by the month.

The black route

In the late 1980s, hundreds of lowbrow titles started to flood the market and put major cracks in the state system of control. Among the most popular types of book were those which featured controversial subjects.

Outside the red route, there are two other ways to get such unofficial books made and sold. The first is the semi-legal way – the 'white route'. This refers to the lesser scam of private entrepreneurs who acquire official permission to print, but secretly branch out to cater to more extreme tastes.

For entrepreneurs and fly-by-nights who have money and contacts, there is another, third channel through which to get a book printed and make buckets of money: the 'black route'. This refers to the shady network of underground printers, distributors and deal makers who publish anything racy enough to grab the attention of the book buyer. They operate without any censorship whatsoever and have profited massively from plugging the vast hole left by the official market.

The people behind this business are known as **shū wáng** 书王 book kings. The illegal book business seems extremely profitable, so much so that the book kings get bolder and their books get more daring almost by the week.

Non-fiction

In the late 1980s **nèibù** 内部 became the genre of choice for book kings. The name means 'internal department' and refers to pieces written by the government for internal distribution only. Such material is not really literature as such, since it consists mostly of government documents, translations of foreign views on Chinese affairs and criticisms of leaders and past actions of the party. Nonetheless, it filled pages and sold like hot cakes.

Since the mid-1990s political books were less likely to make a black route best seller. How-to books became very popular. Titles like *How to Improve your Sex Life* or *How to Improve Your Home* were churned out to hungry readers by the legal and illegal cartload.

Book kings uncovered a gold mine catering to the public's reawakening taste for fortune telling, fashion, the occult, pop music and scandal. Towards the end of the 1990s, they were raking it in from sales of books that claimed to reveal the secrets of successful capitalism. Books about stocks and shares, playing the money markets and gambling continue to sell well today.

Currently, other popular types of book are those which cover the more taboo topics. Nowadays, popular illegal titles are very adult in nature. Copies of Japanese adult magazines are a particularly profitable line, as are raunchy 'true-life stories' as well as the old favourite: foreigners behaving badly. Anything that deals even briefly with sex, crime or money practically flies off the bookstalls that line every major urban street.

Fiction

The legitimate press tries its best with titles such as *I Married a Foreigner* and *Terror of the Gestapo* but cannot match the book kings' list of titles in terms of sheer sensationalism. Recently, the book kings themselves have become powerful figures in the writing of popular literature. They commonly throw large sums of money at a writer to knock out a steamy novel with an eye-catching title in as little time as possible. Writers eager for money can protect their professional reputations through pen names and find their work on Beijing bookstalls a fortnight later.

In the late 1990s, one of the most successful kinds of novel was the crime story. These are written in the slang of criminals, **hēihuà** 黑话 black language, and give a good overview of the increasingly powerful culture of the **liúmáng** hooligan that has emerged in the reform period. The whole crime/violence genre has become known as **Liúmáng Wénxué** 流氓文学 hooligan literature.

The power of the black route is shown by the fact that the popularity of some of their banned titles is so great that TV adaptations have been made!

Wáng Shuò 王朔: modern China's most popular writer?

The writer who championed the hooligan genre has possibly become the most imitated and successful author of 20th-century China. His 20 novels have sold well over ten million copies despite his entire anthology being banned by the government. Many Chinese seem to relate to Wang Shuo's characters who often embody the more brutal aspects of modern urban life in China.

Wang Shuo, like many of his readers and characters, belongs to the 'lost generation' that did not see Mao's violent rise to power but whose lives were hurled mercilessly around by the Cultural Revolution.

Perhaps he took Deng Xiaoping's 'to get rich is glorious' statement a little too far since the money-loving underworld is his preferred setting and his characters are often good guys turned bad by the rat race. The language he uses is appropriately coarse and his style is very simple. This has caused some critics to label his work 'toilet literature' and call it pointless, but to many of his fans these are the very things they love him for. All his stories represent an increasingly vital commodity which modern Chinese appear to be in need of: honesty.

Unlike the government, Wang Shuo is not a dreamer or a jargon dispenser. He shows through his stories that ideals are the talk of poor people and clever people do what it takes to get and stay rich. Wang Shuo's many novels (a number of which are now available in English) give you, in a nutshell, the harsh reality of life in developing China.

Interestingly, after so much successful writing, TV dramatisations of his novels and even a trip to the USA, Wang Shuo has turned his back on worldly matters and has said he wants to retreat to the mountains and live as a monk!

Modern classics

Until the reform period, mainland authors had to be very careful that their work did not offend the authorities. Consequently, post-1949 masterpieces are relatively few and far between. Mo Yan's *Red Sorghum* is one example of a novel that could be called a classic. So few, however, contain the combination of story, political correctness and style that for the best of modern Chinese literature, English-language writing should not be overlooked.

In the early 1990s Jung Chang's *Wild Swans* was a worldwide sensation. The story, the overlapping biographies of three generations of Chinese women, set against the upheaval of China in the 20th century, could not fail as a recipe for success. The style is as straightforward as it gets, but the blend of contradictions, tradition and modern, repression and 'liberation', makes it a fascinating read. The book spawned dozens of imitations, many of them as good if not better.

GLOSSARY

书 **shū** book
翰 **hàn** brush
墨 **mò** ink
翰墨 **hànmò** the scholarly arts (writing, calligraphy and painting)
文学 **wénxué** literature
诗 **shī** poetry
故事 **gùshi** story
作家 **zuòjiā** author
印刷 **yìnshuā** printing
写 **xiě** write
看 **kàn** read
稗官野史 **bìguān yěshǐ** book of anecdotes

正史 **zhèngshǐ** history in the style of biography
传记 **zhuànjì** biography
自传 **zìzhuàn** autobiography
日记 **rìjì** diary
经典 **jīngdiǎn** classics
真实的故事 **zhēnshíde gùshi** true story
我（不）喜欢看 _____。 **Wǒ (bù) xǐhuān kàn _____.** I (don't) like reading _____.
我（不）写 _____。 **Wǒ (bù) xiě _____.** I (don't) write _____.
我看得/不懂。 **Wǒ kàn (bù) dǒng.** I (don't) understand.

Taking it further

Books

Anthologies

An Anthology of Chinese Literature – Beginnings to 1911, Stephen Owen (ed.), W.W. Norton & Co., 1996. The most substantial collection around.

The Columbia Anthology of Modern Chinese Literature, A. Joseph, S.M. Lau and H. Goldblatt, Columbia University Press, 1995. The best of modern Chinese writing inside a single cover.

Seeds of Fire – Chinese Voices of Conscience, G. Barme and J. Minford, Bloodaxe Books, 1996. Post-Tiananmen short stories, poems and articles. Very good.

Seven Contemporary Women Writers, Ru Zhijuan, Panda Books, 1994. A rare anthology of (inoffensive) sentiments, published in China but written in English.

Poetry

The Songs of the South – An Ancient Anthology of Poems, Qu Yuan and other Poets, Penguin Classics, 1985.

Five Hundred Years of Chinese Poetry 1150 to 1650, Yoshikawa Kojiro, Princeton University Press, 1989.

Novels

Playing for Thrills, Wang Shuo, Penguin, 1998. His first translation into English.

The Joy Luck Club, Amy Tan, Putnam, 1989. A very popular title dealing with the emotional issues between first generation American Chinese and their immigrant parents.

Soursweet, Timothy Mo, Random House, 1985. Chinese immigrants adjusting to life in Britain; humourous and sad.

Memoirs/biographies

Wild Swans, Jung Chang, Anchor World Views, 1992.

Life and Death in Shanghai, Nien Cheng, Penguin USA, 1988. An oft-forgotten pre-*Wild Swans* classic.

Colours of the Mountain, Da Chen, Heinemann, 1999. Life in China in the 1960s and 1970s.

The Soong Dynasty, Sterling Seagrave, Corgi Books, 1996. Not a Chinese writer, but a truly wonderful book. The biography of one of the most influential Chinese families ever. Chinese history and traditional culture combined, told through the remarkable story of a modern dynasty.

Websites

A website and periodical devoted to translating modern and historical literature. Includes an enormous database of authors:
http://www.renditions.org/renditions/index.html

Three hundred Tang poems, the entire text of *Dream of the Red Chamber* and much more. In English and Chinese:
http://etext.virginia.edu/chinese/

6 | ENTERTAINMENT

Theatre

When Chinese think of 'theatre', western-style plays do not come to mind. Historically, the Chinese have no comparable theatrical system. The stage and drama consists of opera i.e. Chinese opera, which is very different from European opera and drama.

Plays (spoken drama) are a recent foreign import. Spoken plays (**huàjù** 话剧) began in the early part of the 20th century. Its most successful periods of development coincide with those times when

Beijing opera

interest in western culture was at a high point, the 1930s and 1940s for example. It was also most popular in places such as Shanghai, where foreign influence was most visible.

Spoken drama began around the time of the May Fourth Movement (1919 – see Chapter 1). Its rapid development was due mostly to the work of a single playwright, **Cáo Yú** 曹禺 (1906 to 1996). As we saw in literature, many intellectuals were looking to foreign sources for ideas and the first stage of Chinese drama reflected this. Throughout the 1920s most major productions were translations or adaptations of foreign plays, those by Shakespeare and Chekhov being particular favourites.

Chinese playwrights inserted token common people into the figures of the main characters and this simple idea earned the art many fans since Chinese audiences were unused to seeing ordinary people having their lives portrayed on stage.

Drama as propaganda

The turbulent political scene in the 1950s and 1960s gave playwrights little opportunity to extend their art beyond propaganda plays. During the War of Resistance (against Japan) the medium was a very effective vehicle for propaganda. Dramatic troupes representing Nationalists and Communists travelled the countryside spreading patriotic messages. Since spoken dramas needed very few props and costumes and stages could be easily improvised, they were highly economical and could be staged with minimal preparation almost anywhere.

Following the Communists' takeover of the country in 1949, drama, like all the other arts, had to meet very special criteria in order to serve the people. As in literature, Socialist Realism (propaganda) demanded that plays support some policy or espouse some kind of Socialist virtue. In the 1950s Mao turned on many intellectuals, accusing them of 'counter-revolutionary' sentiment and this foreshadowed the paranoia that would come into full force during the Cultural Revolution.

In this period (1966 to 1976), all the arts were heavily censored and only those that were fully compatible with the ideal of the hour did not land their performers and writers in deep trouble. Playwrights have since described the period as a kind of 'artistic holocaust'. During the Cultural Revolution, **Jiāng Qīng** 江青 (Mao's wife) was the unofficial authority over all the arts but she targeted the theatre in particular (perhaps because she had herself been a second-rate actress at one time). She banned all productions that did not have Mao or Maoism as their central theme. Eventually, only five model works were permitted, all of which recounted heroic tales of the revolution.

Post-Cultural Revolution conditions

After 1976, performing arts companies were among the first to feel the effects of economic reform. The 'iron rice-bowl' (guaranteed income) was withdrawn and companies had their funding cut by an average of 70%. They function today along the wobbly lines of other failing state-owned industries: overstaffed and underproductive. To keep alive they have invested in all sorts of profitable ventures: running restaurants, dubbing companies or making commercials for TV.

Drama today

After Mao's death, theatre began again. The 1970s and 1980s saw more and more foreign works being adapted to the stage (Arthur Miller's *Death of a Salesman*, for example). There is a long tradition of attacking politics through the arts in China and this resurfaced in the 1980s. Playwrights became increasingly bold in their satires and the pointed Social Realism of many popular plays indicated that playwrights and audiences were increasingly disillusioned with many features of modern life.

Drama in the 1990s had less and less importance. As sales of television sets soared and the effects of capitalist forces were felt in many more sections of society, plays had diminished impact. Writers today are unable to attract people away from the glitzy TV commercials and foreign action films that are engaging most of the urban populace.

The government is still providing funds for some authorised productions and these are the bread and butter of many playwrights because, even if they play to empty theatres, there is still a wage packet (albeit a barely adequate one) at the end of the month.

There are, however, a handful of surviving writers who make a meagre living from fringe theatre, but even their titles have to attract increasingly TV-desensitised audiences (as everywhere). In the mid-1990s there was a brief spell of plays that went along the lines of: foreign businessman comes to China, meets a mystical and beautiful

Chinese woman and abandons the vain materialistic American woman back home. This kind of play gets in audiences because many are enchanted by the idea of escaping to foreign lands on the back of Chinese know-how and virtue. There are also the familiar old themes of perceived western (materialistic) society in contrast with the poorer (but infinitely more cultured) east. Such dramas (books, films and TV series) exploit these themes since Chinese audiences seem thirsty for confirmation of stereotypes not reality and there are many young writers who will tailor their art form accordingly. *Woman Left Behind* is one of the better products of this theme (discussed later).

Famous Chinese plays

There are a small number of plays that say a great deal about life in China in the last century. They were and are still famous. They reflect the shifting preferences of audiences as well as the political atmosphere of their times. Recent plays, too, are revealing of current topics of interest to millions of ordinary Chinese.

Cao Yu's first piece *Thunderstorm* (**Léiyǔ** 雷雨) was staged in 1934 and was very successful. The story alone filled theatres: the impending doom of an incestuous industrialist family. This play forces the audience to see the Socialist view of wealth as corrupting and ultimately self-destructive. At that time, many intellectuals were being attracted to Socialism in one form or another. It was popularly and critically acclaimed from the opening night and Cao Yu's subsequent works such as *Sunrise* (**Rìchū** 日出) were equally well received over the next few years.

In 1935, *Sunrise* played to a population becoming increasingly drawn to Socialism. This play contrasts the suffering of the honourable poor with the indulgencies of the idle and corrupt rich. It centres on the archetypal figure of feudal society, the courtesan. At first she lives it up in the city but after a series of tragedies, the death of her patron and a young friend whom she tries to save from a life of prostitution, she kills herself. The Communists loved this play as it clearly showed the futility of chasing non-Socialist ideals. Even during the Anti-Rightist Campaign of the 1950s this play was widely performed and considered very politically correct.

Teahouse (**Cháguǎn** 茶馆) is probably the most famous of all the plays by Chinese playwrights so far. The writer **Lǎo Shě** 老舍 sets this modern three-act play in a teahouse in Beijing that acts as a meeting point for a wide variety of characters. The play's time period covers the final years of the Qing Dynasty up to 1948. Through its characters, the battle between past and future / tradition and change is played out, a dialogue that had obsessed Chinese writers and artists since the turn of the century.

Chinese rulers customarily used history to justify their right to power, showing that their claim was not only valid, but also inevitable. With this in mind, it is easy to see why the Communist Party approved of this play since it appears to serve this purpose nicely. Despite the politics that are associated with it, it is one of very few Chinese works that have been performed in many foreign countries.

The Woman Left Behind (**Liúshǒu Nǚshì** 留守女士) premiered in 1991 at the People's Art Theatre in Shanghai. It is a rather experimental and long play but has nonetheless become one of the most successful of recent years. The story is about a young couple whose partners have joined the thousands of Chinese settling in Japan, the USA and elsewhere. The man and woman fall in love just when he receives his visa to visit his wife in the USA. The woman becomes pregnant and the ending is, of course, very touching. The success of this play indicates the enduring desire of Chinese to move abroad but also acknowledges the painful severing of ties required to make such a move. Sentimentality and emotional themes have become big sellers and all the popular arts have been quick to inject this ingredient and reap the payback.

Film (电影 Diànyǐng)

Film is without doubt a window into any culture. Millions of Chinese are avid moviegoers. Since the economic reforms of the 1980s, foreign films have become particularly popular and, with more and more titles being passed for viewing, they are playing to increasingly packed houses. Recent Chinese films are definitely more popular with critics abroad than with domestic audiences. Chinese audiences are attracted to the flashy and sexy images of American movies much more than they are to the poignant, slow, subtle and comparatively uneventful films made by most mainland directors.

Cinemas (电影院 Yǐngyuàn)

Chinese cinemas show a mixture of both national and international (that is, Hollywood) films. Ticket prices are generally pretty low. There are a variety of seats available. The cinema is a date place for many couples and the theatres cater to this with very dark auditoria and seats with very high backs. There are also special chairs for couples to sit rather snugly together and even box-like booths at the back of many urban cinemas that can completely hide the occupants from view, if that is what they want.

In 1993, 17 billion Chinese went to the cinema. This enormous number continues to rise, despite the TV and video sets to be found in rapidly growing numbers of Chinese homes and the fact that most of the country's 800,000 peasants still see hardly any films at all. Not only is China a great cinema nation in terms of viewers, but also as one of the world's major film producers.

Five generations of filmmakers

Between the founding of the Republic in 1949 and the start of the Cultural Revolution in 1966, film production in China averaged around 35 a year. Most of these were documentary, propaganda (similar in their naivety to old Pathé newsreels) and screened plays such as *Teahouse*. During the Cultural Revolution, cinema became yet another voice for bawling out the party line. Films for the next ten years were limited to 'news' (propaganda) and model stories of Socialist man tirelessly putting the revolution before his own needs. Creativity was heavily restricted but some interesting animated films were made during this period, although these too were political. A favourite of the day was the carefully edited and revoiced foreign 'news': the slums of American cities as the consequences of the ruthless capitalist system and screaming mobs at Beatles' concerts as evidence of a brainwashed youth enslaved by enflamed passions.

Present-day filmmakers are known as the 'fifth generation'. These directors draw much more on western influences for their inspiration and techniques. The first generation refers to the dawn of Chinese cinema during the 1920s when most productions consisted of silent films of Chinese operas and very little else. These led to the development of modern drama films (really just plays before a camera) in the

1930s and 1940s – the second generation. After the founding of the new China, the third generation emerged. These directors were largely preoccupied with producing approved films to help the fledgling Communist government. As a new and powerful medium of ideological propagation, Mao and many other influential thinkers of the day were keen to see the art developed. To do this, several film schools were established, the graduates of these schools became the fourth generation.

Right up until the end of the Cultural Revolution and even into the early years of the post-Mao reforms, the fourth-generation directors strayed very little from the techniques taught to them by their Russian teachers in the 1950s. Overall, the art form had progressed very little and was rather unimaginative. The style was called 'reserved realism' and, not surprisingly, it did very little to capture the interest of the population.

Themes in modern Chinese cinema

Suddenly, in the early 1980s, things began to change. A young director, **Chén Kǎigē** 陈凯歌, produced a groundbreaking film, *The Yellow Earth* (**Huángtǔdì** 黄土地) in 1984. From the outset, it provoked controversy with Chinese officialdom. The film examines the attempts of a young Communist soldier to win over a peasant community (particularly a young girl) to the cause. He fails to do so and ultimately the girl dies trying to sail down the river to join the Communists. The film ends with the peasants praying for rain and harvest as they have done for hundreds if not thousands of years. The story implies the failure of the Communist Party, which, despite the rhetoric and propaganda, was still unable to overcome the fear of change, which is (at least according to the filmmakers) so thoroughly ingrained in the psyche of the Chinese masses. The message of this film ran in total contradiction to all that had gone before it. Its bleakness, minimal dialogue, allusions to feudal customs and the futility of pitting ideology against tradition make the film a bleak but enchanting experience.

The cameraman who shot this film, **Zhāng Yìmóu** 张艺谋, directed his own equally significant film two years later. Historical reassessment was the theme of this piece too. *Red Sorghum* (**Hóng Gāoliáng** 红高粱) is set in two critical periods of Chinese history: the civil war and the War of Resistance against the Japanese. The Chinese authorities accepted this film far more readily, especially the depiction of the peasants' revolutionary potential (they fight back against the Japanese).

Both films and many others by fifth-generation directors show the influence of European cinema, especially Truffaut, Goddard and Antonioni. Chen Kaige admitted he dreamed of completely reinventing Chinese cinema, replacing it with an arty avant-garde that would be profound and politically subversive. The 1980s saw his dream partially realised, but throughout the decade, many artists found themselves drifting gradually away from the general public. The optimism of that decade seems to have ended suddenly, following the Tiananmen crackdown. Some observers called it a period of 'cultural division'.

Soon after the 1989 trouble, many famous Chinese artists appeared to make a trade-off: culture for commercialism, but some very good films were made during the transitional period (early 1990s).

Commercial films

In the 1990s, film production began to slow: from 150 a year to fewer than 90. Chinese national cinema is definitely in decline. Directors are responding by producing big-budget films, funded from abroad but Chinese enough to sell at home too. Many famous Chinese directors have received money from Hong Kong or Japan to make films.

With much more money than they could ever raise in China, film directors are given a far freer hand (although the script of every film still has to be approved by the authorities before shooting).

Commercial films tend to be lavish and colourful but, intellectually speaking, they are rather thin on the ground. Chen Kaige's recent movie *The Emperor and the Assassin* (1999) ran up a production cost of around US $30 million. Two-thirds of this went on a replica of the Imperial Palace! The film is, of course, an epic but makers of commercial cinema often appear to have the foreign, not the domestic, audiences in mind with many of their large scale productions.

In the scramble for box office success, it seems Chinese directors will turn to the most dramatic stories for material. One particularly distasteful example is John Woo's *Nanjing 1937*, which deals with the notorious killing of Chinese civilians by Japanese soldiers. Like many commercial Chinese films, tragedy and melodrama is supposed to compensate for historical inaccuracies, bad acting and cheap special effects. Foreign viewers often come away from such films wondering why subject matter like this is not given appropriately serious attention by the film world. This is, however, only one of many examples of commercial Chinese cinema and whatever such films say about their audiences or makers, they should not be taken too seriously, because after seeing so many, few Chinese feel moved by any films at all.

Hong Kong

Since the 1960s, Hong Kong has been the heart of Chinese cinema. Their primary export, kung fu, is the only major Asian film genre to cross into mainstream cultures outside the Chinese world. In terms of sheer quantity, kung fu films outnumber even westerns. Their famously low production costs, formulaic storylines and technical simplicity made them almost incapable of losing money. In its heyday (the 1970s) the whole industry rested on a very small number of actors who appeared again and again in hundreds of films. Like any other kind of film, there were good and bad. Hong Kong had its own Warner Bros: Shaw Bros. This company made the more expensive films with lots of studio sets, fancy props, costumes and even comparatively imaginative stories! Far more entertaining, however, are the low-budget copies which feature everything the genre is famous for: bad acting, blatant copying, cardboard dialogue, speeded-up action, ridiculous sound effects and atrocious kung fu.

In the mid-1980s, directors in Hong Kong started borrowing many techniques from Hollywood to bring Chinese myths and legends alive in their films. Zombies, vampires and all sorts of strange creatures turned audiences away from their old kung fu heroes to lavish fantasy, horror and ghost stories.

The more successful films combine as many elements as possible: kung fu–horror–comedy, with a bit of romance thrown in too! Science fiction–kung fu seems to have done pretty well in the early 1990s and an enduring popular genre is the sexy action movies that follow similar lines to Japanese mafia flicks, but tend to be more action crammed.

Erotic films are today's blockbusters. Flocking into Hong Kong are thousands of Chinese who were deprived of even slightly raunchy films on the mainland and there is an enormous black market for videos of Hong Kong-made films. Sex seems to be thrown in with everything these days. Although the censorship system is still tight (similar to the British model), filmmakers are forever pushing the limits.

Just like the old kung fu movies which were wall-to-wall brawling, modern films are practically stuffed with non-stop explosions, fights, gun battles and girls!

Reading kung fu cinema!

'Serious' sinologists and critics usually ignore the whole kung fu film phenomenon, but it does say something about China and the Chinese. Today's action films are merely kung fu movies in thin disguise. All the main themes are the same. They usually centre on a noble individual who is reluctantly forced into a situation, which he (or sometimes she) has to fight his way out of. Typically, the action involves the hero/heroine battling their way through scores of lackeys, before getting to the big man himself at the end of the film. The hero will always be ridiculously outnumbered, but armed with the moral upper hand and using the skills taught to him by some honourable old master (who has probably been treacherously murdered, by the way) he overcomes the unthinking thugs who stand in his way.

The concept of the individual standing up for himself against the group is sheer fantasy to Chinese, simply because in real life it is never seen (remember Confucius and Mao?). Moreover, the hero is forced to draw on his kung fu skills to save the day. In times of trouble, the Chinese tend to refer to traditional ways. The first resort is always some attempt at pacification (the hero tries to reason with his persecutors) but the last resort is always violence, although it takes a suitably brutal killing (usually a senior such as a teacher, friend or father – filial piety?) for the hero to take this step.

Many foreigners make the premature conclusion that since there are so many violent Chinese films, the Chinese must be very aggressive or somehow obsessed with fighting, but neither is the case.

Real violence, although often seen in Chinese streets, tends not to be particularly savage, just because most people are afraid of the loss of face involved should they be hurt. Consequently, it seems to be rather ritualistic and involve a lot more shouting and gesturing than fighting. When people do fight, it is seldom two people but a group against a single person; in the movie scenario the lone hero wins. Also, most violence in kung fu films is not realistic, it is stylised to the point it resembles dancing more than fighting (most early kung fu stars were opera performers too). The majority of kung fu films are *supposed* to be unreal – that is why people can leap 20 metres into the air!

Another area to watch out for is the portrayal of foreigners in kung fu movies. It can be hilarious but a little unsettling too. The Japanese are depicted as particularly deceitful and monstrous, while black or white people are always of the most stereotypical sort. Generally, the bigger, hairier and more lustful the foreigner, the better.

This is a generalisation in itself, but it is true that many Chinese feel a kind of inferiority alongside foreigners (most Chinese will never meet a foreigner). Some people say this might be something to do with the colonial history of the country, while others suggest it has more to do with the absence of a Chinese hero (in the days before Bruce Lee or Jackie Chan), but many attribute it simply to old-fashioned racism.

The bottom line is that kung fu cinema allows people to indulge in a bit of fantasy while at the same time turning the tables on tradition and convention.

Television (电视 Diànshì)

More than one billion Chinese have access to television. In the 1980s, a tiny black and white set was a prized status symbol. Now satellite dishes protrude from millions of urban homes.

State TV is a very dreary affair. Lengthy and wordy news reports do little to hold audiences. Although in recent years many TV series have been imported from abroad (*Star Trek* and numerous Japanese soaps are very popular), most of the programming remains unimaginative. From time to time there are variety shows where kids (chubby boys, skinny girls) perform sickeningly cute musical routines to break up the routine of news, soap operas (usually historical and very long running), documentaries (military and war themes are common) and Hollywood films (broadcast from a VHS cassette by the looks of it, soundtrack altered and boring bits cut out). Violence and disaster seem to make up the bulk of primetime viewing. One format features fatal real-life accidents and catastrophes, complete with slow-motion repeat and pop soundtrack. Expect to catch this around five in the evening. Sex, by way of contrast, is never seen. To cater to this there is an illicit but nonetheless thriving industry in Japanese adult videos. Later in the evening there are sometimes sports programmes (presumably stolen from foreign stations).

Satellite dishes have transformed Chinese television. It is possible (courtesy of an illegally manufactured decoder equipped with the right chips) to receive dozens of channels, including many foreign-language services. Star TV and CNN are widely received although its impossible to know by how many people because nobody is watching legally.

Radio (收音机 Shōuyīnjī)

Radio is also challenging the traditional role of the media. There are well over 1,000 talk radio stations across the country. Outside Beijing, they are relatively unregulated. Discussions are extremely controversial (by Chinese standards). This along with the growing quality of independent (and therefore subversive) music that is getting airplay suggests that radio may be the most potent vehicle for change in Chinese society today.

Opera (剧 Jù)

This is the Chinese equivalent of drama and completely unlike opera in the European tradition. Chinese opera is a mixture of music, singing, acrobatics, dialogue and stylised fighting.

Development

Drama began as another form of religious worship, since it was mostly performed at festivals or ceremonies. During the Zhou Dynasty, drama took the form of **shénxì** 神戏 (sacred plays). These developed into a more elaborate style of play that was performed as a feature of court entertainment. During the Tang Dynasty, many of the arts made great progress, including drama. Many great opera dramas were written in the Mongol (Yuan) Dynasty, consequently many authorities cite this period as the starting point of opera in a form still recognisable today. Its subject matter was social life and this earned it great popularity. A small number of these dramas are still performed today.

During the Qing Dynasty, a new type of drama emerged. It was a fusion of earlier, more traditional forms but combined many elements from a variety of regional forms. In 1790, a provincial troupe travelled to the Imperial Palace to perform before the royal family. They pleased the court and stayed in Beijing to play to ordinary audiences. They absorbed techniques from other local forms and, eventually, their style developed a very independent character. This became Beijing Opera (Peking Opera).

Beijing Opera (京剧 Jīngjù)

This is the Chinese national art form. It has both more influence and popularity than any other performed art and is increasingly appreciated by foreign audiences too.

There are four types of character roles in Beijing opera.

Shēng 生 are the male characters. **Lǎoshēng** 老生 are old men, **xiǎoshēng** 小生 are young men and **wǔshēng** 武生 are men with martial skills.

Dàn 旦 are female characters. Like the shēng they are subdivided into **lǎodàn** 老旦 and **wǔdàn** 武旦, but there are also **qīngyī** 青衣 who are virtuous young women (maidens) and **huādàn** 花旦 who are vivacious girls.

Jìng 净 are the painted face characters. **Wénjìng** 文净 are scholarly civilians and the **wǔjìng** 武净 is a warrior.

Chǒu 丑 characters are clownish figures but they too can have martial arts skills (**wǔchǒu** 武丑) or be more cultured characters (**wénchǒu** 文丑).

Female opera characters

Painted face characters

Beijing Opera is famous for the brightly painted faces of its characters. Each colour has a special meaning. Red indicates steadfastness, black is loyalty or ruggedness, yellow is for indecisive, excitable or nervous characters, white is the colour of deceit and cunning. Metallic colours such as gold and silver are used for supernatural beings such as gods and demons. There are over 1,000 types of different painted face, each character having a fixed pattern to allow the audience to recognise them immediately.

Costumes are always very bright, attractive and heavily embroidered. Many of the costumes are modelled on Ming Dynasty (1368 to 1644) fashions and the colours of these have meaning also. The colours signify the character's social status: red for nobility, yellow for royalty, blue for moral men and students, white for elderly scholars. The emperor always wears a dragon robe (in Chinese symbolism, the dragon represents the emperor and the phoenix, the empress).

Some characters are especially acrobatic (the monkey king, for example) and these operas are closer to pantomime and tumbling performances than drama. Fighting involves routines with various weapons that are twirled and tossed around in carefully timed sequences. The whole spectacle is very impressive.

Traditionally, men played all parts, including female characters. Nowadays, it is more common for actresses to play female roles. All characters sing and speak in falsetto voices. Some say the reason for this is because opera was played in noisy teahouses and actors had to shriek to be heard.

Operas belong to one of two broad categories: civil and military. Civil operas might involve the love affair of some effete scholar and a maiden. Military stories focus on generals and their many battles.

Opera used to have no props other than weapons (swords, spears and various kinds of clubs). Since the early part of the 20th century, however, foreign influence has led to the use of curtains and backgrounds, adding to the colour of the stage. Revolving stages have been in use for many centuries but these are seldom seen in modern performances because currently popular operas are of the more acrobatic sort and require as much flat stage surface as possible.

To compensate for the lack of props, posturing and stylised movements symbolise many physical actions. For example, one kind of stepping motion will indicate stepping through a door, while another will mean going upstairs or climbing a mountain. Female characters show their maidenly ways through activities like needlework, but the actress will have neither a needle nor cloth in her hands. Four generals and four soldiers represent an army of thousands. When a lady is being carried in a carriage she has to walk between flags that represent horses. Every movement and gesture of the opera is symbolic and opera buffs enjoyed dissecting and analysing the movements of the greatest performers.

A small (but earsplitting) band produces all the music for the opera. It uses **èrhú** 二胡 (two-stringed fiddles), **shēng** 笙 (reed pipes), **yuèqín** 月琴 (four-stringed moon guitar) and **suǒnà** 唢呐 (Chinese clarinet) as well as various drums, bells, gongs and castanets.

The greatest opera star of all time

Every art has its great masters and Beijing Opera is no exception. **Méi Lánfāng** 梅兰芳 (1894 to 1961) made enormous contributions to the development and promotion of traditional Chinese opera. His roles were all female and he played almost every type of female character: concubines, noble women, martial women and goddesses. He revolutionised the role of women characters by introducing new styles of singing, dancing and fighting skills. He was praised not only for his innovations but also for developing the traditions that defined the characters he played. He was the first person to adopt the **èrhú** (two-stringed violin) into the opera band's repertoire of instruments. Nowadays this instrument is the centrepiece of the band.

He was also the first performer to take Beijing Opera overseas, to Europe, Japan and the United States in the 1920s and 1930s.

Opera today

Many foreigners are surprised to find that Chinese audiences seem to be doing everything but watching the stage during performances. Traditionally, actors and opera stars (along with acrobats, musicians and most other kinds of entertainer) were neither respected nor valued by society. Their skills, no matter how spectacular, were merely physical and their performers were often orphans or other lowly and unwanted members of society. Today, they seem to be faring only a little better. Foreign audiences are the preferred choice: they pay more, are quieter, the surroundings (hotel theatres) are better, the performances are much shorter and the actors have only to perform the prettier or more acrobatic scenes to raise applause. Chinese audiences will talk all the way through the acts (nobody considers this to be rude; after all, they are only acting), rarely applaud and are far more critical of anything they do happen to see when they glance at the stage from time to time.

Most foreigners will be taken to some kind of opera if they are on an organised tour. You should expect to pay between ten and 20 times more than what a Chinese person would pay to see a performance of three or four times the length. There are, however, a number of small consolations to make up for this. One is the lack of distraction and the comfort of theatres designed for foreigners but it is the notes on the opera you will probably be given that make a lot of difference. These will include an outline of the story and an explanation of what you are watching. Without these, even if your Chinese is good, understanding opera is difficult. Some theatres provide subtitles in Chinese and English on screens to the sides of the stage. Typically, these are very literal translations and are often hilarious.

Traditional music

In history, Chinese music occupied an important place in culture. Music was primarily reserved for the accompaniment of court rituals, since it was believed to act as a bridge between heaven and earth. Musical routines were a strong feature of court rites. Each tradition and ceremony had a unique musical element to ensure that the relevant

gods and spirits would observe every significant deed of the court. A scholar's education was considered complete only if he had a good knowledge of harmony. The music of the general populace was far less elaborate and not considered to be real 'music' in the highbrow Confucian sense.

Music had great symbolic meaning. The scale of notation consisted originally of five sounds, believed to represent the five elements (see Chapter 4). They also corresponded to the five planets (from Chinese cosmology), the five colours (feng shui) as well as the five levels of state: emperor, ministers, commoners, politics and material possessions.

In the Qing Dynasty, a nine-note scale was introduced although this was later reduced once more to five. Chinese musical scoring is not directly comparable with the western system. By tradition, music was denoted by vertical columns of characters with a few signs to indicate pauses, rests and so on. Depending on the piece, many notes are flattened or sharpened but no compositions go beyond 14 separate sounds at once.

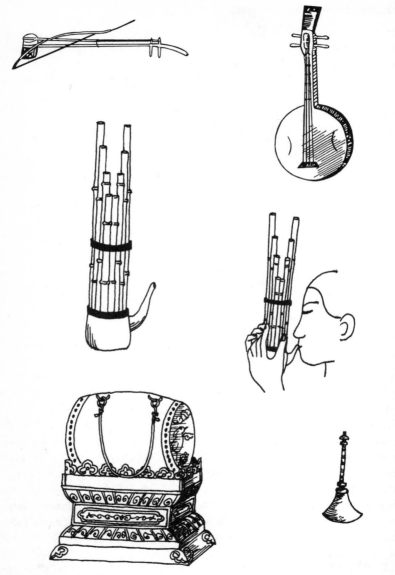

Musical instruments: *ehru*, **moon guitar, reed pipes, small barrel drum, Chinese clarinet**

Musical instruments (乐器 Yuèqì)

At one time there were 72 instruments, but many of these have been lost or are no longer used. Chinese instruments are divided into eight sorts to correspond to the eight diagrams (see **ba gua** – Chapter 4):

1 stone instruments (percussion): stone chime (suspended in a frame and struck during ceremonies to honour Confucius)

2 metal instruments (percussion): bells, gongs, chimes, cymbals and trumpets

3 silk instruments (stringed): lute (**qin**), guitars (including the **yueqin**), violins (the most famous Chinese instrument of all is the **erhu**) and harpsichord

4 bamboo instruments (wind): pipes, ceremonial flute, ordinary flute, small flute and clarinet (**suona**)

5 wooden instruments (percussion): sound box (hollow vessel), musical tiger (tiger-shaped sound box), castanets and wooden fish (fish-shaped sound box)

6 skin instruments (drums): big barrel drum, small barrel drum (搏附 **bófù**), rattle drum and the flat drum

7 gourds (wind): reed organ (**sheng**), which is a cluster of pipes designed to represent a phoenix (the empress)

8 clay instruments (wind): ocarina.

Drums (鼓 Gǔ)

As elsewhere, the Chinese have used percussion since time immemorial. Early drums were made of clay and used in shamanic rituals. Later drums were employed for martial use and there is still a strong tradition of drumming in kung fu clubs. To date there are nearly 30 kinds of drum ranging in size from tiny to truly enormous. Many minority groups have strong drumming traditions to accompany their traditional dances. Even today, forms of drum are used to frighten or summon spirits. It is also a common children's toy. They are still used in many festivals including the Dragon Boat Festival (see Chapter 4) and always accompany a lion dance.

Gongs (锣 Luó)

This instrument is commonly associated with China and East Asian cultures in general, this despite the fact that it is not easily found these days and even in history ranked second to the drum. The large disc shape is said to be a copy of a peasant's round straw hat. The biggest kind of gong is about two feet (0.61m) in diameter, but most are nine to ten inches (23–25cm). Gongs are used by Buddhists to scare away ghosts and are the traditional form of siren in the event of fire. Small gongs (cymbals, really) provide most of the din that accompanies the action scenes in Beijing Opera.

Vocal (声乐 Shēng Yuè)

Chinese singers always sing in a higher than normal voice. Their falsetto also has a rather nasal quality. Even women sing in a very high pitch. The reason may be something to do with old theatres or singing outdoors. Others say it might be because the style is fairly easy to imitate and vocal quality can be better standardised through falsetto. Whatever the reason, in these days of electrically amplified performances, listening to Chinese opera can be excruciating.

Classical music (管弦乐 Guǎnxián Yuè)

China has many good western orchestras, attached, like their western counterparts to big cities. Shanghai and Beijing have their own philharmonics. Many of the senior musicians were trained in the former Soviet Union in the heyday of China–USSR relations, the 1950s. Most of them are now teachers and have successfully transmitted the high standard of classical training they received from the Russians. Like all the arts, western music fell foul of the Cultural Revolution and was effectively shelved for the decade (1966 to 1976). Its popularity was once again revived in the 1980s when it became acceptable to indulge in non-ideological pursuits. Throughout the 1990s China exported many excellent musicians and the traffic has not been all one way. Many foreign orchestras and soloists tour China and are always enthusiastically received.

Pop music (流行音乐 Liúxíng Yīnyuè)

Until the late 1980s, Chinese pop music consisted of little more than badly imitated Hong Kong-style music (not the most productive place in the world for original material, either). 'Formulaic' seems to say everything about Chinese pop music. It all seems to follow a few clichéd lines: the tunes are similar and the singers are all uniformly inoffensive. There are titles like 'Wo Ai Ni Zhongguo' (I love you, China) which get lots of TV and radio play. Most of the officially released songs are still censored for offensive or subversive content but, just in case, the whole market is currently geared towards an age group too young to understand or demand such material anyway.

There is, however, a growing underground music scene, where rock stars who live appropriately rock star-like lifestyles can be found. Until the 1990s they were very deep underground, often performing at secret venues and, not having any official labels, their music was circulated on cassette tape via late teen/20-something friendship networks.

Western pop music is a big seller in China. In the early 1990s Madonna and Michael Jackson were big favourites, the Carpenters had their day in the mid-1990s, so did Led Zeppelin and the Beatles have just kept going ever since tapes were smuggled in during the Cultural Revolution. Foreign record companies are hesitant to try exploiting the Chinese market for a few reasons. The main one is cost: Chinese buyers simply could not afford a foreign compact disc. Other reasons are the medium (people still prefer tapes because CD players are too expensive) and the black market (copies are still the main source of foreign music).

China's greatest rock star

There is only one really big international name in Chinese pop music: **Cuī Jiàn** 崔健 (pronounced 'tsway jen'). Having no footsteps to follow in, he is the pioneer of Chinese popular music. He is also the first artist to come from an independent background and make it into the mainstream without an enormous compromise in style; oddly, his music became more individual as he become more popular (in itself a major achievement for artists in any field and especially in China). He says that his greatest influences were the Beatles, the Rolling Stones, Sting and Talking Heads. Asian countries are full of bands that shamelessly imitate great British and American groups, but Cui Jian is different. His band, Adou, mix all kinds of music and their music features lots of Chinese and Asian sounds that set them apart from the rest of the rock groups.

Cui Jian belongs to the Korean ethnic group and was born in China in 1961. By the age of 20 he was a classical trumpeter with the Beijing

Symphony Orchestra (BSO). After six years with the BSO he decided to go his own way and try his hand at writing and singing his own material. His big break came in 1986 when he appeared in Beijing's One Hundred Singers For Peace concert. His song was a mixture of rock and rap and made him a celebrity the same night.

Soon after he embarked on his own version of the Long March, travelling around the country composing, performing and building a huge and loyal fan base. Gradually, his popularity brought him to the attention of the authorities who became increasingly uneasy with the nihilistic flavour of his lyrics. In 1987, they finally acknowledged his influence by placing a ban on further performances (the hallmark of all the greatest 20th-century Chinese artists). He was peripherally associated with the Tiananmen student movement and this brought him more unwanted attention. In 1990 he was back on the road doing a ten-city tour to raise money for the Asian Games, but this was cut short for similar reasons. Nevertheless his album sales have reached nearly 15 million to date and approximately a billion people have heard his material.

In the 1990s, Cui Jian left China to extend his Long March into Europe (the UK, France and Germany), Japan and the USA. Although it is very unlikely that he will break into the mainstream pop movement in any of these countries, that he has crossed the barriers at all is a success for any artist who began within the confines of the Chinese music world.

An alternative artist: Liú Suǒlā 刘索拉 (Liu Sola)

These days, this lady is almost forgotten by the majority of mainland Chinese, despite having a brief spell of success as both a writer and a musician. Like Cui Jian her music is a hybrid of traditional sounds and more modern styles and she is one of a very small number of Chinese musicians to have carved themselves a niche in foreign music markets. Her music is a fusion of Chinese tones and western blues. Recently, she declared she was 'black' but actually she is descended from the most blues-incompatible background imaginable. She was a Red Guard for a while and her uncle was a famous army general for whom she composed a score as her graduation piece. This brought her fame in 1985 when it was performed on radio by the orchestra of the Central Opera House.

It's very difficult to say how good or even how successful she is (as a writer and musician). Many artists and the companies behind them simply cash in on the novelty factor since there are so few internationally successful Chinese artists. If a non-Chinese artist produced the same material, it would probably go unnoticed. But whatever the conclusion, her music is still worth listening to, even if only because it is unusual. Her most popular works are a bluesy mixture of Asian and African-American traditions. Her first album *Blues from the East* reached an incredible ninth place on the world music billboard chart in 1995. The album is based on two Chinese parables 'Broken Zither' and 'Married to Exile' which is an appropriately oriental tale of a concubine who is betrothed to a Mongolian chieftain as a peace offering.

Some debate exists as to whether the works of artists such as Liu Sola and Cui Jian are real reflections of the historical/cultural consciousness that Chinese people (artists in particular) are famed for or are simply cynical attempts to capture the attention (and wallets) of foreign audiences with a few token Asian flourishes.

GLOSSARY

剧 **jù** theatre, opera, play, drama

剧作家 **jùzuòjiā** playwright

伶 **líng** traditional actor

演员 **yǎnyuán** modern actor/actress

编导 **biāndǎo** direct (a play or film)

武打 **wǔdǎ** theatrical combat

审查 **shěnchá** censorship

宣传 **xuānchuán** propaganda

记实性影片 **jìshíxìng yǐngpiān** documentary

幕 **mù** scene, act

音乐 **yīnyuè** music

谱写 **pǔxiě** compose music

班子 **bānzi** theatrical troupe

录像机 **lùxiàngjī** video recorder

录像带 **lùxiàngdài** videotape

纪录片 **jīguāng chàngpiān** compact disc

歌手 **gēshǒu** singer

乐队 **yuèduì** band

Taking it further

Books

Chinese Drama: A Historical Survey, Colin MacKerras, New World Press (China), 1990.

Chinese Cinema, Chris Berry (ed.), British Film Institute, 1991. A good introduction to the subject.

Peking Opera and Mei Lanfang, Wu Zuguang and Huang Zudin, New World Press (China), 1980.

I am Jackie Chan: My Life in Action, Jackie Chan, Random House, 1998. Autobiography of the world's most daring action hero.

Asian Pop Cinema, Lee Server, Chronicle Books, 1999. Fairly lightweight but well-illustrated. A good book for appreciating modern Chinese cinema compared to film in neighbouring countries.

Music

Blues from the East, Liu Sola, Island Records, 1994.

Spring Snowfall, Liu Sola and Wu Man, Also Productions, 2000.

Power of the Powerless, Cui Jian, World Beat, 1999.

Fable, Faye Wong (Wang Fei), EMI, 2001. China's answer to Madonna, the nearest thing to an international Chinese pop diva.

Websites

Every Chinese star you could ever want, their biographies, works and pictures. In English and Chinese: http://1chinastar.com

Chinese music – instruments and history: http://chinesemusic.n3.net

Links to Asian cinema sites (particularly China and Hong Kong): http://www.arches.uga.edu/~yomi/film/filmlinks.html

Ten great Chinese films

Everybody has their own idea about what makes a good film, but with so many Chinese films made, where do we start? The following films are all good for one reason or another and you should find them both entertaining and educational. All these films are available on video, both in the UK and the USA.

Fifth generation

The Yellow Earth (1984, directed by Chen Kaige) is the story of a young soldier sent to live with a peasant family, in order to spread the Communist creed. The film angered censors because the end is tragic and ideology proves to be no match for tradition. Some interpreted the ignorance of the peasants to be an attack on party rhetoric. It is slow paced but loaded with cultural references and food for thought.

Red Sorghum (1986, directed by Zhang Yimou) consists of two stories set during crucial periods of Chinese history: the War of Resistance against Japan and the civil war period. The point of the film is open to question, but the revolutionary potential of the peasant masses is central. This film features a very young **Gǒng Lì** 巩俐, a support actress who would later prove crucial to the very best works of the fifth generation.

Ju Dou (1990, directed by Zhang Yimou) this time Gong Li carries the whole film, which is set in the early years of the 20th century. She is sold off to the wealthy owner of a dye works and falls in love with his assistant. The film is deeply atmospheric and gives a good account of the conditions faced by many peasant women under the traditional system.

Raise the Red Lantern (1991, Zhang Yimou) starts similarly: once again, Gong Li is sold as a concubine to an ageing landowner. Both these films give a good outline of many traditional Chinese values, but despite their historical settings, many critics read them as commentaries on modern society too. The film is as visually rich as it is poignant.

Farewell My Concubine (1993, Chen Kaige) has been called the greatest of all the fifth-generation films and I agree. The powerful storyline charts the fates of two Peking Opera actors across many decades. The sad ending angered the authorities, since the final tragedy takes place *after* the Cultural Revolution, when things were supposed to be so much better.

All these films reveal the overwhelming preoccupations of the fifth-generation filmmakers: reappraisal of history, popular resistance to change and fatalism. They are fine examples of the historical consciousness that characterises all great Chinese films and modern literature.

The Story of Qiu Ju (1992, Zhang Yimou) differs from other fifth-generation films in that it appears less critical. The story is simple: Gong Li is a peasant woman who seeks some kind of justice for her husband after he is assaulted. She wades through many levels of bureaucracy before the perpetrator is finally arrested, but by which point, things have changed. The film is interesting because it uses many non-actors and gives a very realistic treatment of the lives and difficulties of rural people.

Hong Kong

No venture into Chinese cinema would be complete without at least one kung fu movie. **Bruce Lee (Lǐ Xiǎolóng 李小龙)** in *The Big Boss* (1970, directed by Lo Wei) could be regarded as the father of them all. The genre was already underway, but this film was something special. From the opening night it was an explosion. At last there was a genuine Chinese superstar and he became the yardstick for every kung fu star ever after. The film has virtually no special effects (or acting for that matter) but the action skills of the hero were more than spectacular enough to make it not only a classic but a legend.

A slightly more recent example of Hong Kong action cinema is **Jackie Chan**'s *Police Story* (1985). Jackie (**Chéng Lóng 成龙**) started off in the standard kung fu mode, following the craze that was started by Bruce Lee. This film was the pioneer of countless scores of fast-paced comedy–kung fu–stunt action movies that has become the trademark of Hong Kong cinema.

The stunts are amazing and it is funny enough to appeal to audiences all over the world.

Foreign

Occasionally, foreign films can do Chinese stories sufficient justice to make them essential viewing for sinophiles (China lovers). The best example is Bertolucci's 1987 epic, *The Last Emperor*. It is one of the few films that is every bit as good as the hype. The story is based on the story of the child emperor 'Henry' Pu Yi, who was the last monarch to reign under the imperial system. It gives an outline of China in the 20th century, in all its glory and sadness.

Soursweet is a British film (1988) based on the novel by the popular novelist, Timothy Mo. It is about a Chinese immigrant family and their experiences as they try to settle in London. Strangely, it is a very Chinese film, combining both drama and comedy, but ultimately ending sadly. Sometimes it is easier to understand Chinese when they are not in the surroundings of their native culture (Chineseness becomes more visible) and this film allows this, as well as giving the viewer the Chinese perspective on British life.

7 | ART AND ARCHITECTURE

Painting (绘画 Huìhuà)

Chinese painting has a very long history. Pots decorated with pictures of animals were discovered in the 1920s and date back around 6,000 years. These artifacts revealed that even at this early time, Chinese artists were already familiar with brushes and basic painting techniques.

Chinese tradition states that a recognisable art of painting started around 3,000 years ago. It is said that it reached its greatest height in the Song Dynasty (960 to 1280 AD). Its contribution to both Chinese (and world) culture has however, been relatively consistent. Foreigners have prized Chinese art ever since they first saw it and Chinese too, from the time they first picked up the brush.

Throughout the world, Chinese painting is known for its brush techniques and expressive yet simple compositions. The greatest works of Chinese painting belong to the **xiěyì** 写意 'drawing meaning' school. There are others schools but the flowing brushwork of the xieyi made it the most beautiful and famous style.

Technique (技法/技巧 Yìshù)

The xieyi technique is Chinese painting in a nutshell. Its theory is that art should express emotion and feeling and not be restrained by reality. In ancient times too, Chinese artists seldom tried to depict real scenes with photographic accuracy. **Gù Kǎizhī** 顾恺之, a famous artist who lived in the 4th century AD was the first artist to promote the theory of 'making the form show spirit'. To him, a painting need not convey a form but should show how the artist perceives that form. His other famous quotes include 'likeness in spirit is found in unlikeness' and 'a painting should be something which expresses something between likeness and unlikeness'.

Subsequent artists followed these recommendations and experimented with proportion and perspective to communicate their feelings about the subject matter.

This is where Chinese painting differs enormously from classical western painting. There is no fixed or standard viewpoint or perspective. Chinese painting is far less concerned with notions of symmetry, balance and proportion than its European counterpart. Because it lacked a single focal point, Chinese artists were free to paint on long strips of paper (or silk) and could compose pieces of amazing complexity in a rather comic book-like manner (not unlike the Bayeux Tapestry). Artists could paint a whole chain of pictures to depict continuous scenery, like all the scenes along a riverside for example.

Another contrast to western painting is the use of changing perspectives. For example, many pictures include objects that are both far away and near, but they are depicted as being of the same size. The reason is a cause of much debate. Some people read Daoist and Buddhist concepts into the art, saying that it represents the artist's elevation from the normal notions of space and time which confine the perceptions of ordinary people. It is more likely to be that the artists were trying to paint life exactly as they saw it. That is, people view the world from constantly changing angles and painting, like the eye, could not be restricted to a single perspective.

Shading does not feature strongly in Chinese painting, neither does colour. Colour was reserved for less philosophical subject matter. Scholars generally stayed with (black) ink painting. Oil colours were unheard of until the beginning of the 20th century, except in the very south of China where artists had access to foreign materials.

The coloured painting that was produced was done with great care and there were many schools of ornamental painting. They painted large, intricate and colourful paintings of everyday scenes onto scrolls of silk or paper, but these were seldom taken seriously by the lettered members of society since they lacked substance and were considered therefore to be something more of a 'craft' than a real art.

Painting and calligraphy (字画 Zìhuà)

These two are very closely related since the skills required to do one would almost certainly be transferable to the other. Both use lines as their primary means of expression (by contrast, some western traditions use blocks or grades of colour). In calligraphy and most types of painting, the artist has only one colour of ink (black, although there is a range of hues) and uses this not only to give the elemental form (outline) but also to give contours, concepts and feeling to the picture. In both forms the lines are curved or straight, hard or soft, pale or dark and thin or thick. The ink may also be dry (to give a scratchy look) or runny and watery (to give a soft, water colour-like effect).

The key concept behind both is simplicity and harmony. Just as a few lines drawn in a flash depict the profoundest character, a few strokes of the painter's brush may represent a figurative or philosophical universe in a single painting.

Poetry as a picture

Traditional Chinese painting had a definite objective: to combine four related arts into one medium. The four arts it attempted to embody were calligraphy, seal engraving (the forerunner of calligraphy), painting (i.e. pot painting etc.) and poetry. Artists believed that through painting, the essence of each form could be extracted, merged and magnified.

The earliest great painters were all poets too. The Chinese today still say 'poetry in painting and painting in poetry'. This has been the guideline for judging painting for two millennia. All the most excellent works of art were likened to poems.

People often wonder what the writing is that can be found in many examples of Chinese painting. This writing is usually the artist's attempt to explain the ideas and feelings that he was trying to convey through the painting. Sometimes they are quotes from philosophical texts. Whatever they are, the artist probably included them to add a decorative effect to complement the rest of the painting, rather than explain it. This often seems strange to western eyes only familiar with posters that have text running over pictures, but not classical painting. To the Chinese artist, however, the two are hardly separable (remember the graphical nature of Chinese characters, Chapter 2).

Painters (画家 Huàjiā)

An old saying succinctly describes the archetypal painter in traditional China: 'When a man has read hundreds of books, studied the works of old masters and travelled the world then, and only then, can he pick up his brush and try his hand.'

Drawing and its cousin, painting, stemmed from writing. Not only philosophically, but practically because they were both taught in the same way. Scholars would teach writing methods to budding sketchers and painters. They were taught to perceive and portray the world as they would the lines and components of Chinese characters, with their set proportions and directions. By breaking the subject down into pieces, the painter was trained to treat the parts separately and then group or arrange the sections to fit the higher message he wanted to convey. Needless to say, to be a proficient painter, an artist required a solid grounding in calligraphy. Therefore, most of China's greatest artists came from the scholarly classes.

Symbolism

Ancient artists liked to use symbolism and painted nature to represent virtuous qualities. Favourite subjects were things like bamboo, plum blossoms and pines. The artists often added captions such as 'perfect etiquette', 'exemplary conduct' and 'the utmost nobility of character' to their paintings. Eventually this evolved into a vast symbolic language. People today still like to dissect pictures for hidden or subtle meanings but what it really means is usually open to wide debate. However, one thing is sure: Chinese artists liked to use nature to represent virtuous qualities that man could aspire to. Nature was, of course, perfectly in line with the order of the Dao and Daoism (itself strongly connected to poetic traditions) influenced painting heavily.

Subject matter

Choosing what to paint was not based on what was pretty or what would sell in the market. Artists tended to be reclusive types who had spent many years in scholastic or spiritual disciplines and subjects were chosen to embody the philosophical musings of their (usually) well-educated minds. Consequently, everything in Chinese painting seems to make allusion to something or other. Symbolism and subject matter overlap constantly. Certain animals represent Chinese characters or personalities. Landscapes (probably the favourite subject of all the greatest artists) are full of philosophical references, even if the picture itself seems a little empty. The various manifestations of nature correspond to aspects of the human body and soul. Water is the blood of the world, the rivers are its veins; mountains are its faces; grass and trees are its hair. There are figures wandering around or sitting in these landscapes, they could be interpreted as meaning many things: a lone scholar, for example, could represent the spirit of natural order.

In order to do his lofty subject matter justice, the artist would spend many days (sometimes weeks and even years) immersing himself in the spirit of his subject. If he was planning to paint a landscape, he would climb a mountain and spend days meditating on the view. Again, like calligraphy, painting was believed to be a spiritual discipline, a kind of meditation through the brush. Once the artist had received the spirit of the landscape, his painting would reveal the true nature of the land and the clear mind he had attained through his meditation would make the picture all the more truthful.

Since it was associated with spiritual forces, learned Chinese believed that painting was not to be debased through the depiction of inappropriate subjects. There was a strict value placed on subjects. Artists, perhaps influenced by the Buddhist notion of 'merit' (good karma), often chose their subjects for the spiritual rewards they stood to reap by depicting them. They were:

1 **Gods, demons and saints.** Any kind of divine being would help remind people of the spiritual consequences of their actions. Artists and rulers thought such pictures would help society at large.

2 **Portraits and historical pictures.** Following the prestige attached to history writing, painting important people and scenes from history helped keep the past alive, a high priority in Confucian society.

3 **Architecture.** Evidence of the triumph of the scholar and the Confucian principle of working together to achieve a greater goal. It was also an early form of technical drawing.

4 **Flowers and animals.** Probably for their symbolic more than decorative value. (The popular willow pattern found on ceramics was the invention of an Englishman, Minton, in 1780.)

5 **Landscapes.** This was a favourite, probably for symbolic purposes too. Chinese artists (past and present, including filmmakers) have been fascinated with images of huge expanses of land or sea.

The art of the state

Right up until the beginning of Communist China, there had been little development in painting but things changed very quickly when Mao instructed artists to 'serve the people'. Socialist Realism was the result and painters like writers were forced to conform. Thereafter, until around 1980 painting consisted basically of ruddy-cheeked peasant girls joyfully bundling bumper harvests, beefy soldiers ruggedly defending their honourable homeland and the ever-grinning, happy-go-lucky father figure of the dictator himself, surrounded by adoring legions of lovingly overfed, patriotic, Socialist youths.

Traditional painting today

In China today, the whiff of foreign money has effectively disposed of a hitherto undiluted tradition of classical Chinese painting. Many paintings these days are done for sale to foreigners. They tend to be of the simple, archetypal landscape and mountain/landscape and pagoda/landscape and mystical figure sort. They are painted to what their artists perceive to be foreign taste and are sold at various prices, depending on the artist. Despite the sell-out, all the technique is still there and even before dollars drifted into China, there was a long tradition of not exactly copying, but sticking with the winning formula. So maybe today's paintings are traditional after all. Businesses, shops and offices may have paintings hung on the walls, but generally people prefer calligraphy because its easier to come by, cheaper and usually contains well known proverb-like snippets of wisdom. For their homes, ordinary people prefer modern posters (girls, motorbikes and American cities).

The state of the art

Art, whether classical or modern, foreign or Chinese attracts few crowds in modern China. Of course, there are many thousands of talented painters (sculptors, writers etc.) but the only way to get known is by being subversive, yet to do so would get them banned or thrown in prison, so they often find themselves in something of a catch-22 situation. Chinese artists go abroad to sell their work, or they move to a part of the country where they are less likely to disturb the authorities. Recently, many artists are taking the latter option, since for most it is simply too expensive to leave (ideally for the USA). Beijing and Shanghai are the places where an artist can make his or her name (big exhibitions, foreign buyers) but they are also places where the government is most paranoid.

There is a small city in the south of China which has recently become a Mecca for growing numbers of artists who are uneasy about the prospect of censorship in the bigger Chinese cities. The city is **Kūnmíng** 昆明. Artists here produce sculptures and paintings that would get their studios shut down or earn them a place in jail if they were found in Beijing.

In Kunming, the authorities are far more concerned about the mass poverty and drug-trafficking problem in their city than they ever could be about a few bohemian types painting nudes and queues of laid-off workers. Many of the artists are yet to become well known outside their little haven, but a few have exhibited in Europe and the USA and they are attracting more and more foreign attention (and money) by the week.

If you want to see good modern Chinese art, mainland China is not the place to go: artistic freedom is still a long way off.

Architecture (建筑学 Jiànzhùxué)

Buildings reflect material wealth and taste. They are a good measure of the development of a civilisation. Chinese architecture has a long and rich tradition.

Building in history

The earliest dwellings were natural caves. Such a shelter was home to Peking Man who lived about half a million years ago. Many thousands of Chinese today still live in caves (although they are fitted out in a style far more suited to 21st-century living!) around the loess plains of north and northwestern China.

As people learned to interact and cooperate, communal tasks could be undertaken and more sophisticated dwellings were built. The very earliest buildings were called 'nest residences' which were made from shallow round holes dug into the ground, the earth acting as both floor and walls. Their round roofs were made of thatch and strong poles were used to stop the sides falling in. These supports were covered with earth to stop them catching fire. The occupants would build fires inside the houses to keep themselves warm and cook food. Fumes were released through small holes in the roof.

In southern China where the ground is too soft and wet to live in, houses were constructed on platforms which rested on upright poles driven deep into the ground. This style of platform house is still common in many parts of Southeast Asia (particularly Vietnam) and is still used by a number of minority groups in the south of China. Although these houses are extremely lightweight (they are made of bamboo, wood and other kinds of grass) they are incredibly strong. Primitive people used stone tools to make beams and supports and even had chisels to hollow out mortise and tenon-type joints (these have been found in remains of houses which were built over 7,000 years ago).

This simple joining technique (like a peg in a hole) became the starting point for much more elaborate buildings made in later centuries. During the Xia and Shang Dynasties (21st to 11th centuries BC) many great advances in building design occurred. Slaves still lived in pit-style nest houses, but their masters lived in houses on the surface, built on foundations of compacted earth. Their walls were made from rammed earth and some homes had up to three rooms. Rooms had hard and smooth floors from being heated by fires. In these times, masters demanded many sacrifices of animals and humans so many slaves were buried in the foundations of their owners' houses.

The greatest architectural achievement of the Shang Dynasty was an enormous palace built in Henan. It covered 32,810 square feet (10,000 square metres). There was a vast central hall surrounded by galleries and elaborate gates.

The beginning of classical architecture

The Zhou Dynasty marked the beginning of sophisticated architecture. Noble families were given land on which they were free to build as they saw fit. Archaeological excavations tell us that a distinct pattern of grand building emerged around this time. Main buildings had front and back courtyards and porches. Earthenware roof tiles were used to cover gutters, drains and roof ridges. Plaster made from soil, sand and lime was applied to the rammed earth walls and floors to give the interiors a very flush appearance. Geomantic (feng shui) principles began to influence building design. Architectural plans sought to align the buildings with the most favourable directions in order to benefit the occupants. On a more practical level, buildings were given thicker north-facing walls to withstand the cold winds blowing down from Mongolia.

The Great Wall (长城 Chángchéng)

After the country was united in 221 BC, architecture became even more extravagant and Qin leaders were very ambitious. Their grand palaces were erected on elevated stone platforms to express power, wealth and inspire awe in visitors. The most incredible achievement of the Qin (see Chapter 1) was the Great Wall. This was built to stop marauding northern tribes from penetrating into the newly unified Chinese empire. The wall is really more of an incredibly long, stretched castle. It was the home to hundreds of garrisons along its vast length of 1,500 miles (2,414 km) (practically the entire span of the country) housing armouries, look out towers and living quarters. It rises and dips at very acute angles (it follows the jutting contours of the mountainous land) and makes for a very challenging walk/climb. It is still one of the world's most wonderful and spectacular ancient monuments; but it is a myth that it can be seen from space!

The Tang Dynasty

As with all the other arts, this dynasty was a period of enormous productivity (Chapters 1 and 5). Architecture prospered immensely. Glazed tiles and carved stones were introduced, permitting a far more decorative effect. Brick walls were a strong feature of Tang architecture. These replaced the earlier hardened-earth material and allowed for much more standardisation. Despite the robust simplicity of brick structures, grand building design deviated little from the basic tenets of Chinese architecture: namely the timber columns, beams and brackets which supported the enormous flared hip roofs. There is an old saying which testifies to the reliability of the traditional technique: 'The walls may collapse, but the roof will never topple'. Earthquakes proved that this saying was quite true. Since tremendously strong posts

The Great Wall

supported the roofs, walls were never load bearing, so doors and windows could be placed for decorative effect. Aristocrats played an architectural equivalent of 'keeping up with the Joneses'. The rivalry quickly became absurd and at times dangerous, so eventually standards for construction were introduced to limit the number of bays or arches a person's house had. This may have been because scholars thought it wrong that their merchant neighbours should literally be able to look down on them (they were, after all, a lower social class!).

The greatest accomplishment of the Tang was the construction of their great capital city **Cháng'ān** 长安 (present-day **Xī'ān** 西安). The geometry and orientation of the city was decided on feng shui, numerological and astrological principles. The design was added to by rulers of later dynasties, but never bettered. To varying degrees, the basic layout of the city was the model for many imitations. Two of the most famous are the beautiful cities of Kyoto and Nara which were havens of Chinese culture and early capitals of Japan.

The Song Dynasty

Designs became more flexible and elegant during the Song (960 to 1279 AD). Polygonal, multi-eave roofs became the fashion. Interior decorating seems to have been popular too. Intricate ceiling structures and heavily carved doors, windows, columns and brackets made this period a little like a Chinese rococo. Lattices on windows with silk in place of glass gave homes and palaces a more civilised appearance.

Palaces (宫殿 Gōngdiàn)

As in any country, royal homes were the finest examples of architecture. China has literally tens of thousands of exquisite buildings, but nothing comes near to matching the splendour of the two royal palaces to be found in Beijing: the Forbidden City and the Summer Palace.

The Summer Palace **Yíhéyuán** 颐和园 is the smaller. The royal family built it during the Qing Dynasty as a spacious and breezy place in which to relax during the hot summer months. It has probably the largest number of pavilions and pagodas to be found in any single place in China. The palace is not a single huge building, but a collection of smaller, connected halls and rooms spaced by courtyards

Exemplary grand Chinese architecture: the Temple of Heaven

The Summer Palace

and connected by miles of ornate corridors, all brightly painted with classical scenes and rich symbolism. The bigger buildings epitomise the ultimate in 'oriental' architectural beauty: the multilevel pagodas and great roofed halls sit on top of high stone terraces accessed by steep staircases looking down onto artificial boating lakes and ornamental gardens.

The Imperial Palace/Forbidden City **Gùgōng** 故宫 located in central Beijing is these days reduced to its basic structure; the details were looted and vandalised during the various turbulent periods of the 20th century. Despite this, it is still magnificent. Today the Forbidden City lacks the colour and intricacy of the Summer Palace but more than makes up for this in terms of sheer size and splendour. Building was started by the Mongols, but owing to its geomantic (feng shui) properties, the site was considered sacred since antiquity. Construction continued during the Ming and Qing Dynasties as each ruler competed with his predecessors for glory. The enormous site covers an area of over 72 hectares, and is believed to contain 9,999 (and a half) rooms. It is a series of huge halls, protected at both ends by enormous gates that are more like tunnels through houses than doors. The most famous of these is **Tiānānmén** 天安门, the Heaven and Peace Gate, which is

The Imperial Palace

the entrance to the palace, overlooking the square of the same name and adorned with a giant picture of Mao's friendly face.

An unbroken wall encloses the whole palace to keep people out, hence 'forbidden'. During the Cultural Revolution the palace was practically gutted. Most of the finery and fixtures that had survived earlier unrest were vandalised or stolen.

Consequently, most of the halls feel very empty but to keep people coming, restored and mock pieces of furniture and finery have been installed. Overall, the Imperial Palace is still overwhelming, both in size and beauty.

Ordinary houses (房子 Wūzi)

Historically, there were many varieties of house for everyday people. Many of these still survive today, but are completely eclipsed by the far less interesting but much more numerous high-rise tower blocks which house most urban Chinese. In the past, however, things were a little more colourful. In the Inner Mongolia area of northern China, Mongol yurts are still a common sight on the grasslands. These are large (around 15 feet (4.6 m) in diameter), high-walled, round tents with a centrally placed stove and chimney for cooking and warmth. Genghis Khan's army carried their homes wherever they went, making camping and living very economical. The roofs are supported by 108 wooden poles (a number of great significance to many Asian cultures) and the whole house can be put up inside one hour.

The Hakka people of southwestern China have a form of communal house, sometimes called the Hakka roundhouse **yuánwū** 圆屋. They are seldom seen nowadays, but their design is unique: a kind of multilevel coliseum shape. The rooms are built into the rim of the building, as many as 900, but there are very few windows opening outward; so from the outside, the roundhouse looks a little like a fortress. In the centre is an open space that can be as much as 230 feet (70 metres) across.

Beijing is the home of alleys **hútòng** 胡同 and courtyard houses **sìhéyuàn** 四合院. The famous alleys of Beijing can be found in the old inner city area, the ramshackle sprawl that clings to the outside of the Forbidden City. These alleyways date from the Yuan (Mongol) Dynasty when Beijing became the capital. The area was a ghetto of nobles and merchants living at very close quarters, but there are many stories of more unsavoury characters who inhabited the alleys. There are still many miles of alleyways, but they retain little of the history they are often praised for.

The wealthier inhabitants of the capital lived in courtyard houses (quadrangles), so-called because they consisted of a number of rooms built around a central open courtyard. The orientation of the house was crucial. The man's bedroom was at the head (north side facing south) and the lesser members of the household were allotted rooms according to the Confucian pecking order (servants were put in the east or west wings with the storerooms and toilets; wives and children in the southern rooms).

Modern housing

Beijing, like all modern Chinese cities, is suffering from a chronic shortage of space. To make way for ever-growing numbers of city dwellers, many excellent examples of historical housing have been bulldozed. Eighty-five per cent of urban Chinese live in apartments and condominiums, the average household has eight members (grandparents, aunts and uncles). In Beijing, it is estimated that there is only 7.2 square feet (2.2 square metres) of space per person, about the size of a single bed! Naturally, the answer is high-rise building. The design follows the old Soviet style very closely, so it is not surprising that the tower blocks are stark and dull, usually built in uniform rows and patterns reminiscent of the British inner-city housing projects of the 1960s and 1970s, but much greater in scale. The majority of apartments are spacious by comparison to many Asian countries but house twice as many people.

Rural people rarely have it better. Few homes in rural China are connected to water and electricity. Houses are typically of brick or stone structure and are difficult to heat or insulate. They have few rooms (two is normal) and very rarely have more than a single level, although some peasant homes use the upstairs portion for storing produce or even keeping animals in.

Modern architecture

Showpiece skyscrapers have been the fashion ever since economic reforms began to take effect in the early 1980s. On the whole they stray little from the block-with-glass formula. They are big, compared to the surrounding buildings but reflective windows aside, are practically featureless. Occasionally there will be a traditional roof sitting on top of one of these faceless monstrosities, but there is little else to catch the eye. Many of the buildings are half-empty, because, as yet, there are not enough businesses to fill them, but this situation is changing.

Public buildings receive far less attention. Libraries, schools and dormitories are crudely practical and seem to have been designed along the guidelines of Communist functionality (the bare essentials only). They certainly do the job, but often lack indulgences such as fire escapes and safety fittings like handrails and fire doors.

Museums, halls and squares were in favour with Communists all over the world and China seems to be no exception. Most of the best museums and government buildings look as if Stalin himself designed them. They have huge doors, high ceilings and broad open foyers and long corridors. The intended effect is to dwarf the individual and celebrate the greater whole, but actually the staff just have more places to hide from guests and everybody has further to walk.

Safety

Shoddy workmanship appears to be the hallmark of Chinese building. Windows don't shut, doors are flimsy, furniture collapses, plugs flash and handles snap. Everything looks as if it was made in ten minutes, with very little attention or consideration for safety. Businesses and factories are a law unto themselves. In recent years there have been a number of fatal incidents involving fires in nightclubs and factories. In many of these places, fire escapes (if there are any) are used as storage spaces. Sadly, building collapses are also common. Second and third storeys are regularly added to buildings that were designed to support only a single floor. Predictably, the results of such practices are often tragic.

GLOSSARY

国画 **guóhuà** traditional Chinese painting
画笔 **huàbǐ** paintbrush
画卷 **huàjuàn** picture scroll
画屏 **huàpíng** painted screen
展览 **zhǎnlǎn** exhibition
画绢 **huàjuàn** silk (for painting on)
画布 **huàbù** canvas
纸 **zhǐ** paper
风景 **fēngjǐng** landscape
漫画 **mànhuà** comics, cartoons
我画漫画画得很好。 **Wǒ huà mànhuà huàde hěn hǎo.** I draw comics very well.
建筑 **jiànù** building
房子 **fángzi** house, room, apartment
公寓 **gōngyù** flats/apartments

公寓大楼 **gōngyù dàlóu** block of flats/apartments
摩天大楼 **mótiānlóu** skyscraper
楼房 **lóufáng** multi-storeyed building
平方 **píngfáng** single-storey house
屋顶 **wūdǐng** roof, top of a building
寮 **liáo** shack, hut
门 **mén** door, gate
我住在 _____。 **Wǒ zhù zài _____.** I live in _____.
我在日本住了两年。 **Wǒ zài Rìběn zhùle liǎng nián.** I lived in Japan for two years.
她住楼房还是平房？ **Tā zhù lóufáng háishì píngfáng?** Does she live in a single- or multi-storeyed building?

The lotus motif

Taking it further

Books

Through The Moon Gate: A Guide to China's Historic Monuments, Oxford University Press, 1986.

The Ming Tombs, Ann Paludan, Oxford University Press, 1991. Tombs are another area of architecture and this book is a good introduction.

Imperial China: Architectural Guides for Travellers, Charis Chan, Penguin Books, 1992.

Art of China, Korea and Japan, Peter Swann, Praeger, 1964 (many editions of this book are available). A thorough and accessible reference (now a classic). Shows the influence of China on her neighbours.

Chinese Art and Culture, Robert L. Thorp and Richard Ellis Vinograd, Harry N. Abrams, 2001. A survey of 7,000 years of Chinese art from cave paintings to video.

Websites

Good basic architecture site:
http://www.sec.nl/persons/stals/nns97/grp03/htdocs/chinese/Architecture.html

A well-illustrated and detailed site:
http://leather.pages.com.cn/chinese_culture/architecture/architecture.html

Calligraphy, paintings and a helpful glossary:
http://www.metmuseum.org/explore/Chinese/html_pages/index.htm

Plenty of information and examples of traditional painting:
http://www.gio.gov.tw/info/culture/culture4.html

8 | CREATIVITY IN OTHER SPHERES

Food

The Chinese are rightfully proud of their rich culture of food and drink and not without justification claim it to be the finest in the world. They also take their food very seriously.

Nǐ chī fàn le ma? 你吃饭了吗？ 'Have you eaten?' is another way of saying 'hello' and Chinese hosts will always stuff their guests to demonstrate their hospitality. Every form of social behaviour centres

Eating and drinking, Chinese style

on some kind of food and all the major festivals are associated with a specific snack or dish (see Chapter 4).

Everybody who has visited a Chinese restaurant knows that there is a very varied menu to choose from. As we have seen from the geography of the country, China was (and still is but to a lesser extent) home to a wide range of flora and fauna, fruits and vegetables, animals and grains. Chinese food reflects this diversity but can be broken down into a few broad categories:

1 **Staples** (主食 **Zhǔshí**). The most famous is, of course, rice (米 **mǐ**), but this is not as popular in the north of China, where the climate is less favourable for rice growing. Wheat, maize, buckwheat and sweet potatoes are the other staples (in roughly that order).

2 **Beans** (豆 **Shū**). China's most famous bean is the soybean (where soy sauce and thousands of other products come from). Broad beans and mung beans are the other most commonly used beans. China is also home to many varieties of nut, which are used to great effect in cooking (cashews and peanuts, for example).

3 **Vegetables** (菜 **Cài**). Chinese (white) cabbage, mushrooms, turnips, onions and radish. Certain kinds of soft bamboo are eaten too.

4 **Meats** (肉 **Ròu**). The Japanese say that their Chinese neighbours eat anything with legs, except tables and chairs. On the face of it, this seems true. Meat from exotic animals has fascinated wealthy Chinese for centuries and continues to do so. The most popular meat consumed by Chinese is pork (dishes that do not specify what kind of meat they contain will *always* be pork based). This is because much of China's agricultural area is not suited to grazing for other animals. Chicken is probably the second most easily acquired meat, followed by mutton, beef and duck. Seafood is popular in the cuisine of coastal areas. Dog meat is on the menu in many cities but is expensive. (It is thought by many to be something of a traditional form of Viagra!)

5 **Fruits** (水果 **Shuǐguǒ**). China has just about everything in this department. Peaches, apricots, lychee, crab apples,

oranges, lemons and pineapples are available. Until recently, fresh produce could not be transported very far from the area where it was produced, so city streets were often lined with the rotting surplus of fruit crops while it was difficult to find fruits grown in other areas. These days, it is much easier to come by tropical fruits in colder parts of China and sometimes even see them added to local recipes.

6 **Spices** (调味品 **Tiáowèipǐn**). These are the ingredients that really bring Chinese food alive. There are an enormous number of spices to choose from, but most households prefer ginger, garlic, cinnamon and red peppers making these the most frequently used spices. Restaurants and takeaways inside, but more especially outside, China add liberal amounts of monosodium glutamate (MG) to their food as a cheap form of flavour enhancer and this can cause health problems for many people.

Preparation

Since a good meal is supposed to balance various elements, it is easy to read a lot of (perhaps too much) yin and yang philosophy into Chinese cooking. Food is divided into two broad types: grains and other starchy staple foods on one side and meat and vegetables on the other. A good meal should contain a harmonious mixture of these two types of food.

Grains are always cooked whole or as flour, so that half of the meal could be made up from rice (usually boiled) or noodles **miàntiáo** 面条 (fried, crispy or cold). Vegetables and meats are cut up. Meat is sliced, cubed or chunked and vegetables are cut into edible proportions, but not chopped up like they are in many European cuisines. Chinese cooks cut vegetables into strips or broad, thin slices because they believe that if more of the inside is exposed more flavour will come out.

Some meals (like dumplings **jiǎozi** 饺子) appear to mix the two, but really the opposites are only put together, not mixed (mashed) because that is the job of the digestive system and the essence of the food (as well as the taste) would be lost. With this basic separation as a guideline, cooks will use as many ingredients and mixtures of spices as it takes to give a good taste.

Mixing flavours and cutting up ingredients is the rule of Chinese food. Meat is rarely cooked as a single whole piece (duck is, however, one notable exception) but shredded, diced or ground so it can be put into a rice dish (a fusion of opposites to make a whole).

Utensils

A Chinese kitchen has two essential items: a rice cooker **fànguō** 饭锅 and a wok **càiguō** 炒菜锅. A rice cooker is simply a dish inside a heating device. A quantity of rice is added and then covered with water. To the eye, the ratio is approximately two parts rice to three parts water, so the water level will always be higher than the rice. The rice is normally washed beforehand to remove excess starch. A household rice cooker looks like a squat kettle, but industrial cookers can be up to 3.3 feet (1 m) in diameter.

A 'wok' is simply a frying pan (the word is Cantonese). It has high walls and a round bottom. Until very recently, there was no such thing as non-stick, hence the development of the technique of constantly tossing the contents during cooking. Chinese cooks say that the highest temperature is best because food can be cooked in a flash, preventing its taste and goodness from being heated away. Since most meat comes in small pieces, even with pork there is only a very small danger of feeling ill afterward.

The cleaver **càidāo** 菜刀 is the Chinese chef's favourite utensil. The traditional style consists simply of a handle and a broad, rectangular blade. Despite progress in knife technology, many Chinese still prefer the lethal-looking old style. The weight and size of the knife makes chopping through bone and harder material easier. They are highly durable, easy to sharpen and simple to use. The broad sides of the blade make chopping vegetables quick, as slices tend to stick to the knife rather than fall off into the uncut portion.

Chopsticks (筷子 Kuàizi)

Since records began, Chinese people have eaten with chopsticks. There are many legends about the origins of these tools, but it is probable that they developed from some kind of long tongs used to extract things (such as food) from fires. It is feasible that food was manipulated during cooking using sticks of some sort and these gradually became shorter and more delicate until two could be held in the same hand to pinch and lift food.

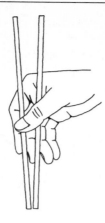

Chopsticks

These days they are made from plastic since these are easier to clean and last longer; a typical length is around 10.5 inches (27 cm). Wooden chopsticks are still in use and tend to be of the shorter 8 inch (20 cm), disposable kind. These are being phased out due to concerns over deforestation.

The upper portion of the chopstick is square and the eating section has a round cross-section. There are no real reasons for this, but this is standard for both wooden and plastic. Spoons are used too, for soup and loose rice, but the chopstick is more versatile: closing the ends of the sticks is the primary technique. This way food can be squeezed with enough force to be lifted to the mouth. When the ends are closed, they can be used like a shovel to eat rice from a bowl that is lifted, like a cup, up to the mouth. Food can be split with chopsticks too (no need for a knife): the ends are inserted together, like a point, and then separated to push away to the sides.

There are a few basic mistakes people make when using chopsticks. The first is grip: it is easy to grip too tightly. If the points are not holding the piece properly, you can send it flying through the air if there is too much pressure. Similarly, you can cut through whatever it is you are trying to pick up and make the pieces smaller and smaller! Also, where to grip is a problem for beginners. Halfway and below is a bad position, the sticks will simply keep crossing; too high and it becomes difficult to be dexterous. People all differ, but the best place is two-thirds of the way up.

Skinning and de-boning a soft cooked fish is just about the most difficult thing to do with chopsticks, but even this can be done with only a few hours' practice (honestly!)

Regional varieties

The Chinese say there are four main varieties of cuisine: northern (Beijing area), southern (Canton), eastern (Shanghai) and central southwestern (Sichuan). Food is almost as varied as dialects, so you can safely expect to find a great deal of variation and crossover in any given area.

Northern (北方 Běifāng)

Northern food is renowned for its thick rich sauces and meats. Mongol influence is evident in the preference for hot meat dishes and relatively little rice. Mongolian hotpot is a winter favourite in the north. It consists of slices of meat and vegetables that are dipped into water (which is boiling in a heater on the table) to cook. After no more than a few seconds, the pieces are taken out of the water, dipped in one of the many condiments on offer and then eaten. Another classic (and slightly more Chinese food) is Beijing (Peking) Duck. A duck is force-fed until its bloated body (full of oil) is cleavered into pieces. The method of eating is simple: the pieces are wrapped in a floury pancake and mixed with a few slices of spring onion and sauces. Restaurants rarely present the same food to foreigners that Chinese customers would expect. In China, very few parts of the duck's anatomy escape the pancake. Chinese diners consider brain especially good; but to many foreign palettes, even the meat itself is simply too oily to stomach.

Southern (南方 Nánfāng)

Southern Chinese food is far more familiar. Sometimes it is known as 'Cantonese' food because (for historical reasons) the largest percentage of Chinese to settle abroad came from the Canton area. The western version is highly modified and many dishes served in western restaurants are very recent inventions (fortune cookies and chopsuey, for example). It is reputed to be the most refined of all China's cuisines. There is a distinct preference for fresh vegetables, seafood and lighter tasting sauces. Black bean sauce, oyster sauce and garlic are used to give flavour. Sweet and sour dishes are perhaps the most famous. This sauce is made from a mixture of vinegar (sour) and sugar (sweet) which is added to a vegetable (usually tomato) or fruit base. Southerners are considered omnivorous even by Chinese standards. They are said not only to eat anything with legs, except tables and chairs, but anything that flies except planes and anything underwater, except submarines.

Eastern (东部 Dōngbù)

This is probably the least exciting of the four main varieties. Flavours tend to be milder and the dishes slightly more vegetarian friendly. The diversity of vegetation in this part of the country might explain the greater use of bamboo and mushrooms in local dishes. Freshwater fish, eels and crabs are heavily used, as is tofu (bean curd). On the face of it, this cuisine appears ideal for people with a sensitivity to strong spices or not keen on the idea of sweet and sour gerbil, but the food in this region has one major drawback: oil. Practically everything is made and served with three times the amount of oil you would find (on even the same dish) elsewhere in China and probably five times more than in a foreign Chinatown. Fried rice can be drunk straight from the bowl (it would probably be too slippery to pick up anyway) and Beijing Duck Shanghai style is to be avoided unless you find the thought of swigging the contents of a bottle of vegetable oil attractive.

Sìchuān (四川)

This is the land of spicy food. Northern influence can be seen in the use of garlic and ginger, but red chilli is the characteristic spice of this region. Not all of the dishes are spicy, but the tastiest are (that is if you like hot food!). The area is mercilessly humid in the summer and some people argue that this climate made preserving meat a high priority. Consequently, to hide the bitterness of the preservative (salt), extra strong flavourings were developed. Most of the dishes are at least a little peppery and some are so hot they will have you howling and crying (but probably going back for more). Street stalls sell an assortment of flattened and skewered animals and animal parts (such as chicken feet) that are deep-fat fried and rolled in spices that are so hot, the devil himself couldn't eat them!

Tea (茶 Chá)

The legend goes that long ago, two men (variously identified as scholars, adventurers or philosophers) were travelling and stopped for rest. To refresh themselves, they decided to heat water, perhaps for soup or maybe simply to drink. A leaf fell into one man's cup just as he was about to drink and tea was born! Whatever the origin of this drink, the Chinese have enjoyed it for a very long time. The varieties are infinite, ranging from green (like Japanese) tea to shades so dark they can stain the inside of a cup black. It is drunk on almost every occasion or meeting of people. Tea is more of a token of Chinese etiquette than a simple drink.

Peasants still 'clean' their teeth by swilling tea around their mouths and rubbing their fingers against their teeth and gums. It is drunk both hot and cold. A peek into a teapot will show you that the leaves are not thrown away the instant one cup is poured; they are normally left to accumulate in the pot for days. A workman will drink tea from a jar that he will refill with cold or hot water many times a day, never changing the leaves. There are three basic forms of tea:

1 Red teas 红茶 **hóngchá**. Leaves are roasted to give them a flavour that would be familiar to most English people.

2 Green teas 绿茶 **lǜchá**. These leaves come straight from the tea bush, via a drying-out process that preserves all the flavour. Some foreigners find green tea a little bitter.

3 Flower teas 花茶 **huāchá**. These are very fragrant since flowers or other scented flavours are added to give taste to the red tea base. Chrysanthemum tea is a famous example. These teas may also be sweetened and some even have daisy-like flowers floating around in them.

Crafts (工艺 Gōngyì)

China has few rivals when it comes to crafts. Both in quality and variety, Chinese crafts are of an excellence that is rarely equalled.

Cloisonné (景泰兰 Jǐngtàilán)

This is a colourful type of ornamental enamel that is used to decorate vases, pendants, figurines, brooches, ashtrays, jewellery boxes and even glasses cases. The process is complicated. The body of the object is usually made of brass. Tiny, thin strips of brass are bent into patterns and stuck to the surface, to form little walls. The walls make sections and these are filled with a single colour of enamel. Patterns can be as intricate as the dexterity of the craftsman's fingers, floral and animal scenes are popular. The object is fired to seal the colours, then glazed to harden and add brightness. Cloisonné is prized for its bright colours and highly detailed designs.

Pottery and ceramics (陶器 Táoqì)

Hasn't everybody heard of Ming vases? Pottery and porcelain has been made in China almost since records began. China has its own version of Stoke-on-Trent, **Jǐngdézhèn** 景德镇, which is still the porcelain centre of the country (if not the world). The Ming Dynasty (1368 to 1644) is considered to be the great period of pottery because potters learned to apply colours to unfired pieces using cobalt (bright blue) and high-temperature kilns. The result is the famous creamy or white colour vases with beautiful blue designs that are still popular 700 years on.

Carpets (地毯 Dìtǎn)

Northern China has a long heritage of carpet making, probably because of the shepherd influence of Mongolia. Woollen carpets are still made by hand in areas around Beijing and further into the northwest of the country. The minority people of Xinjiang make carpets with geometric designs that are very similar to the carpets of Pakistan and Persia. Beijing and nearby cities such as Tianjin produce carpets that are far more sinitic (Chinese) in their preference for larger blocks of colour and pictorial patterns. Silk carpets are still made too. These are highly detailed and colourful, hung in frames and treated with the same respect as oil paintings in Europe. A good indication of quality is the underside of the carpet: it should be difficult to know which side is the display side, because a good piece will be almost as beautiful and detailed on the underside.

Lacquerware (漆器 Qīqì)

Painting many layers of lac tree resin onto wooden or copper objects creates lacquer. The finished product has a glossy, durable, reddish or black coating. Vases, plates, trays and ornaments are the most typical forms of lacquerware. Another form of lacquerware is made from cinnabar lacquer (it has a matt red colour). Over 100 coatings make it thick enough to carve relief patterns into.

Jade (玉 Yù)

It surprises some people to learn that no jade in the world originates in China. The Chinese word for jade is **yù**, but this covers a variety of stone, not just the glossy green type. The stone is a connoisseur's item due to its rarity (no jade has ever been mined in China) and hardness that makes it extremely difficult to carve. A single piece may take many years to craft and the design would be chosen to suit the colour and quality of the stone. In tradition, the stone was associated with all sorts of mystical powers; it was often powdered to make longevity potions. These days, to cater to the tourist and mass market, modern cutting techniques and large quantities of cheap, fragile jade (mined on the Canadian coast) have brought the quality and prestige of jade down to the level of any other mass commodity.

Batik (蜡防印花法 Làfáng yìnhuāfǎ)

Several minority groups in China practice this folk art which is a combination of painting and dyeing cloth. A kind of knife is dipped into melted wax and used to paint designs on white fabric. When the wax cools, it sets and hardens and the cloth is dyed with the wax design in place. The dye seeps through the cracks of the wax to make fine lines. The cloth is then boiled and all the wax disappears leaving fine patterns imprinted on the cloth. Batik designs are used to decorate clothes, bags, tablecloths and bedspreads.

Ingenuity

The Chinese have a well-deserved reputation for ingenuity. They have shown remarkable resourcefulness in virtually every aspect of civilisation. As we have already seen, in terms of historical development, Chinese society was (at times) thousands of years ahead of other cultures. In the fields of education and the arts (the hallmarks of a truly advanced society) China was without rivals: we saw earlier (Chapter 6) how paper helped to popularise learning and how teaching was considered a science even in the time of Confucius (Chapter 3).

Military

More than 1,000 years before tanks rolled across the Somme, the Chinese had armoured vehicles. They were, of course, horse drawn, but protected their crews from arrows and spears much the same as their modern equivalents and proved very effective on the battlefield. Another famous example of Chinese military science was the use of powered rockets, the technology of which came from fireworks that were in use in the 7th century AD. Like modern armies, ancient Chinese troops were equipped by science: rockets armed with explosive heads and hand grenades were used. Fortunately, perhaps, the formulae were lost but the technology re-emerged in the Middle Ages. Espionage and spying was recommended by Sun Zi in the *Art of War* (see Chapter 5) and ancient Chinese armies even used men carried by kites high into the air to gather intelligence on the enemy.

Agriculture

Long ago (that is, over 1,000 years), Chinese farmers were irrigating their crops with machines that lifted water in buckets from streams and rivers. Sometime around the 18th century, a system of planting crops developed that gave rise to drastically increased harvests. Much of China's rural land is mountainous and hilly leaving the flat land necessary for growing rice in very short supply. Cutting steps into the hillsides offered the solution. Hills were converted into multilevel rice paddies. There is some debate as to where this technique began. The Chinese almost certainly borrowed it from the Vietnamese, but northern Vietnam at that time was little more than a southern extension of China. Wherever it came from, it is probably the single most important innovation in Chinese agriculture and was possibly the original factor behind the sudden population explosion that began around the same time.

Domestic

Long ago, wealthy men were wall papering their houses and sleeping on heated beds. The world's first flushing toilet was another Chinese innovation. Silk (although not really a purely Chinese innovation) was loved for its feel, look and durability. Chinese people exploited the versatility of silk to make clothing, coverings for windows, rugs, brushes, paper and many more items.

Scientific

Parachutes and pistols are among the large number of lesser known Chinese inventions. Map making and navigation techniques were widely employed centuries before they were in Europe. Mathematics and astronomy were also developed long before they reached a comparable level of sophistication elsewhere (this was partly due to Arab influence). Chinese scientists developed the atom bomb not through ingenuity but from sheer effort and resourcefulness. The story goes that in the golden age of Sino–Soviet relations (the 1950s) Russian scientists were lending China the knowledge to build nuclear weapons. Halfway through this era, however, there was a breakdown in the relationship between the two countries and the scientists were ordered to return to the USSR and shred all the documents and blueprints for the bomb before leaving. Chinese agents retrieved the shred and scraps (presumably there would have been thousands) and after many weeks of effort succeeded in arranging them into recognisable form. The rest, as they say, is history and China has the third (or perhaps second) largest nuclear arsenal in the world today.

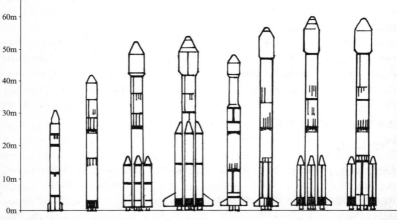

The Long March rocket family (unmanned satellite launchers)

Chinese space rockets carry most of Asia's satellites into orbit. Space technology is, of course, a highly profitable spin-off from missile technology and the Chinese have not been slow to capitalise on this. Japan and South Korea are very good customers. The systems and materials of the rockets have changed little since the days of the space race and cost a fraction of their American rivals. Chinese rocket technology is still based on the costly but effective system of huge powerful rockets (the single aspect of the space travel in which the Russians stayed ahead of the USA).

Transport

China has a vast rail network, constructed on the pattern of the Soviet train system. The engines are of the old diesel locomotive sort and the carriages are fairly simple affairs. There are no classes in Socialist China, so grades of luxury are described by the kind of carriage you pay to ride in. The lowest class consists simply of hard seats that do not recline and bright lights, which do not turn off at night (to deter thieves). The next class up is hard sleeper. This is good for long journeys; it is a communal dormitory carriage. It is also dark at night to allow people to sleep (usually padlocked to their valuables). Just like their Soviet parents, Chinese hard class toilets will be little more than a hole with a view of the track racing beneath. Soft seat class is a comfortable air-conditioned carriage with big, soft chairs and plenty of leg space. The highest class is the very deluxe soft sleeper class. It is a four-bunk compartment with a little table, hot water, adequate beds and a lockable door. The soft class bathrooms are perfectly acceptable by western standards. Although the trains chug, puff and sometimes stall for hours for no apparent reason, timetables are very accurate and trains are seldom late and always depart promptly.

Air travel is another story. Many Chinese pilots are not trained to international standards and this is one reason why Chinese airlines fly to only a very small number of foreign countries. Often Chinese pilots are recruited on their connections. Like so many other occupations in China, tests can be bypassed by those who have contacts. Also training is, on the whole, inadequate. A small number of pilots are trained abroad (in the USA, for example) and return to train the others. Ground and maintenance crews are only a little better. The result is often tragic. Internal Chinese flights crash regularly.

The road network in China is a very haphazard affair. Big city roads are adequate but out in the country dirt tracks are normal. To cope with the economic changes, enormous intercity highways have been built. For the moment these are still very quiet. Traffic accidents are very common in China, road safety is not a high priority as long as car ownership stays low (around one in 20, but rising). Roads built during the 1960s and 1970s resemble runways: dead straight and practically featureless, save for the splitting surfaces and regular ridges. With masses of surplus labour at hand, roads and bridges can be built in only a few weeks. They are not pretty (few safety barriers and minimal lighting) but they do the job.

Fashion and fads

China seems to be trying everything and all at once. In its haste to catch up with the rich countries of the world, fads have come, gone, stayed and even transformed into a few bizarre hybrids. Fashions are similar yet varied, both outrageous and conservative. Some are indescribable.

A lasting favourite for men is the suit. Whether you are running around a track or labouring on a building site, suits are a safe bet. They are another symbol of western culture and believed by many to be the only thing worn by European and American men. To set it off, white tennis shoes go nicely (apparently). There also seems to be a preference for having the trousers a little short (wafting around the lower shin is ideal) and for keeping the label stitched to the sleeve. For boys, a slightly more casual look can be achieved with denim. It appears that the white-out acid wash variety is best. Girls can get the same trendy effect with pink denim.

Women have to be a little more careful, since modesty is always a priority. While Chinese women like to wear very short skirts or shorts, it is thought indecent if a foreign woman does the same. Low necklines will make people stare, but they will be staring whatever you wear. Chinese women consider it more decent to wear a semi-transparent blouse. Frills, wrinkly tights and loud colours seem to constitute feminine dress.

Every imaginable fashion can be seen on the streets of Chinese cities. The rich go in for designer labels on the same lines as wealthy people anywhere. For younger women, copies of Japanese trends (from a few seasons back) seem popular, particularly in the more style-conscious south. For middle-aged women the uniform of choice consists of leggings and big shirts. There are also a few interesting combinations of traditional and modern styles to keep an eye out for.

Makeup has come back with a vengeance, after being abandoned for most of the 1960s and 1970s in the attack on capitalism and traditional femininity. Face-whitening cream is a big seller. It can be bought in department stores (look out for the hilarious 'before' and 'after' photos) and boasts a variety of exotic ingredients, such as human placenta. Goodness knows what else is in the stuff, but it certainly works. Ghostly white faces are the mark of sophisticated women; sun tans are the curse of peasants. Whereas ladies in Taiwan and Hong Kong follow the expensive tastes of Japan, mainland women definitely have their own style when it comes to dressing up. Makeup (I'm no expert) is severe and hair often looks dyed with less than considerate chemical recipes.

Han Chinese women used to pride themselves on their blacker-than-black hair. Comb-in blackening powders were one of the few cosmetic items to survive the Cultural Revolution. Hair of all colours can be found these days. Like everywhere else, girls love to experiment. Sometimes, a bright peroxide blonde can be seen bobbing amid the sea of dark brown heads. Far more popular, however, are subtler browns and reds; again such styles follow Japanese trends. Chinese men like to dye their hair, too, but usually to a more natural shade. Perhaps this is because greying is more visible in darker hair or because silver heads are the cause of great amusement. Chinese men prefer to keep their hair black, even if they are very advanced in years.

Things are improving rapidly, but until Chinese people are able to afford clothes and cosmetics of a quality comparable to those sold in developed countries, they are making do with what is available in China. Low-quality copies and modifications of foreign products and ideas make up the bulk of the market. No matter how strange the design or how badly made the garment, it will sell, simply because there are so many people swarming from the countryside into the cities and in need of such things. Until this changes, expect to be surprised by the imagination and variety of Chinese style.

GLOSSARY

吃 **chī** eat
喝 **hē** drink
厨房 **chúfáng** kitchen
炊具 **chuījù** utensils
作饭 **zuòfàn** cooking
丝绸 **sīchóu** silk
农业 **nóngyè** agriculture
兵力 **bīnglì** military strength
火药 **huǒyào** gunpowder
武器 **wǔqì** weapons
科学 **kēxué** science
公路 **gōnglù** highway

铁路 **tiěguǐ** railway
汽车 **qìchē** car
飞机 **fēijī** aeroplane
宇宙火箭 **yǔzhòu huǒjiàn** space rocket
核能 **hénéng** nuclear energy
核武器 **héwǔqì** nuclear weapon
时尚 **shíshàng** fashion, fad
化妆品 **huàzhuāngpǐn** cosmetics
化妆 **huàzhuāng** put on makeup
衣服 **yīfu** clothes
时装 **shízhuāng** fashionable clothes
西服 **xīfú** men's suit

Taking it further

Books

Food

There are so many books available on this subject! The following all contain easy-to-follow instructions and a variety of recipes (too many Chinese cookbooks contain the same dishes!)

Chinese Cooking For Beginners, Su-Hei Huang, Wei-Chuan Publishing, 1994. A good place to start for novices.

Martin Yan's Culinary Journey Through China, Martin Yan, Bay Books, 1997. I recommend any of this author's books (he is the star of the TV show *Yan Can Cook*). This one is particularly useful for the regional slant and extra information, as well as the usual clarity of the explanations and instructions.

The Chinese Way: Healthy Low Fat Cooking From China's Regions, Eileen Yin Fei Lo, Hungry Minds, 1997. Chinese food is not as healthy as people think but this book provides some recipes for dishes that are both delicious *and* healthy.

Tea

Tea in The East, Carole Manchester, Hearst Books, 1996. A close look at tea-drinking culture across Asia (not only China). The book describes many customs surrounding tea drinking and the various methods of production and preparation across the continent.

The Japanese Way of Tea: From Its Origins in China to Sen Rikyu, Sen Soshitsu, V. Dixon Morris and Paul H. Varley, University of Hawaii, 1998. Discover how a tea-drinking culture began in China and developed into the highly elaborate 'tea ceremony' of Japan. A superb book.

General

The Genius of China: 3000 Years of Science, Discovery and Invention, Robert Needham and Joseph Temple, Prion Books, 1998. Excellent detail, but not too academic for the general reader.
Made in China, Cornelia Spence, Harrap, 1947. An old book but contains lots of China-first information.

Other

The Chinese Space Program, Joan Johnson-Freece, Krieger Publishing Company, 1998. A good account of the programme and a thorough review of the political and economic aspirations of the regime behind it.
China Chic: East Meets West, Valerie Steele and John S. Major, Yale University Press, 1999. A beautifully illustrated book describing Chinese costume, from silk robes to Mao suits.

Websites

Thorough and well designed, presenting ancient Chinese technology and knowledge under a number of headings (everything from warfare to mathematics). Very good photographs:
http://library.advanced.org/23062/index.html

About tea in China, not a big site but it contains some interesting text and photographs: http://desires.com/1.4/Food/Docs/tea.html

A good place to start if you are looking for Chinese recipes:
http://www.globalgourmet.com/destinations/China/

| **THE BASICS FOR LIVING**

Education (教育 Jiàoyù)

This is the one aspect of life that Chinese are openly fanatical about. Nothing else is held in such high regard. Today, as in the past, the Chinese have a ruthlessly pragmatic approach to education. Most families would (and often do) sell everything they have to support their child's learning, especially if the child is a boy. Parents push their children into higher learning for several reasons. The most obvious is, of course, money and the higher standard of living that will bring. Prestige is another reason. In the past, scholars were regarded as superior to men of much greater wealth such as merchants. Underlining these two factors is the historical conscience that is at work in the thinking of most Chinese. For the vast majority, poverty and the stagnant cycle of peasant life is only two or even one generation behind. Education is the way out.

For overseas Chinese it is a way of getting out of the takeaways and restaurants of their immigrant parents. Like people everywhere, Chinese parents want their children to have more than them and to help them get it they are willing to make great sacrifices. Filial piety (the Confucian code of respect among family members) also plays a major part, although not on a conscious level. Parents follow the Confucian recommendation that they give their children as much as possible and, later, the children return the favour by taking care of them when they are too old to work. The better educated they are, the more money they will have. The more money they have, the better the parents will be looked after. This kind of long-term, practical thinking is a strong characteristic of the Chinese psyche.

The system

The law in mainland China requires that every child receive a minimum nine years of education. This law was passed in 1995: the

Educational Law of the People's Republic of China. Shocking as it seems, prior to this no comprehensive law existed; administrating the education system was done through notices, instructions and official announcements. Prior to 1995, the 'system' was a monumental mound of bureaucracy operating on a number of laws that covered only very specific areas of teaching, but failed openly to enforce the right to education for everyone.

Elementary schooling

Schooling begins with kindergartens **yòuéryuán** 幼儿园 (nursery schools) when children are about three years old. Most will attend local schools. In the cities these are common enough for about 50% of urban families to send their children to. In the countryside, the figure is around 12%: kindergartens are unusual in rural places. Children are taught basic-level language, mathematics, arts and sciences. These schools are not compulsory.

When children reach six years, they will enter local elementary **xiǎoxué** 小学 (primary) schools. Generally, the nearest school is the automatic choice, but many better-off or ambitious parents try to send their children to 'key schools'. These can be fee paying or work on an entrance through (very competitive) examination method. In elementary school, there are six grades (academic years) to complete. Schooling at this level is almost universally received (the figure for enrolment is 98%).

High school

High school has two parts: junior high **zhōngxué** 初中 (初等中学), which everybody goes to and senior **gāozhōngxué** 高中 (高等中学). Junior high school consists of another three grades (seven to nine). Schools are entered on an examination system and this is a highly important stage in the sequence of schooling. Students are put into a class (average size 50 students) and stay with this group over the three years.

In junior high students study the sciences, history, geography and languages (Chinese and foreign, usually English but Japanese is an additional possibility in many of the bigger urban schools). Physical education and sport is encouraged but always takes a back seat to academic subjects. There is little association between team sport performance and school prestige (as there is in the USA, UK and Japan).

At the end of junior high, the compulsory system expires. If a student (now aged around 16) has performed satisfactorily in the examinations set at the end of each year, they can attend a vocational school **zhuānkē xuéxiào** 专科学校 or continue in academic subjects based on their examination results and preferences. Approximately one-third of students enter this stage of schooling. Since university exams are of two types, science/engineering and humanities/arts, learning at this stage centres on more specific fields and all students are channelled into one or the other subject streams. The whole purpose of senior high is to coach students for entrance to universities. Vocational schools teach trades or workplace skills and graduates expect to find employment around the age of 19.

University (大学 Dàxué)

Around 4% of the population receive education beyond the age of eighteen. Every year, in the first ten days of July, nationwide examinations are held. Candidates are offered places in the universities of their choice if their results and details are acceptable to the department in which they want to study. Undergraduates are posted to that department for the four years of their studies. It is almost impossible to change course once a place has been accepted. Professional courses in law, medicine and business are offered at this level. Chinese universities tend to be very specialised, far more so than most foreign universities. There are, for example, language universities, universities of social sciences and even universities that offer four-year undergraduate courses in sports and martial arts.

University courses are no longer fully funded for all students who are Chinese citizens. Foreign students are admitted but have to pay their own way. Entrance into native student courses is easiest for overseas Chinese and difficult for foreigners unless they have had at least one year of intensive Chinese language study (preferably at the same institution). On paper, special allowances are made for minority people but they are proportionally underrepresented at the better universities (with the notable exception of ethnic Koreans). Enrolment is determined not only on examination results: prospective students are investigated and their moral and social conduct especially is looked into. It is a popular belief among Chinese academics that certain kinds of people make better students and, as in many areas of Asian social life, a face simply has to fit. This aspect of the

Chinese educational system appears unethical but is perhaps no more prejudicial than the more subtle ways the same end is achieved in many foreign institutions.

Student life

Conditions for Chinese university students are Spartan by western standards. In some universities, six or eight students may share rooms which most foreigners would consider cramped with only two occupants. Dormitories are never mixed although some campuses have dorm buildings in which there are male and female floors. For some privacy (and protection from the insects) students hang sheets from their bunks as makeshift curtains. If they need some time alone with their girlfriend or boyfriend, it is customary for students to pay their roommates to leave them alone. Otherwise couples have to resort to a night in one of the campus parks.

Dormitories (like fees) are free but typically squalid. Light-starved corridors are packed with bags of rubbish, junk, refrigerators and bicycles. Sanitation and food hygiene are poor. Summers are too hot and winters too cold. Hot water for washing is available for only a couple of hours a day. Only the millions of cockroaches enjoy the physical side of dorm life. Campus dormitories are run by student societies and these form a key part of undergraduate life.

Things are getting better slowly. The numbers of paying students are increasing and to attract this much needed source of money, the major universities are attempting to improve student living conditions.

Chinese universities can provide subsidies, loans and grants to students whose families cannot contribute anything to help them. These are given only in cases of extreme hardship (poverty). Education funding offers very little in the way of living expenses since it is expected that parents will subsidise their children's education. Students have very little money to spend and never miss even the blandest canteen meal that is dished out in military fashion three times a day.

Teaching and schools

Strangely, despite all the glory given to academic success, teaching is not a respected profession. It lacks status and funding, conditions are poor, pay is inadequate and student dissatisfaction with courses is high. Most developing countries spend far more on education than China which, at best, allocates only 2% of the GNP (gross national product). Primary and secondary school teachers are in very short supply since it is very hard to attract talented individuals away from better paying jobs in the private sector. It is common for entire classes of undergraduate teachers to fail even to appear at the schools they are assigned to. So severe is the problem that now they are awarded their qualifications only when they have begun teaching. Universities have problems too. Due to money problems, scholarship funds are very tight and dropout rates amongst poverty-stricken students are dangerously high. Currently, universities are graduating about 700,000 students a year, but this is a drastically low figure for a country with a population of 1.3 billion. Less than 1% of Chinese receive a university education (compared to the USA which is 22%).

A teacher's salary (around US \$50 to \$100 per month) is rarely enough to afford a decent standard of living, despite some university teachers living in subsidised campus homes. To make ends meet they take part-time jobs. Music teachers play the piano for foreigners in hotels, for example. This has a direct effect on the quality of instruction and research. Teachers lack the time and motivation to bring new ideas or techniques into their work.

In rural areas, the situation in schools is worsening. The dropout rate among girls is high. The main reason for this is money: it is expensive to send a child to school because when the child is learning their family is losing the money they would be earning from the child's contribution to the family labour force. High school diplomas are simply of no use to a young person whose only option is to work in a factory or a field and a daughter will leave the home once she is married anyway.

Studying overseas (留学 Liúxué)

Every young Chinese person wants to study abroad, ideally in the USA where there are over 100,000 government-sponsored Chinese students. Practically every student is sent away to study sciences, technology, engineering, business or computing. If China is to reach its goal of becoming an advanced nation within 50 years, experts in these fields are vital.

However, most students who are sent abroad don't want to go back to China and never do. Around 70% never return. In the 1990s, the figure was nearing 80% so the government decided to extract the cost of a stay-away student's education from their family. But even this has had little effect because most people believe that when their children become rich in the USA, they will rescue their families too. The brain drain is costing China a fortune.

For Chinese who have already settled in foreign countries, the subjects they favour are those that will bring them the most in terms of social and material benefits. Chinese are first and foremost practical and even though art subjects might appeal to the individual, within the Chinese community they will never be the equal of law, business studies, economics, computing or the sciences. As a result these are the areas young Chinese are drawn to. Not only is this for the status and money they stand to gain from these fields, but also because such studies are far closer to Confucian concepts of learning than are art subjects. Chinese by and large feel uncomfortable with the idea of analysing and criticising conventional wisdom, as they would be required to if they studied philosophy, for example. Moreover, following is much safer than leading and Chinese students are seldom interested in actually developing their fields but look on their studies more in terms of what they will be enabled to do by their degrees once they leave university.

Politics and education

When the Communists took power in 1949, there was no solid educational model either to improve or reject. Generally, education had been the exclusive pursuit of wealthy families. Following the revolutionary mood of the May Fourth reformers, the Nationalist government had attempted to make education more accessible but the upheaval and warfare of the 1930s and 1940s prevented any serious improvements in mass education. The Communist Party adopted the Soviet model with the idea that in order for China to become a Socialist paradise, education was a top priority. As a result, education has a very political flavour in China, even today. Propaganda, ideology and education are part and parcel of the same deal.

The Education Law passed in 1995 states that 'education must render services to the establishment of Socialist modernisation'. This basically means that education must support government policy and aim to give children not only knowledge, but a world view based on the party line.

For the last decade 'patriotism' has been a strong theme in many aspects of Chinese life. The reason being that since China has been developing more and more contact with the west, interest in potentially subversive ideas has grown. Also, the fragmentation of countries like the former USSR has worried the government for many years. 'Patriotism' has become another term for 'Nationalism'. In 1995, the National Education Committee (the government department that controls schooling) issued a directive that every school make efforts to commemorate the 50th anniversary of Victory Over Japan Day. Song contests and lecture meetings were held and over ten million students participated. The Leninist idea of education as a vehicle for ideology is still strong, except in private schools where there is much less political influence. 'Patriotism' entails studies of other cultures. One particularly interesting textbook gives a breakdown of all the important nationalities (American, French, British etc.) and the physical traits and mental strengths and weakness of the typical man or woman from these countries. In short: how to spot them and how to understand them. The tone is very much of the 'blacks make good dancers and runners' sort. Consequently from a young age children are presented with very incorrect descriptions of foreign countries and ways of life. The goal of such education is to hold China together (especially to hold onto the minority peoples and the lands they occupy) by contrasting the familiar with the strangest aspects of foreign life as a way of praising the wonders of Chinese uniqueness.

Health (健康 Jiànkāng)

The Chinese people are unhealthy and the health system is grossly inadequate. Cigarettes are cheap and it seems that every male over the age of 16 smokes (it is unacceptable for women to smoke in public). Spitting is a habit of young and old, male and female, indoors and out. This spreads diseases such as bronchitis (which makes people cough, so they spit more). Public hygiene is poor and food hygiene little better. Expect to find toilets that are no more than holes (don't look down), stones in your rice and kitchens that look as if they have been vandalised by blind men with grime hoses.

Sexual health is a major problem. Using prostitutes is not taboo for any man with enough money. Sexually transmitted diseases are far higher than official figures suggest. Because of sensitivity about these matters, statistics are inaccurate and education has to be done through euphemism and insinuation. Blood is another area for concern. Many rural families make a living from selling their blood to travelling tycoons who sell it on to hospitals. Infected blood gets through and both donor and recipient pay a very high price for the shortcuts of middlemen and their dirty equipment.

Like everything in the public sector, hospitals are overstaffed, badly organised, underequipped, underfunded and inefficient. Medical insurance was guaranteed under the work unit scheme which offered this as well as other benefits to everybody who belonged to the official organisation representing their workplace. These days the system has collapsed since it is almost impossible for people to join a new unit once they have left their area. So, as the rural population converges on the cities, the health service has become a pay-for-what-you-can system. Ambulances are hardly ever seen in Chinese cities because only the richest members of society can afford the bill that is promptly presented to them on arrival. It is normal to see road traffic accident victims thrown into the back of taxis and then dumped in a hospital waiting room.

Communal living is particularly hazardous. Cramped living conditions and unclean washing facilities spread diseases such as colds, flu and athlete's foot through student populations in days. Hepatitis, tuberculosis and typhoid are also growing problems. Recently, fouled water sources have led to whole town and village populations being poisoned.

'Psychological illness' seems to equate to 'personality problems' which is a label quickly slapped on anyone (usually children) who exhibits eccentricities or behaviour that is not approved of. Curiously, such cases are on the increase. Real psychological problems go unchecked, because the Chinese have deep-rooted fears about them. They are considered tremendously shameful for a family, so sufferers rarely receive treatment. Overall (but perhaps not officially), mental illness is still considered to be a product of capitalist societies (as used to be believed in the old USSR) and simply too rare in China to warrant serious funding. Mental patients are often put into prison with criminals. Even in the biggest cities, there are only a handful of mental clinics that are adequately staffed and equipped to deal with this growing problem and in rural areas, the situation is particularly bleak.

Perhaps because of the appalling lack of public health resources, millions of ordinary Chinese have a love affair with pills, potions and medicine of all kinds. Accidents aside, health, the Chinese believe, is a question of what you can afford and the sum total of your own efforts to preserve it. No matter what their ailment, many Chinese, especially in rural areas, demand an injection of some sort before they leave the doctor, nurse or hospital. In the minds of many, injections represent real treatment, since they are the symbol of modern scientific medicine. But, in the intrinsically dualistic Chinese world, traditional medicine still has a major role to play. Since the end of the Cultural Revolution Chinese medicine has been creeping toward a synthesis between western and Chinese medical science.

The basis of Chinese concepts of health

Chinese philosophy consistently emphasises the existence of a subtle but mighty force that unites and determines the creation of all things. Daoists describe this as the Dao, but this belief was widely held long before the birth of the 'ism'. Central to this theory is the universal force **qì** 气. This is sometimes called 'ch'i', 'chee' or 'ki'. The Chinese believe that this energy governs the well-being of all living things as well as giving shape to inanimate phenomena. Qi is sometimes described as the stuff of the Dao. The natural state of qi is motion. It flows in the most efficient manner possible and interruptions in its circulation give rise to problems. In the case of buildings and furniture, qi must be allowed to flow naturally to preserve the health of the living things in the environment (see feng shui section). If a person suffers health problems, the Chinese look at many lifestyle factors to diagnose and find a cure for the ailment. Their approach is generally holistic, since not only the physical environment is taken into account, but many other things as well. Whatever the problem and whatever the cure, the Chinese base most of their understanding of health and long life on the maintenance of good qi flow.

What is qì 气?

First off, it is important to pronounce the word correctly: it is said as 'chee' and written with the Chinese character 气 (the traditional character is more commonly seen than the simplified one) which is often defined as 'spirit', 'air' or 'breath'. Many cultures have names for a subtle energy, which despite being normally invisible (although some people can apparently see it) is said to be critical to health. The Indian yogic concept of *prana* is possibly the closest to qi.

The Chinese generally tend not to attempt to define it in a manner which suits most western scientists and sceptics. Instead, its existence is implied through the observation of certain physical phenomena. For example, acupuncture is said to have evolved after seeing how the ailments of some people who suffered arrow wounds were relieved even though there were no perceptible links between the injured area and the recovery. Early Chinese physicians concluded that lines of energy (meridians) ran over the body and these could be interrupted to produce injury or strengthened to give a curative effect. The energy flowing down these meridians was identified as qi.

Principles of traditional Chinese medicine (TCM)

TCM is really Chinese philosophy in practice. It fundamentally accepts that the human body is the result of a balance between two polar forces (yin and yang) and seeks to maintain or recover that balance. To the Chinese doctor, the principles of TCM are universally applicable, but every patient requires unique treatment. This is because no two human bodies can ever have exactly the same physical or psychological experiences which have led to the disharmony.

The Five Elements of the body

The Chinese believe that the body is a world in miniature and has its own version of the Five Elements (see Chapter 4): qi, blood, moisture, spirit and essence.

Qi is the breath of life itself, that energy which allows us to breathe, think and feel. Blood **xiě** 血 is a broader term for the physical matter that makes up our bones, nerves, organs, skin and muscles. Moisture **shī** 湿 is the liquid matter that lubricates the many tissues of the body. Spirit **shén** 神 is the non-physical aspect of the individual, the expression of the unlimited and timeless soul. Essence **jīng** 精 refers to the regenerative and reproductive powers and substances of the body.

The organ networks

Just as the Five Elements work together, the human body is believed to be governed by a network of five systems: the organ networks, namely the heart, lungs, spleen, liver and kidneys. Each organ has unique yin and yang properties and is responsible for governing the qi of one of the body's Five Elements. For example, the kidney is said to be in charge of the essence and the liver stores the qi for the blood.

Body climates

Early Chinese doctors were intrigued by the way temperature and climate affected the natural world. In TCM, the body is believed to have its own five types of climate, these are: heat, cold, dampness, dryness and wind. Dampness causes phlegm and mucus to be produced in excess (as in the common cold), so the cure must produce dryness to counteract this. Too much dryness causes chapping or cracking of the skin (eczema, for example) and the remedy for this would require a moisture-producing medicine.

Channels (经络 Jīngluò)

Qi, blood and moisture flow around channels in the body. These channels (meridians) act as pathways, linking all parts of the body into a network. Health is achieved when the qi, blood and moisture flows in the most natural way. Since all parts of the body are mutually dependent, the channels are critical. Typical symptoms of channel disruption would be things such as headaches, high blood pressure and indigestion.

All ailments originate from depletion or congestion of qi, blood or moisture in the channels. Depletion is inferred from symptoms such as lethargy, poor immunity and general weakness. Congestion manifests as pain in certain areas, poor mood and aching.

Diagnosis

Chinese doctors recognise many types of pulse and interpret this in relation to the patient's other complaints. Doctors of TCM deduce the cause of an illness not only from obvious symptoms but also from observations of a patient's lifestyle, posture, psychological factors, odour, breath, complexion and so on. They use this information to prescribe a course of treatment.

For example, patient John comes to the doctor for help with recurrent bronchitis. His eyes have a slight redness and his tongue has a yellowish colour. To the practitioner of TCM, these indicate a congestion of qi and excess heat. The treatment will concentrate on reducing that heat.

Treatment (治疗 Zhìliáo)

The harmonising of the body's yin and yang energies is the ultimate goal of all TCM treatment. This involves the balancing of opposite energies, for example: heat with cold, dryness with dampness and mind with body. This is done through the regulation of qi, moisture and blood within the organ networks.

Weak organs are hardened (toned), tightness is relaxed, congested channels are expanded, irritation is calmed, heat is cooled, cold is warmed, dampness is drained and dryness is moistened.

TCM has two main forms of treatment: acupuncture and herbal medicine, as well as a supplementary but equally sophisticated system of massage.

Acupuncture (针刺疗法 Zhēncì liáofǎ)

This method is based on the assumption that qi runs in lines over the surface of the body, just like water runs in rivers over the surface of the earth. Each organ network has a corresponding set of channels. Small stainless steel needles are placed into specific points in the channels (穴位 xuéwèi), opening and closing them to interrupt or stimulate the flow of qi. The piercing of the channels is believed to allow stagnant qi to escape or improve the circulation of healthy qi.

Acupuncture mobilises not only qi, but blood and moisture too. In turn this leads to invigoration of the muscles, nerves, glands and organs.

Some people find acupuncture completely painless. Others feel a slight pinch followed by numbness. It is not unknown to experience sensations of tickling, aching, warmth or heaviness either. Some patients even say they can feel the qi travelling from point to point. Whatever the physical sensation, insertion of the needles is rarely painful and usually produces relaxation and a slight elevation of spirit.

Symptoms acupuncture can treat

Infections	Internal	Eyes, ears, nose and throat	Musculo-skeletal/ neurological	Dermatological (skin)	Genito-urinary	Mental/ emotional
Colds	Hypoglycemia	Hay fever	Sciatica	Eczema	Menstrual irregularity	Insomnia
Flu	High blood pressure	Sinus infections	Arthritis	Herpes	Morning sickness	Stress
Hepatitis	Asthma	Earache	Neuralgia	Acne	PMT	Depression
Bronchitis	Colitis	Ringing ears	Sprains		Pelvic-inflammatory disorder	Addictions
			Cerebral palsy		Vaginitis	
	Ulcers	Dizziness	Bell's palsy		Impotence	
	Diabetes	Bad eyesight	Headaches		Infertility	
	Constipation	Sore throat	Stroke			
	Diarrhoea	Deafness	Backache			
	Haemorrhoids		Stiff neck			
			Tendonitis			
			Bursitis			

Needles stay inserted typically for between 20 and 40 minutes. Some patients notice symptom relief immediately but usually the best results come about through a course, not a single session. Symptom relief is more likely to occur in the days following the treatment and people often feel very energetic following acupuncture therapy.

In the language of TCM, acupuncture is the most effective method of dealing with ailments that originate in dysfunctions of qi, blood and moisture or complications involving the organ network. In western terms these translate to conditions such as stress relief, post-surgery recovery, addictions such as smoking or alcohol, chronic fatigue and poor immunity.

The World Health Organization has acknowledged acupuncture as effective for the treatment of several common conditions, as shown in the table on the opposite page.

Herbal medicine (中草药 Zhōng Cǎoyào)

TCM uses herbs as another powerful tool of medicine. Although it shares a few parallels with western pharmaceutical methods, it is overall quite different in that TCM herbal medicine targets the underlying cause of the disease. By contrast, western drugs control symptoms, but do little to alter the process of the disease significantly. For example, antibiotics remove bacteria but do not strengthen the patient's immunity. Generally, Chinese herbal medicines give priority to improving the patient's ability to fight disease and seldom have harmful side effects.

To the TCM doctor, the fluid substances of the body (qi, moisture and blood) are similar to soil which, through overuse or neglect, loses its vitality and becomes barren. Qi, blood and moisture can become eroded too, through overuse, underuse, inadequate rest, bad diet or psychological problems. As a result, the organ networks cease to function productively.

Herbs that boost the strength of qi would be prescribed for patients suffering from conditions related to fatigue as these are interpreted as evidence of poor qi. Blood-enriching herbs are given in cases of insomnia, blurred vision and irritability because these are traditionally associated with undernourished blood. Moisture-replenishing herbs are given to treat conditions such as dry skin or dehydration.

Herbal medicine works by helping the organ networks to do their jobs. Some herbs can assist the heart in pumping blood to ease circulatory disorders. The lungs can be strengthened by herbs to build immunity and improve breathing. Herbs can vitalise the liver to ease muscular stiffness or empower the spleen to manage digestion. The kidneys are the seat of the reproductive and sexual functions, problems with which can be treated through herbs.

Herbal medicine is particularly effective in alleviating the symptoms of many common illnesses such as colds or flu. Herbs that support the flow of qi and the functions of the lungs will help increase immunity to these ailments. Cramps, allergies and inflammation can be treated with herbs and these often produce dramatic results.

To achieve maximum results, Chinese herbs are mixed in formulae to meet a patient's needs. Symptoms are matched against a herb's effects and prescribed accordingly. Formulae come in a variety of forms. Some herbs are boiled into teas or fortified soups (many Chinese like to do crude home saucepan formulae for themselves too!), some come ground and packaged like western medicine and some come as raw, ground powders, still others come as liquid concentrates.

Chinese people often regard herbal medicine in a similar way to dietary supplements, i.e. more like food than drugs. Milder herbs and popular cure-alls such as ginseng (人参 **rénshēn**) are found in many supplements and are consumed daily as a preventive rather than curative measure.

Massage (推拿 **Tuīná**)

The TCM method is the oldest discipline of massage in existence (it is mentioned in a medical manual said to have been written in 2300 BC!). Like acupuncture, it is based on improving the flow of qi to produce a therapeutic effect. It is like a needleless acupuncture in that it utilises the principle of meridians (channels of qi) to allow the body to heal itself.

The technique involves using the arms and hands to manipulate the soft tissue of the body (muscles and tendons) and the many acupressure points of the body. When such places are pressed or kneaded, qi flow through the meridians is greatly enhanced and the overall condition should be improved.

Acupressure points correspond to acupuncture points which are simply points on the meridian lines that are believed to be particularly important to the flow of qi down that meridian.

Key acupressure points, like acupuncture points represent the organs of the body. Therefore, once a patient has been diagnosed and the weak organ identified, the doctor can then go to work on the area of the body's surface that corresponds to that organ, and thereby treat the patient's illness.

To help them further, practitioners of TCM massage uses compresses, liniments, herbal poultices and salves.

There are four major schools of Chinese massage. One is the rolling school, which concentrates on soft tissue work and is particularly good at treating joint injuries and sprains. There is also the one-finger-pushing method school, which emphasises more acupressure techniques for the treatment of internal problems. Another system concentrates on skeletal alignment for the relief of nerve, muscular and joint-related pain. The last is a slightly more specialised school involved with using massage as a system of revitalising the qi of depleted energy systems. On top of these there are literally hundreds of family systems, which have been passed down from generation to generation.

In a typical session of TCM massage, the patient wears loose-fitting clothes and no shoes. He/she will lie on a mat on the floor or a specially designed massage table with a hole for the face to rest in. After a few questions, the masseur will begin the procedure and focus initially on painful areas. More advanced practitioners will use massage in conjunction with herbal medicines, especially in the treatment of more serious problems.

Normally sessions will last between 30 minutes and one hour. Depending on the patient's condition, further sessions on a regular basis may be advised. After massage, clients feel deeply relaxed but also very energised.

The pillars of Chinese massage (musculo-skeletal knowledge and acupressure points) support hundreds of more modern schools such as *reiki* (a Japanese system of foot massage) and provide the substance of many martial disciplines that focus on attacking the critical points of the body. Many Chinese are familiar with the basics of acupressure and it is certainly growing in popularity both outside and inside China.

GLOSSARY

学生	**xuéshēng**	student
老师	**lǎoshī**	teacher
学校	**xuéxiào**	school
学习	**xuéxí**	study
数学	**shùxué**	mathematics
英语	**Yīngyǔ**	English (language)
日语	**Rìyǔ**	Japanese (language)
课	**kè**	class, subject
留学生	**liúxuéshēng**	foreign student
毕业	**bìyè**	(verb) graduate
论文	**lùnwén**	thesis, dissertation
织业	**shēngyá**	career, profession
医学	**yīxué**	medicine
国药	**guóyào**	traditional Chinese medicine
医治	**yīzhì**	cure
西医	**xīyī**	new (western) medicine
病	**bìng**	disease, sickness
精神病	**jīngshénbìng**	mental illness
性病	**xìngbìng**	sexually transmitted disease
爱滋病	**àizī bìng**	AIDS
癌症	**áizhèng**	cancer
理气	**lǐqì**	regulate the flow of qi
气滞	**qìzhì**	stagnation of qi
气郁	**qìyù**	obstruction of qi
气虚	**qìxū**	deficiency of qi
气血辨证	**qìxiě biànzhèng**	qi and blood analysis
气逆	**qìnì**	flow of qi in the wrong direction

Taking it further

Books

In Their Own Words: Profiles of Today's Chinese Students, Tony Gallagher, China Books & Periodicals, 1998. Beijing University students speak out about their education, lives and politics.

Broken Portraits: Personal Encounters With Chinese Students, Michael David Kwan, China Books & Periodicals, 1990. A penetrating insight into China's education system, disillusioned youth and society in general.

The Complete Illustrated Guide to Chinese Medicine: A Comprehensive System For Health and Fitness, Tom Williams & Han Liping, Thorson, 1996. The basics behind TCM and simple fitness routines and tips to improve and maintain health.

The Chinese Way To Healing: Many Paths To Wholeness, Misha Ruth Cohen and Kalia Doner, Berkley Publishing Group, 1996. Lots of background, case histories and healing programmes for a variety of common complaints.

Websites

Links to every Chinese university on the web and information for people who want to study or teach in China:
http://hong.commerce.ubc.ca/www/shen/univ.html

A serious English-language publication dealing with every aspect of TCM. There is an annual subscription fee but the quality of the material makes it worth it (it is also a good way of bypassing much of the nonsense about TCM that is on the internet): http://www.jcm.co.uk

10 | WORK AND PLAY

On paper, China is a Communist country, run by its people. In practice it is a capitalist state driven by an elite behind a barbed tangle of bureaucracy. The government still holds the reins on industry, agriculture and the economy even though increasing numbers of private enterprises 私人企业 **sīrén qǐyè** have entered the arena.

At present, the state owns approximately 100,000 enterprises that employ about 50 million workers. Most of these operate as individual, semi-autonomous companies. The workforces can make up whole communities and some factories are big enough to employ entire populations (half a million for example) of small cities and towns. The emergence of joint private–state-owned industries 公私合营 **gōngsī héyíng** is the principle factor behind China's economic growth.

Most state industries were at one time (in some cases until very recently) under direct state control 国营 **guóyíng**, but authority has become gradually more localised so that, nowadays, managers are effectively owners. However, in typically have-your-cake-and-eat-it fashion, the state still retains the authority to override any management decision, but empowers the managers to make decisions at other times (as well as take the blame for failed initiatives).

The days of the iron rice-bowl are long gone. Prior to Deng Xiaoping's economic reforms of the late 1970s and early 1980s, everybody was practically guaranteed an income no matter how shoddy their work or how badly run their organisation. This was a matter of Socialist principle. To control productivity, the state requires that managers ensure that their factories produce a certain amount in a specified time. However, capitalism has proved a dangerous gamble, both for state and managers. Before the reforms, all profits went directly to government coffers but, nowadays, factories are taxed instead.

This means that as long as they pay their taxes, managers can skim enough off the extra to make themselves very comfortable. Not everybody is better off, however; workers foot the price of these changes. China has an enormous population and factory jobs can be filled in minutes. Like any business, profits require saving money and making shortcuts here and there. Exploitation of a cheap and disposable workforce seems to be the rule of thumb.

Despite the reforms and semi-independent state of government industry, the entire state-owned sector is in big trouble. With each year, the percentage of industrial output from state-owned enterprises is decreasing. Two-thirds of state-owned businesses are operating at a chronic loss. To avoid filling the streets with millions of discontented unemployed, factories are under pressure to keep their workforces by granting them reduced pay and hours or very long holidays. Women have been hit hardest by the crisis. Maternity leave is given, often whether a woman is pregnant or not. Durations as long as five years or more are not unheard of. Subsidising this is very costly.

Industry (工业 Gōngyè)

Whether private or state sponsored, all industries have to pay their own way. The passage from the old system in which everything was state run to the new liberalised approach continues to be very hazardous. The traditions of the old system are still strong. After the Soviet model, production was achieved, but usually in the most inefficient manner. The very costly heavy industry that came to China on Stalin's recommendation was never more dynamic than a lumbering dinosaur that, these days, is all but extinct. For the worker, it is arguable that things were better under the old system. A job was pretty much for life. The work unit a worker was attached to provided them with medical insurance, housing and sometimes even a say in how things were run. This has gone the way of the dinosaurs too. Because of the iron rice-bowl system, everybody was paid roughly the same income, nobody worked harder than the next man and everybody did the bare minimum required by the job. Consequently, details like quality control, research and development and worker initiatives were close to non-existent. Of course, things worked out but rarely as well as they could have.

Nevertheless, China has sprinted ahead in the race to be the workshop of the world. The main economic goal of the Chinese Communist Party since the death of Mao has been to acquire foreign money. Light industry and a low-waged workforce is the formula. Plastics, textiles and metalware can be produced at costs which simply cannot be matched elsewhere in the world, even in countries such as Thailand. Working conditions are hard. A normal factory is of the deathtrap sweatshop variety. Typically, workers are young people attracted from rural areas to the bright lights of the big cities. A good wage is about $30 a month. Work is often dangerous. The laws passed in the 1990s concerning private ownership of factories comprehensively neglected to include safety regulations. Beyond plaques on walls and headed paper, trade unions do not exist since China is a Communist country and everybody is really in one big union. The unions that do dare to complain are very reluctant to do so for fear of scaring away desperately needed foreign capital. When strikes do occur (there were many in the early to mid-1990s), they are desperate and violent, especially in rural areas where there are even fewer alternative sources of income for everyday people.

Resources (资源 Zīyuán)

China is well stocked in a few key natural resources, namely iron ore and coal. By industrial standards their quality is low but they are adequate. Until the mid-1980s, China was a significant exporter of special metals for use in aviation and technology (tungsten, for example), but supplies seem to have run dry. China today is one of the world's biggest importers of steel, pig iron, copper and aluminium.

Manufacturing (制造业 Chūchǎn)

State-run factories use badly outdated equipment and methods. Most are highly labour intensive. In many cases they are kept this way to prevent mass unemployment. The government still considers steel production to be the key to economic advancement. Output is estimated at around a million tons per plant, but with only 20 or so plants capable of such production, China still has to import, usually from Japan. Electric power and machine technology is for the large part still of 1960s and 1970s vintage and highly energy inefficient. The electronics industry appears to be ten to 15 years behind most of the world, but enormous progress has been made in domestic appliances as demand for things such as televisions and radios continues to soar. Much of the industry is devoted to copying and modifying old Japanese appliances. Production of electronic consumer goods is probably the biggest growth industry today.

The majority of industrial bases are on the eastern coast of the country. A number of industrial plants (such as car factories) can be found in more inland areas, but, naturally, rural places are the home of agriculture. Coastal areas are also where China's textile industry can be found. The heart of textile manufacturing is the Shanghai area. China is today one of the biggest producers of cotton, wool and silk.

Agriculture (农业 Nóngyè)

China has been an agrarian society for more than 4,000 years. Today agriculture is taken more seriously than ever and the government is just as sensitive about it as ever and probably more. Economic relaxation means that it is subject to the ups and downs of buying and selling just as any other business. However, since China is a big country and people have to eat, the gamble seems to be paying off. Today's China is the world's biggest agricultural economy, feeding roughly 23% of the world: easily ahead in production of cotton, rice and tobacco; it is also very competitive in wheat, millet, hemp, tea and corn.

Approximately 800 million people make up the country's rural population, with about 500 million directly engaged in agricultural work. 'Peasant' is a broad term used by the Chinese government to describe people who live in rural areas, not just those who work the fields. Modern agriculture with its chemicals, mechanisation and market forces has changed peasant life enormously.

There have been three stages of development in agriculture since 1949. The first stage was collectivisation. In the 1950s, the land was returned to the people. Prior to this, peasants were tenant farmers, most of the land being owned by wealthy individuals, warlords and aristocrats. In the 1950s, this all changed and former owners were put into peasant communes alongside regular folk working the fields. The people/state owned, ran, worked and at best scratched a meagre subsistence living from the land. Wonder harvests lovingly produced by honest, Socialist toil were pure fiction. In the very worst period, the mid-1950s, up to 30 million died of starvation. The era was more of a gigantic stumble backward than the 'Great Leap Forward' as it was called.

The second stage was reparation. From 1961 until Mao died in 1976 changes were made to undo the damage done in the previous decade. China looked to the Soviet Union (another big fan of make-believe harvests) as well as to her own experts and scientists for new planting techniques, chemicals and systems of farm planning. More significantly, other areas of the economy such as industry were used to subsidise agriculture. Things were put on hold for much of the late 1960s when the insanity of the Cultural Revolution was at a zenith, but improvement was rapid during the 1970s.

The economic reforms that began in the late 1970s and continue today ushered the most far-reaching changes to agriculture seen so far in modern times. Peasants are now allowed to grow and sell their produce as they wish. Such decentralisation has had many effects. Now that the responsibility for production has shifted from the collective (commune) to the household the number of labourers has dropped and production has increased rapidly. Farmers and their families are free to bring their produce to the cities and sell it in competitive market fashion. As a result, the household income of rural families has generally increased (US $10 to $25 a month). The casualties of the reforms include children and a massive labour-starved workforce. Children of poorer families leave school to help with the family work because in the capitalist world it is sink or swim. Urban society is feeling the effects of rural unemployment as millions of unemployed fill the streets of the big cities like Shanghai. Urban workers find themselves unable to compete in the job market against the inexhaustible numbers of peasants who accept much lower wages and local councils are intimidated by their readiness to riot and vulnerability to criminal activities.

Distribution

Of China's enormous area 88% is unsuitable for cultivation. Most of the western part of the country is at best suitable for grazing livestock, not growing. Technology has helped irrigate high-altitude areas of the far west (like Tibet) and, further, enabled them to grow specially developed strains of wheat, barley and rice.

The semi-tropical south is the heart of production. The growing season here is very long and water in the form of rainfall and rivers is fairly abundant. These are ideal conditions for growing thirsty crops such as rice which is predominant in this region. Potatoes and wheat are also grown as winter crops. The land is naturally acidic red clay; with the help of heavy fertiliser use, as many as three crops a year can be cultivated on the same land. Cotton and tea are also grown in the south of the country.

In the dryer north, wheat is the traditional crop. Ninety per cent of China's winter wheat comes from this area. The area is characterised by dryland crops: sorghum, millet and corn. The success of these crops is due to the soil in the area being much richer than that of the south. Irrigation is, however, the major limiting factor in these parts. The area is blighted by regular flooding (see Chapter 1) and droughts, but water conservation measures have improved the situation. Mechanisation is lending a hand too. Northern growing areas are easier to plough and the cropping patterns are less labour intensive.

Leisure (余暇 Yúxiá)

As in other developing countries, the lives of most Chinese are relatively limited in terms of leisure and free time. The majority of ordinary people simply lack the money to spend on recreation and have far less time to indulge in activities that do not bring in money. This is particularly true for the two-thirds of the population that live in rural areas. There are virtually no facilities for sport such as leisure centres and athletics tracks. The situation is improving in the cities, but since only a tiny minority of people have the disposable income and time necessary to enjoy recreation the way people in developed societies can, there is still no comparable leisure industry. As we saw in the last chapter, Chinese people like to think of themselves as health conscious (even if they smoke like chimneys). Old and young are fond of exercise and traditional forms are still popular: they are free, require no great physical exertion and are easy to learn.

There are a number of foreign sports that have captured the interest of young Chinese.

Soccer (足球 Zúqiú)

This is currently the fastest growing sport in Asia. China has tried hard in recent years to come up to the level of its diminutive neighbours Japan and South Korea which both have very strong national teams and leagues. The Chinese league is improving very rapidly, but since the sport still lacks serious interest from sponsors, there is only a very small number of foreign players bringing their skills into the leagues. Travelling away to matches is practically impossible for most because their incomes and jobs would not allow it. Despite these problems, it is growing in popularity, both as a played and watched sport.

Schools and universities have leagues but the sport in general has yet to become as competitive as in foreign countries. Television provides coverage of major foreign games, particularly the Italian and English leagues. Manchester United has an enormous following.

Athletics and recreation (运动 Yùndòng)

Facilities for athletic sports are available in all the big cities. Although only a small number participate seriously, China's population is so big that even a tiny percentage translates to millions. China has produced many great athletes, but seems to have followed the Russian model a little too closely. As in most other competitive countries doping is the norm but Chinese teams seem particularly vulnerable to testing that often leaves them in disgrace. In their defence, the Chinese claim that the highly contributing USA is let off lightly for fear of withdrawing funding from bodies like the International Olympic Committee.

In terms of popularity, track and field events are behind sports such as basketball and table tennis. Non-competitive activities such as recreational tennis, squash or jogging are the reserve of those with enough money to use the minute number of sports clubs that are prohibitively expensive for most people.

University and school running tracks offer an alternative. First thing in the morning (before the smog gathers and makes breathing unbearable) these places are filled with people, young and old. Many will be doing stretches and warm-ups, some will be jogging casually, others sprinting as if from a burning building. Strange though it sounds, few will be wearing sports clothes or running shoes, some will be running backwards and others puffing cigarettes as they do their laps.

University campus grounds offer free facilities such as outdoor basketball courts and weights for lifting. Many Chinese are self-conscious when it comes to physical exertion so bodybuilding is something of a nocturnal affair. Many public places have table tennis tables made from concrete. If people can provide their own bats, balls and nets they can play free of charge for as long as they like. However, because the surfaces are bad, they often lie unused like solemn grey tombstones.

Dancing (跳舞 Tiàowǔ)

Sometimes it seems the Chinese are allergic to sleep, especially the elderly who are up at the crack of dawn. They can be found waltzing away with their friends in parks and public squares to crackly classical music blaring from pole-mounted speakers that once barked out propaganda night and day. Chinese people have a fondness for old-fashioned social dances, seeing them as both a dignified and relaxing pastime. Some youngsters are keen too. On many university campuses entry-by-ticket improvised dance nights are regular events.

Traditional dances survive but these seem to be enjoyed by the elderly alone, although grandchildren and other curious kids sometimes join in too. A big drum is beaten and people march round in a large circle, sometimes waving coloured scarves and handkerchiefs as their hands swing in time to the beat which is slow enough to keep it gentle.

Nightclubs and discos can be a little strange to foreign eyes. They are certainly less fancy and fairly small, but are just as loud. Some are very dark: to lessen the dancers' inhibitions. Perhaps Chinese youngsters are more modest than Europeans or Americans, so dancing in big groups is preferable, particularly for girls. This said, Chinese dancers are as energetic and imaginative as anybody else. At some time during the night there may be an hour set aside for slow smooching. The pop will scratch to a sudden stop and the lights go up a little while the couples take to the floor and everybody else gets a breather.

Violence in nightclubs is fairly rare and is generally a problem only in places that cater to foreign customers. Drugs have yet to invade the nightclub scene, but limited quantities of Ecstasy are finding their way in from Vietnam.

Martial arts (功夫 Gōngfū)

These are nowhere near as popular as the film industry suggests. Even though martial arts of all kinds have very strong traditions in China, today they are in a pitiful state. Teachers were driven from the country during the Cultural Revolution and today the arts are considered little more than a relic of history or something on the cinema screen. There is only one recognised system of kung fu/**gōngfū** (martial art): **wǔshù** 武术, which is a demonstration art combining acrobatics and dance-like fighting routines. It has no combative component.

The arts are divided into two broad categories: internal and external. These correspond to yin and yang respectively. The external embodies action and the use of aggression, muscular strength and speed (yang is the male aspect). The internal (yin) stresses the cultivation of qi (subtle energy) and higher states of consciousness to avoid rather than meet conflict.

In any park or open space, you can find groups of people moving their bodies with gentle but precise movements. They are doing taiji quan or another form of qi gong.

Qì gōng 气功

This practice could be described as TCM without medicine, as such it represents the internal school. It means *qi work* or *qi practice*. It is pronounced 'chee gung'. The term is very broad, covering many old aerobic, martial and yoga-like systems (over 3,000 in fact!)

The idea is that through set patterns of motion the flow of qi in the body can be controlled. Qi gong has a variety of movements, breath-control and meditation techniques. Each induces the other i.e. controlled breathing leads to a state of meditation or vice versa.

Movement

This is the starting point. The body is moved in ways designed to improve the flow of qi. These are gentle, slow and rhythmical movements that focus on the arms more than the legs which remain relatively static, although usually bent and relaxed as if in a state of readiness. The arms swing and make patterns which are usually symmetrical. The goal is to energise the body's various qi centres

Qi gong movements

(there are three major points). Since the lower belly is said to be the main seat of energy, many exercises involve moving the arms around or holding this area. The whole practice is pleasing to watch and not very complicated (at least as far as the basic physical movements are concerned) so it can be learnt in a short time. Some groups like to perform their routines to background music (although this is often blaring and very distracting to non-Chinese ears!). Normally, people wear loose-fitting clothes and use public places. Qi gong is learnt and taught by watching other practitioners.

Meditation

This takes many forms but is based on controlled breathing. After the movement routines have been completed, many classes finish their qi gong sessions with a form of sitting relaxation.

Postures vary: some schools recommend yoga-like positions like the lotus while others allow sitting in chairs. Generally, cross-legged, straight-backed sitting postures are best, since these require some effort and should stop people falling asleep. Most qi gong practitioners close their eyes, but some prefer half closing, again to prevent sleepiness. The hands rest somewhere in the lap or on the legs. Breathing is all done through the nose. The word qi itself can mean 'air' so they are closely related (the term 'qi' at one time referred to all invisible physical phenomena such as air, heat and cold). Qi gong meditation is believed to promote a healthy flow of qi because regulated, deep breathing is supposed to invigorate the organs, releasing stagnant (i.e. bad) qi, re-energising the meridians. Sunrise is the best time to perform qi gong.

Tàijí quán 太极拳

By far the most famous internal/soft art is taiji quan (pronounced as 'tie jee chew-ann'). The name means 'great eternal fist' since *taiji* refers to the symbol of yin and yang (see Chapter 3) and *quan* means 'fist'. It is commonly known as 'tai chi' (incorrectly pronounced as 'tie chee'). It is most popular with women and the elderly both in China and abroad.

Taiji quan develops qi through techniques very similar to those of qi gong (in fact, taiji quan is a valid form of qi gong in itself), but it differs in that each movement has a subtle martial application too.

Taiji quan does not permit the practitioner (boxer) to use force against force when fighting; it advocates that redirecting an attacker's own force will be sufficient. The taiji boxer is grounded by qi, remaining supple yet stable, physically and emotionally. Some schools practise with swords but you will never hear the crashing of blades, because actively fighting is completely contradictory to the philosophy of the internal arts: their objective being to preserve life and *stop* fighting, ideally in the most economic manner possible.

Taiji quan is often described as a kind of yoga-in-motion and this is very accurate. Like yoga, breathing and suppleness is developed and the benefits of yoga can be reaped by taiji quan boxers too. In taiji quan theory, a boxer's power is drawn upward from the earth through the feet, goes through the waist (energising the *dan tian* on the way) and goes out through the arms. In the beginning, concentration is required as the boxer tries mentally to control (visualise) the flow of energy through his body. The slow, continuous, rhythmic movements and controlled breathing lead to higher levels of focus so that, while performing their routines, some boxers become totally oblivious to the world around them!

Through practice, the boxer is no longer only moving his arms and legs but synchronising himself with the universal life force and his movements are expressing that energy. In time, there is no need to

Taiji quan movements

concentrate, since practice leads to a state of no-mind, where thought is replaced by clarity. Taiji quan is said to be flowing more or less of its own accord at this point.

Mahjong (麻将 Májiàng)

Gambling is a magnet for millions of Chinese. The preferred game is mahjong. China has an enormous chest of traditional games, but none is more passionately (obsessively?) played than mahjong. Like all great games, the idea is simple: collect the tiles to make up suits. There are 136 tiles. To start the game they are arranged into a square of four walls: 17 long and two high. The tiles have numbers and belong to suits: dragons, Chinese characters, winds, bamboos and circles. Like poker, players take turns selecting and discarding tiles to build their suits. Points are won based on the value of the tiles and the sets and sequences built.

In southern Chinese villages, elderly people play this game fanatically, winning (but more often losing) lots of money. Jewellery, watches (Rolexes are a favourite), cars, houses and even women have been won and lost at the mahjong table. Overseas Chinese are just as keen, but with loan sharks lurking to help someone whose luck and wallet has run dry, it can be a very costly and sometimes dangerous pastime.

GLOSSARY

工作 **gōngzuò** work
工厂 **gōngchǎng** factory
工人 **gōngrén** factory worker
轻工业 **qīng gōngyè** light industry
塑料制品 **sùliào zhìpǐn** plastic products
重工业 **zhòng gōngyè** heavy industry
钢 **gāng** steel
生铁 **shēngtiě** pig (raw) iron
煤 **méi** coal
矿业 **kuàngyè** mining (extraction industry)
农民 **nóngmín** peasant
农场 **nóngchǎng** farm

农业技术 **nóngyè jìshù** agricultural technology
工资 **gōngzī** wages
移居 **yíjū** migrate
流动人口 **liúdòng rénkǒu** floating population (unemployed rural workforce)
外来妹 **wàiláimèi** migrant country girls
玩耍 **wánshuǎ** amuse oneself, have fun
乒乓球 **pīngpāng qiú** table tennis
跑步 **pǎobù** running
锻炼 **duànliàn** exercise
纸牌 **zhǐpái** playing cards
夜总会 **yèzǒnghuì** nightclub

Taking it further

Books

Work and Inequality in Urban China, Yanjie Bian, State University of New York, 1994. A deep analysis of the inequalites of the pre-reform era system and the more modern work situation in Chinese cities.

Sport and Physical Recreation in China, James Riordan and Robin Jones, E. & F.N. Spon, 1994. A historical and contemporary survey of sport in China, very thorough.

Ki: A Practical Guide for Westerners, William Reed, Japan Publications, 1986. Probably the best book of its sort: principles, practice and the cultural applications of qi.

Mah-Jongg: Basic Rules and Strategies, Dieter Kohen, Sterling Publications, 1998. A solid introduction to the game.

Chinese Gung Fu: The Philosophical Art of Self-Defense, Bruce Lee, Ohara Publications, 1988. An overlooked classic on the art of kung fu, written before the author became famous.

Acrobats and Ping Pong: Young China's Games, Sports and Amusements, Isobel Wilcox, Dodd, Mead and Co., 1981. An excellently written and illustrated book, covering just about everything.

Websites

All about the most famous Chinese game of all, includes tournament information, clubs, rules and history: http://www.mahjongg.com

11 POLITICS

The party: peasants in power?

In 1949, after a long struggle, the Chinese Communist Party (CCP) came to power. At the helm was a charismatic new leader, Mao Zedong. Chiang Kaishek's Nationalist forces had fled to Taiwan (taking the national gold reserve with them). The Communists came to power in the only way that gave their claim to government traditional credence: they had endured, fought bravely (and usually victoriously) but, crucially, they had won the hearts of the populace. 'Democratic' countries have demonised Communism ever since the Soviet Union flexed its muscles during and after World War II and while it is true to say that Socialist countries were and still are propaganda-driven societies, the Chinese revolution was nevertheless a genuinely popular movement.

As we have seen, there is no tradition of government by the people in China, no common belief in the right of the majority to have a say in how things are run. Democracy is alien to Chinese history and life (how can you elect your parents?). Even where it does exist, it is a matter of which of a small number of very similar parties or individuals to choose from, rarely a platform for competing ideologies (look at Japan for an example of democracy in the Confucian world).

China was and is still a peasant society. For all its mobile 'phone wielding, designer label flashing and deal clinching, it still operates on peasant values. First and foremost to anyone who lives off the land is food. A full bowl at the end of every day is the least a peasant can ask and still a luxury to millions. Who fills the bowl, how it is filled or what kind of people fill it are questions that need be asked only when one's belly is too full, as a popular saying has it.

The Chinese Communist Party understood this and knew too that peasants would shape and hold the country if united. Once they had won the countryside, victory was only a matter of time. Sure enough it came. Even Mao himself came from a peasant background, albeit one more comfortable than most.

The state (国家 Guójiā)

The CCP is the only political party in China. The laws it wrote for itself suggest that this will be the way for a long time. Like the old USSR and other Communist countries, the party is acting a little like a caretaker, guiding and educating the population toward an unfolding Socialist state which will, since it will be free of a class system based on the vested interests of competing groups, be truly democratic. People being what they are could easily forget their natural Socialist leanings and be seduced by unnatural systems like capitalism. To avoid this and ensure that the population receive the only government the future will thank them for, politics, for the time being, has to be the responsibility of a single party.

The CCP is not the Big Brother entity that some people imagine. One person out of 20 is a member of the party (although most join for perks like cheap train tickets and other discounts). Government positions are filled by people who are selected on their political correctness. Candidates must have a sound understanding of the current party line and steadfastly endorse it. Unlike in the 1960s when fanatical commitment alone could open doors, in recent years technical and entrepreneurial knowledge have become desirable qualifications for would-be statesmen.

In theory, the government and party are two separate bodies. Each has its own system of structure and organisation, but the government serves to implement the policies set by the party. All state leaders (mayors and ministers) are high-ranking party officials and therefore duty bound to serve the party. This kind of arrangement makes it possible for the most senior party official (like Mao or Deng) to control, through legions of loyal lieutenants, the entire governing of the country.

The structure of government

The Chinese people have a form of parliament. It is not a democratic body but is designed to represent every region and nationality in the country. It is called the **National People's Congress** (NPC)

人民代表大会 **Rénmín Dàibiǎo Dàhuì**. It meets every five years with the purpose of serving the groups it represents in matters of constitution. It also selects officials to fill high positions in the offices of state (although these are mostly ceremonial and do not involve any real power). At the core of the NPC is a standing committee, which regularly meets between assemblies of congress.

It sounds good enough but the whole NPC seldom does anything more than approve decisions and changes already made by the party. Members of the NPC are constitutionally free from accountability to the people they represent. At best its role is symbolic, the relic of a well-meaning Socialist principle.

The NPC and its standing council gives the nod on directives passed by the **State Council** 国务院 **Guówùyuàn**, the highest administrative body in the government. This is where the real power lies. The State Council works like an overseer, operating through the various ministries that are the limbs of party control. Ministries are responsible for implementing Communist Party policies on education, defence, the health service and so on. The State Council is also deeply (and increasingly) involved in economic matters and setting up new organisations to deal with the changing times. The special economic zones 经济特区 **Zhuānshǔ Jīngjì Qū**, for instance, are model industrial and financial areas, designed by Deng Xiaoping to attract foreign investment.

Next is the CPPCC the **Chinese People's Political Consultative Conference** 政治协商会议 **Zhèngzhì Xiéshāng Huìyì**. Like all organisations that include the word 'people' in their names, the CPPCC is undemocratic and answerable to nobody. This body is a collection of the eight approved 'democratic' parties 民主党派 **Mínzhǔ Dǎngpài** that are permitted to 'help the organs of state implement [Communist] Party policy'. They are not allowed a say in how things are run (in fact, most people have never heard of them) neither do they exert any kind of moderating influence over the Communist Party (in House of Lords fashion). This organisation is completely unconnected to any of the real democratic parties that operate outside China (in Hong Kong and Taiwan), or any other groups that push for democratic changes from the bottom up.

Local administration is the most significant level beneath central government. The country is divided into four urban municipalities

(Beijing, Shanghai, Chóngqìng and Tianjin), 22 provinces and five 'autonomous regions' 自治区 **zìzhì qū** (including Tibet). Each acts like a minor version of the greater government, but policy is always decided centrally, in Beijing. Lower levels have a certain freedom to resist directives or modify them to fit local conditions, but when push comes to shove, Beijing always has the last word.

Inside the CCP

The CCP began in 1921 and up to the present day has worked through congresses that are held to debate policy and steer the government through announcing major decisions or changes affecting the running of the country. The Chinese Communist Party likes to present itself as a unanimous organisation (that is, everybody is permanently in a state of agreement), which of course it is not. To help keep up the image, all the infighting, rivalries and compromises are made long before each congress starts.

Two bodies form the heart of the CCP: the **Central Committee** 中央委员会 **Zhōngyāng Wěiyuánhuì**, which meets periodically to discuss major motions and the **Politburo** 政治局 **Zhèngzhì Jú**, which meets a little more often. This is where only a very small number of people make the most significant decisions.

The title no longer exists, but for 40 years the 'chairman' 主席 **Zhǔxí** was likened to a fatherly caretaker figure. Because of his vast experience and unshakeable principles, his wisdom guided the party and the country towards Socialist transformation. After Mao, Deng held the title. In theory, the chairman is a uniting force, gently steering the party; in effect, he can rule like a dictator. The chairman could hold all the strings of all the puppets in the government and manipulate them as he saw fit. The new name for the head-of-party position is 'president' 总书记 **Zhǒngshūjì**, currently held by **Jiang Zemin** (see Chapter 1), who has demonstrated only a fraction of the dictatorial tendencies of his predecessors.

Economics (经济 Jīngjì)

In 1978, Deng Xiaoping returned from a visit to Japan committed to initiating major changes in the running of the Chinese economy. China was way behind the industrialised nations of the world.

The answer was simple, the planned economy had to be abandoned and the realities of market capitalism embraced. The experts in charge of the transformation tried a number of methods but from the outset agreed that the switch should not be big-bang style (as would later happen in Russia) but incremental and methodical. Despite the slowly-slowly approach envisaged, the changes have been swift. The reform process has completely overhauled not only the economy, but the lives of millions. Currently, the increase in the annual value of China's trade is 17 times what it was in 1979.

The agricultural collectives were among the first to feel the winds of change. Land was contracted to single households that were suddenly given the freedom to grow and sell how they wished. The result? A vast improvement in output, household incomes more than doubled and the food shortages that have plagued the Chinese peasantry for centuries came to an end, practically overnight.

Marketisation entails open-door policy to foreign investment. Foreign capital is pouring in. China's dirt-cheap manufacturing is hard (if not impossible) to match. Consequently, China has become a very convenient workshop crutch, its products supporting the economies of the richest countries in the world (the USA in particular).

Decentralisation has helped attract foreign business. Nowadays, significant decisions can be handled at lower levels of government, loosening the tangle of officialdom that used to deter foreign companies. But, since virtually every legitimate business is somehow connected to the government, there is still interference from the state but this can be overcome (see section on corruption).

There has also been a major shift towards handing over responsibility for the economy to business itself rather than government. As a result, market forces are now truly running the country. In this sense, the economy has outgrown the various schemes that were meant to shape it and has itself become both politics and ideology. Of course, the government will never admit this; it is too great a loss of face, but the evidence is everywhere. Millions are flocking into the cities, people save more than ever before (on average, 40% of their income) and displays of personal wealth are increasingly conspicuous. Not to mention the state-owned enterprises that are puffing uphill like overweight joggers while the entrepreneurial skylines of cities like Guandong and Shanghai are elevating by the week.

Bureaucracy (官僚主义 Guānliáo Zhǔyì)

Bureaucracy is as central to Chinese politics as the vote is to British parliament. Abundant quantities of red tape ensure that everything moves in the most inefficient manner possible. This is for a number of reasons, the first being the iron rice-bowl. Working for the government is like riding the gravy train. Why work hard when you will see no personal benefit? If there is always work left to do, nobody can work himself out of a job. Bureaucracy equals job security. Because the bureaucratic chain of command is so complex, it is very unlikely that any individual will be singled out for responsibility or asked to point the finger at others. In short, a self-perpetuating system striving to keep things the way they are, justifying and ensuring its own existence. It is the modern-day equivalent of the scholastic civil service that controlled imperial China.

However, the entire bureaucratic mountain can be leapt over provided you have the necessary contacts (see next chapter for an introduction to this very important aspect of Chinese life). If you are connected to the right people and prepared to lubricate the cogs of officialdom with a little currency, papers can be processed with astonishing haste and your problems solved in a flash.

Corruption (贪污 Tānwū)

This is the cancer of the Chinese government. It is important to say here that corruption does not carry the stigma that it does in most developed countries. As in Africa and other parts of Asia, it is the norm not the exception and, indeed, is legitimate practice in many situations. If an individual does not make the very most of his position, he is considered odd. Bribery is a custom, used like grease to get things in motion. It takes many forms. Teachers might receive gifts from a student's parents around exam time; university professors may, for a fair-sized sum, pass a student who has not attended classes for four years; officials might forget to enforce a few laws to help a local factory. Practically everything and everybody is for sale if you know who and how to ask and have the money.

Local authorities are particularly susceptible to bribery. For a cash incentive, they can turn a blind eye to almost anything. The environment is often the victim. Politicians are in the pockets of big business and profiting immensely from being there. The government, if not directly involved, has permitted a whole range of illegal ventures to thrive in changing China. Bribery (taking and offering), embezzlement, sale of contraband items, production of fake goods and prostitution are just a few of the symptoms of the disease.

Every now and again, the government has a crackdown and its inevitable success is celebrated all over the newspapers. The big fish always seem to escape, only to set themselves up somewhere else or in a new line of work. They have paid the right people. The scale of the problem becomes obvious when you consider that even the People's Liberation Army (PLA) is implicated in gun and drug-running scandals. Forged documents entitling people to obtain visas to leave China are a hot commodity these days. The issue of such documentation is impossible without the cooperation of influential individuals.

The military (军队 Jūnduì): then and now

The Gulf War woke the Chinese military's top brass like a very rude alarm clock. Much of China's war technology and strategy is of Korean War vintage, despite massive spending on arms and personnel. To acquire high tech, the PLA has moved into a number of profitable sidelines. They have properties in the most lucrative locations (Shanghai, for instance), own and run factories and even dabble (mafia like) in protection rackets and nightclubs (again in Shanghai).

The army was once a big player in politics, but this is not the case so much anymore, now that economics (not ideology) is the law of the land. The military used to have an air of prestige that made it an icon to many (it had delivered them from the Japanese and freed them from the tyranny of Chiang Kaishek). This went up in smoke when Deng called in the tanks to drive protesters out of Tiananmen Square. Since then it has become a quasi-criminal lackey, being drawn towards the magnet of capitalism.

China in the world

China will soon be a member of the World Trade Organization (WTO). The benefits will be great: China can borrow more money than ever before, receive investment with more ease and generally have a more significant place in the global economy. Chinese products have been steadily improving in quality and now new markets must be found to sell them in. Unfortunately, the Chinese leadership is not eager to toe the line where it does not suit them. While the advantages of participation in the WTO and the UN are great, the government is not keen to follow laws relating to human rights and environmental issues. The Chinese government maintains that their country has to be run in such and such a way because conditions in China are unique. In their defence they argue that nobody criticised western countries during *their* periods of industrial transformations. Environmental concerns and human rights problems were not obstacles to *their* industrial advancement, so why should China's be hindered?

China's UN image is very much one of China-focused self-interest. China has a permanent seat on the Security Council but (unlike the others) takes no comparable interest in matters that do not directly affect China. Deng Xiaoping summed up the Chinese stance when he said: 'The stronger China becomes, the greater the chances of world peace'. In other words, the economy has top priority, until the time comes when China can afford to dabble in foreign affairs. Although China unashamedly shirks on its UN responsibilities, it is just as eager (probably more so) than the other members to enjoy the status and privileges of permanent membership. Money is a good example. The United Kingdom contributes seven times the amount given by China, yet what China currently receives in the form of financial and technological help far outweighs its input.

In terms of participation too, the Chinese offer little. Very few UN reforms or proposals have either Chinese sponsorship or initiative. The Chinese government is very fond of the term 'sovereignty' 主权 **zhǔquán**, the argument being that each country should be allowed to decide for itself what constitutes law and human rights. 'Sovereignty' translates to non-interference. 'Asian values' are, they argue, that unique set of China-specific circumstances, that exempt it from universal laws that are, on the whole, decided by much wealthier countries that are much further along the road of development.

Foreign problems

This term refers not to problems in international relations, but to problems in other societies that do not exist in China. Not only does the government spout the idea of foreign problems through the media, there is a popular belief among ordinary people too that Chinese society is free from certain woes found elsewhere. The government is in a state of permanent denial. Racism does not plague China. The official stance is that everybody of every race within the Chinese borders has lived peacefully alongside one another for centuries (the Great Wall was built to keep northern tribes out, but that is overlooked), bound together by shared history and interdependence. Tibetans, however, do not agree; neither do the Turkic-speaking peoples of the far west, nor the Mongol minority of Inner Mongolia. Homosexuality is another famous foreign problem. While Chinese people on the whole are modestly reluctant about admitting its existence, the government is adamant. When alternative lifestyles run contrary to conventional thinking, the authorities get very paranoid. Currently, homosexuality is regarded (with humour) as a form of affliction. Connected to this is, of course, HIV. Much ignorance about this disease persists. It is now so serious that the government has taken action to educate people on the dangers. Drugs are a favourite foreign problem. There is no mention of the international drug-running adventures of Shanghai crime gangs (all with official connections) or the enormous heroin trade in big Chinese cities, but there is always a lot of interest in wealthy foreign addicts and drug-related crime on American streets.

'Spiritual pollution' 精神污染 **Jīngshén Wūrǎn** is the label branded on foreign ideas that the government consider politically unsafe. In the 1990s there were a number of campaigns to cleanse China of this. Concepts like democracy, feminism, freedom of the media and political curiosity usually earn this label with the most speed.

The media (传播媒介 Chuánbō Méijiè)

There is no censorship in China. All the newspapers rewrite stories that are printed in the *People's Daily* 人民日报 **Rénmín Rìbào** (the official voice of the Communist Party). Everybody who works for the paper is housed, salaried, pensioned and insured by the state. Writing anything even remotely controversial would be very risky. The government hatches ideas and the media sets about broadcasting them in various forms. If news items do not fit the agenda, they are simply left out. The same goes for films, books and TV. There is no need to censor what does not exist, so omission is by far the best method of information control.

Provincial papers are the most likely to speak out, but even then, in only the subtlest way. Outright criticism would land the writer and editor in prison.

Speeches (讲话 Jiǎnghuà)

Nobody escapes hearing them and everybody who is somebody is expected to make them. Politicians love them (if you talk forever, no one can question you) as do academics and everybody involved in officialdom. Foreigners should expect the classic 'when in Rome' (do as you are told) speech early on if they are spending time in Chinese institutions.

Chinese like to think of themselves as shy, modest people, but it seems this is suddenly abandoned when it comes to getting up on stage to make a speech. Students are expected to do it on important occasions, usually on some nationalistic/political theme. It seems that the actual content of the speeches (mostly waffle) is of less importance than the delivery, which has to be very passionate (and loud). Political speeches are merely hymns to the party line and student speeches are seldom more than rhetorical chants.

Sport and politics

Sport says a lot about society and the Chinese government employs it with great craft to serve patriotic ends. From the mid-1980s to the present day, foreign soccer teams have been invited into China to play a handful of showpiece matches during the summer months. Before they started to wise up, big teams like AC Milan and Arsenal came to China under the illusion that they were the guests of a welcoming crowd, eager to see some pretty football. What they discover is an atmosphere like a Roman circus. After their Chinese hosts have performed a synchronized warm-up routine, a very aggressive match begins. Referees seem to suffer from selective blindness and a compulsion to blow the whistle every time the foreign team looks dangerous. In the event of 0–0 draws, Chinese refs like to end the game with a penalty shoot-out (to the amazement of the visitors). If they win, players do laps of honour and sometimes receive medals (on one occasion they were even awarded a car each!). For months prior to the match, the game is hyped on the theme of 'Foreigners vs. Chinese', if not directly then by implication.

Up until the mid-1970s China had a very Socialist attitude to sport; it was the participating not the winning that counted. Things changed in the 1980s, however, when Chinese athletes (blatantly assisted by the men in white coats) started collecting medals in international competitions. Since then, the hunger for glory has become ravenous.

China fought hard to win the 2008 Olympics for Beijing. After ranking third in the Sydney Games medals league and making promises to clean up the air and be more approachable on touchy subjects like human rights issues, it succeeded. Heavy-handed superficial measures that are the hallmark of the present Chinese leadership were in full bloom: the 'grass' was sprayed with green paint and hundreds of tramps and assorted undesirables were bussed out of the city when the International Olympic Committee (IOC) paid a visit in early 2001. Meanwhile, every Chinese person you meet seems delighted by the prospect of the Games in Beijing. The reason for this is politics.

Chinese sport is a very nationalistic affair. Like everything else in Chinese life, it has to serve a purpose other than simply being a visual spectacle. Whereas in developed countries modern sport is embedded in advertising, sponsorship and multinational business deals that make notions of nationhood increasingly vague, the very opposite is the case in China. Athletics is not about the races that are run, but the races that are running. As we saw earlier, the Chinese Communist Party is trying to push the idea of nationhood and sovereignty, both in its international relations and at home. The underlying belief is that, by doing so, China can be left alone to do her own thing, entering and participating in international events and politics in a pick and choose manner, if and when Chinese interests are involved. Moreover, a sense of shared identity makes it less likely that the country will fall apart, like the former USSR.

It sounds sensible enough for a developing country to be cautious, but every organ of the media follows this principle with the result that international affairs and sports have a very us-and-them slant. So much so, that it simply seems to boil down to racism.

GLOSSARY

民变　**mínbiàn**　mass uprising
革命　**gémìng**　revolution
政府　**zhèngfǔ**　government
政策　**zhèngcè**　policy
民主集中制　**mínzhǔ jízhōngzhì**
democratic centralisation
自由主义　**zìyóu zhǔyì**　liberalism
保守主义　**bǎoshǒu zhǔyì**
conservative (politics)
资本主义　**zīběn zhǔyì**　capitalism
愚民政策　**yúmín zhèngcè**　policy
of ignorance (to keep the masses
uninformed)

民主　**mínzhǔ**　democratic rights
人民币　**Rénmínbì**　Chinese
currency
政治改革　**biànfǎ**　political reform
新闻　**xīnwén**　news
言论自由　**zìyóu yánlùn**　freedom
of speech
牵线　**qiānxiàn**　to control from
behind the scenes
商业　**shāngyè**　trade and
commerce
外贸　**wàimào**　foreign (external)
trade

Taking it further

Books

Politics and economics

The China Reader: The Reform Era, Orville Schell, Vintage Books, 1999. An extremely informative description of the changes in China since the reforms. The book covers politics, society, the economy and the media and has many translations of official speeches and papers.

Understanding China: A Guide to China's Economy, History, and Political Structure, John Bryan Starr, Hill and Wang, 1997. A look at modern China's problems (and achievements) through its recent political and economic history.

After the Propaganda State: Media, Politics and 'Thought Work' in Reformed China, Daniel C. Lynch, Stanford University Press, 1999. A very complete and up-to-date account of today's Chinese media.

Behind the Myth: Business, Money and Power in Southeast Asia, James E. Clad, Unwin Books, 1989. An assessment of the factors behind the economic growth of China's neighbours (interesting to see China's progress relative to their decline during the last decade).

The Four Little Dragons: Inside Korea, Taiwan, Hong Kong and Singapore at the Dawn of the Pacific Century, Brian Kelly and Mark

London, Simon and Schuster, 1989. Good as a pre-Asian economic crisis/China economic explosion examination of China's small but influential satellites.

Political unrest

Rebellions and Revolutions: China from the 1800s to the 1980s, Jack Gray, Oxford University Press, 1990. The story of two centuries of struggle for freedom and power.

Tiananmen Diary: Thirteen Days in June, Harrison E. Salisbury, Unwin Books, 1989.

Voices From Tiananmen Square: Beijing Spring and the Democracy Movement, Mok Chiu Yu and J. Frank Harrison (eds), Black Rose Books Ltd, 1990.

Websites

China's only daily newspaper in English, there is a special Hong Kong edition too: http://www.chinadaily.com.cn/news/index.html

From China's official news agency, get the 'facts' and opinions straight from the source: http://www.xinhua.net.com/english/index.html

12 PEOPLE AND SOCIETY

Family (家 Jiā)

Nothing is more central to Chinese life than the family unit. Confucius taught that the family was the most essential component of society; indeed society itself was merely one big family, with the emperor as the ultimate father. The Chinese word for 'everybody' – **dàjiā** 大家 – means literally 'big family'. Although less so today, the concept of family extended across national boundaries too. If China were the father, Korea was the elder son and Japan the younger. This is one reason why defeat in war at the hands of a neighbouring Confucian culture (like Japan) was so much more humiliating for the Chinese, compared to barbarian civilisations (like Europeans) over whom the Confucian sphere does not extend.

Family is first for the Chinese, but all relationships are perceived in terms of family whether there is blood involved or not. For example, an older male friend will be addressed as 'big brother' but to a child he will be 'uncle'. Within the family, parents call children by nicknames like 'Little Fatty'. First names are very rarely used; they are considered too personal. If they cannot be addressed by profession ('Teacher Wang', 'Master Chan' etc.), everybody outside the family is 'big sister', 'aunty' or 'grandfather'. This is both polite and friendly. Polite because social position is being declared, in other words 'by calling you 'big brother' I give you respect and you be nice to me in return' – which is Confucianism in a nutshell; and friendly because the family represents the closest bonds between people that exist.

Paradoxically, it is not the family name per se that is of importance, but how the family members act in relation to each other (see section on Confucius in Chapter 3). Until very recently Chinese women, on the whole, retained their family name after marriage (although children always take their father's name; double-barrelled names are unheard of). Recently increasing numbers of women are taking their husband's name. Maybe this is because of the almost obsessive desire of many Chinese to experiment with western (and therefore modern) ways of life. In traditional (pre-1911) China it was common for people to take the name of other families to forge allegiances. For this reason, families became very big and whole towns and villages shared the same name. This was done for protection as much as anything else. If a family united itself under a stronger family, they were contracted to subservience yet at the same time became valid family members and were treated as such.

Family commitments and loyalty are extended to ancestors as well as the living. Although this is not ancestor worship as such (they are not thought of as gods), a great deal of superstition is centred on the belief that the dead continue to influence the fortunes of the living. For this reason, many Chinese (even if they have adopted Christianity) still revere their ancestors' spirits.

Groups

Chinese like the safety of numbers. In western societies individuality is lionised, we read in it the qualities of strong personality, self-reliance and confidence. To the Chinese it is simply non-conformism, the mark of an individual who is somehow unacceptable to others. Groups and group consciousness are a strong feature of Chinese identity. If someone has no group to back them up, things will be difficult. Family is obviously first and foremost, but there are several other groups that Chinese people find themselves attached to:

1   The Chinese community. In the case of overseas Chinese, the group is the Chinese minority living in that area. Most will be related, if not through blood and marriage, then certainly through business and social contacts.

2   Roots of the community. When they left their homeland, they never went alone, but with their friends and family. Consequently, Chinese in certain areas could be made up of a group whose roots go directly back to small villages in southern China. Although this is not the case in big cities anymore, it does explain why most of the Chinese population of cities like San Francisco speak Cantonese

and a large section of the restaurant business in the UK is run by Hakka families.

3 Secret societies. Known in the west as 'triads'. The name comes from an early group that interpreted creation as consisting of three separate but linked elements: heaven, earth and man. They are the most influential group to which any individual can be affiliated. Although they are fond of justifying their past with mystical mumbo-jumbo and legends about toppling tyrannical rulers, they are little more than a criminal version of the freemasons. They grew out of guilds and families, attracting disgruntled individuals and running rackets everywhere they could. Their strongest base is southern China, both today and in the past. The triads arrived on foreign shores along with the rest of the package. Not every Chinese family is connected to them directly, but everybody knows where to find them and most takeaways and restaurants will have some kind of dealings with them.

4 Religious groups. This is not a recent addition to the list but one that is becoming increasingly prominent. Filling the spiritual vacuum brought about by Communism, millions of Chinese have taken a sudden interest in religion. Muslims and Christians have resurfaced now that it is relatively safe to do so and the numbers attending mosques, and particularly churches, continue to swell. Christianity has caught on among mainlanders and overseas Chinese alike and is expected to grow. How this will alter the structure of Chinese society we do not know, but we can safely assume there will be space to accommodate it without too much need for change.

Contacts (关系 Guānxi)

If the groups we have just examined form the backbone of Chinese life, we could say for sure that **guanxi** is the nervous system. Everything works through unofficial interrelated networks of contacts. Jobs are given, money is lent and favours exchanged on the basis of guanxi. Having no influential contacts reveals a lack of ambition, inability to network or utter insignificance. Contacts lubricate every motion of the Chinese world. Without them there are no shortcuts and you will have to wait for nine hours to buy your train ticket, just like everybody else. The system is simple: befriend someone who has what you want and, in time, he may need something from you and you something from him. People introduce each other to their own contacts, earning them both a favour in return and face (see next section). The system is very effective. On the downside it is very useful for the triads to run things without recourse to direct force. Contacts can also be good for sticking one's nose into other people's affairs and leaves people wide open to corrupt practices, whether in business or politics.

Face (面子 Miànzi)

Not unique to China, this is the Asian answer to the western term 'ego'. If the Chinese find the tendency of foreigners to self-flatter unbearable, the foreigner is equally affronted by the Chinese sensitivity to face. The concept is related to respect. In much the same way that children are supposed to listen to their fathers' lecture at the dinner table, the Chinese man expects to hear his opinions go unchallenged. The terms 'losing face' 丢面子 **diū miànzi** and 'saving/gaining face' 爱面子 **ài miànzi** reveal the character of the obsession. A man loses face when his opinion is challenged or contradicted. Even an innocently posed question can knock someone's face. The question reveals a lack of respect, not only of the opinion but towards the individual too. Even though the question may be sensible and even justified, it is not the Chinese way to make someone explain himself. If people disagree (and, of course, they do) very often the Asian solution is to nod, not say anything, accept and then do the complete opposite once the situation permits it.

Saving face is the sequence of complicated verbal gymnastics somebody does when they know they are wrong, but cannot admit so for fear of losing face. This can involve bizarre scenarios such as taxi drivers who don't know where they are going saying they do for hours as they drive round in circles and people giving you wrong directions because they don't want to say 'I don't know'. Saving face is what counts, especially in public. Most fights (and there are many to be found on the Beijing streets at night) come from people trying to keep face. The Chinese government has provided scores of excellent examples of desperate attempts to keep face. The best (worst?) is probably the Tiananmen incident rewrite which involved a ludicrously fictitious yarn along the lines of: 'Everything was going peacefully, some of us even sympathised with the protesters, but then some radicals started attacking the military personnel (sent there just to keep an eye on things) who were forced to defend themselves, of course in the most limited manner.'

Face and business

Some old China hands reckon that face is one of the biggest problems facing foreigners in their dealings with Chinese. For example, a loss of face at the hands of a woman is far more offensive than from a man, so it is not a good idea to have a female deal with a male executive. The Confucian social order might be one explanation for this. Foreigners are excused if they cause someone to lose face (it is a strongly held belief that no codes of respect exist outside the Confucian world) but in business, wires often get crossed so the Chinese take many precautions. Chinese companies often insist on providing the interpreters (always Chinese people) to avoid such problems. But this also supplies them with several strategic advantages (they can speak freely knowing that their interpreter will reveal an appropriately edited version).

Among Chinese, face can be both useful and dangerous. Gambling involves face. Chinese men (face is a predominantly masculine obsession) can be driven to ruin trying to keep face at the mahjong table.

Sexuality and marriage

Even by British standards, the Chinese have a repressive approach to matters of sexuality. At home, such subjects are very rarely raised and if they are it is usually with some feigned innocence. Public displays of sexuality such as holding hands still turn heads. Kissing is done openly only if there is enough darkness to hide the daring couple. Even into their twenties, young Chinese are discouraged from sexual behaviour. Paradoxically, childishness (in women) is regarded as a sexual characteristic. Perhaps it is for this reason that cuteness (as opposed to mature feminine beauty) is preferred in many Asian cultures. This takes the form of squeaky high-pitched voices, giggles and girlishness that tend to disappear in Jekyll and Hyde fashion once the boyfriend is no longer present.

Sex is a taboo subject but young Chinese are not persuaded by abstention any more than people in other Asian countries (although they like to say that pre-marital sex is a purely foreign indulgence). When compared to other developing countries, the Chinese are relatively permissive. In Chinese society, however, sexuality is hidden. Cohabiting couples are extremely rare.

Concepts of masculinity are closely connected to material wealth and influence more than good looks or manliness as we identify them in western cultures. Face seems to grow on a diet of big spending, flashy watches, powerful contacts, designer suits and cars. Thus, it is the primary platform for attracting women. For less affluent Chinese men, we can only assume that (to their credit) less superficial virtues express their manhood.

Men do not like to compliment their girlfriends on their appearance since this is not considered masculine, yet the beautiful girl is a mark of a man's success as much as any other possession. Today as in the past, Chinese men will more often than not find themselves marrying the woman they can afford. Although he is not purchasing her directly, since no money passes to her parents (at least not normally), his financial status is of utmost importance to any prospective bride. The Chinese are open about this. Although true love marriages are increasing due to foreign-style dating getting more common, Chinese women like to be practical in their selection of a husband. Foreigners often find such hard-headed thinking difficult to relate to. We have to remember that in the developing world bad decisions in such matters can have far more serious consequences. The country is vast and its population unmatched by any other nation. Chinese people calculate all their prospects in terms of what will get them ahead of everybody else. This kind of pragmatism is an enduring trait of the Chinese and probably the only reference they base their lives on with any consistency.

Population control

Reluctance to discuss sexual matters creates a number of problems. The hazards of prostitution are beginning to be felt in Chinese society. HIV is becoming a major concern. Contraception, although available everywhere and often free, is not widely understood or used. The cause is rooted in ignorance through inadequate sex education and conflicts between methods and traditional notions of masculinity (in the case of condoms). The one child policy as put into effect by Mao encouraged Chinese couples to take contraception very seriously. Mao believed the main problem with China was its deep-rooted obsession with fertility and big families. (He thought that the selfish nature of Chinese people was the second biggest problem.)

Mao was probably right about the fascination with fertility and the issue of overpopulation. A man can become a laughing stock if he fathers only daughters. Sadly, a bad son is always better than a good daughter (even many good daughters). A good wife gives birth to sons; it is popularly (and erroneously) believed that it is the woman's contribution to the conception that determines the sex of the child.

Economic changes have destroyed the effectiveness of the one child policy. Although the 1980s and 1990s brought about a very serious epidemic of little emperor (小皇帝 **xiǎo huángdì**) syndrome (sons were spoilt into fat, selfish brats) the effects of economic push and pull factors are changing everything. Nowadays, the average woman gives birth twice in her lifetime. The reason is that people are now more mobile than ever before. Whereas most would have stayed in their villages three decades ago, millions are being drawn to the sweatshops of the big cities. People rely much less on their work unit to provide medical care, preferring to take their chances paying out of their own pocket. Mobility also removes the consequences of having more than one child. In the past, couples who conceived for a second time would get a lecture and possibly a fine, a third time would be very serious and beyond that sterilisation, or worse.

Women

Chinese people like to paint a romantic image of their women. She is both the embodiment of femininity and the product of the world's richest and most sophisticated culture. The reality is, of course, very different. In southern parts, Hakka women swing picks in the road almost as much as they work the fields. From the start of their lives, women are less likely to be as welcome in society as men. Because of the acutely patriarchal nature of the traditional Chinese social order (see section on Confucius in Chapter 3) a woman's main function was to provide sons. No sons – no continuation of the family. A man could have as many women as he could provide for. To allow a man a greater chance of many sons, concubinage was the custom. A girl from a poor family would be bought and brought into the household to live harem style and give birth (to sons). A concubine who provided a son could become a wife and would certainly move up the household hierarchy.

Nowadays this is no longer possible, but the preference for boys continues. Advertising hammers home the concept of the perfect family as much as it does in other cultures, but the Chinese family is unlike the westerner's 2.4 children, suburban living, estate car-owning ideal. In the place of two blonde kids is a single rotund little emperor (the one child policy is still running, in theory), his parents practically fighting with one another to stuff him with 'healthy' foods.

Illiteracy is highest among rural women. Very few (around 10%) receive education beyond 15 or 16 years of age. When industry has to shed some of its huge surplus workforce (as the state-owned sector is trying to do now) women go first, no exceptions. Alternatively, they can be given *very* long holidays.

Emotion and expression

Many foreigners are confused by Chinese habits of expressing emotion. Whereas northern Europeans may find the body language of Italians or Spaniards a little excessive, they can easily identify the emotion being conveyed. Chinese body language is a little different. Chinese laugh when westerners would not consider it appropriate: when giving bad news, for example. The laughter is intended to disguise feelings of nervousness or embarrassment. Grinning can also reveal nerves or a sense of awkwardness. In many Asian cultures, to resist revealing emotions is interpreted as a sign of maturity and dignity. Confucian societies are famous for their ability to suffer stress yet not exhibit discomfort. Displays of anger and frustration are thought of as undignified. Perhaps like the British, Chinese families do not like to discuss emotion with the intimacy found in other cultures. Emotional issues are played down, both at home and outside. Chinese believe that emotion distracts from cool-headed thinking, which Confucius said marks the difference between man and animal. So, to many foreigners, Chinese appear cold and rather deadpan in their expressions. However, after spending a little time with Chinese, every emotion becomes visible, once the new body language is learnt.

The Chinese are admittedly repressive when it comes to the question of emotion, probably because they are actually *very* emotional people. When emotion does surface, it is far stronger (and louder) than most will admit or reveal, especially to foreigners. It is common to see 20 family members wailing with frightening abandon in the Shanghai airport departure lounge, but far less common to see the same sight in the London Heathrow departure lounge.

Etiquette

Emotional issues tend to be avoided. This is another reason why many Chinese are reluctant to 'get to the point' as we say in the English-speaking world. When complex matters arise, Chinese people are hesitant about spelling something out (conversely, in simpler matters, they seem reluctant to do anything but bawl it out). In important conversations and with influential people, they prefer not to call a spade a 'spade', but 'a sort of long-handled digging thing'. Their language is vague; probably to avoid insulting someone's intelligence by black-and-white clarity and to hide from responsibility should their words have bad consequences. To western ears that are obsessed with getting the bottom line, negotiating with Chinese can be very frustrating.

Senior men expect to be treated tactfully and to cruise through every encounter with their face unchallenged. In characteristically Chinese I-scratch-your-back style, good etiquette is based on what to say and do to avoid having your opposite number feel any embarrassment. Foreigners are in the habit of overlooking such considerations (to their cost) when they are doing business with Chinese. As much as the Chinese are wrong to expect Chinese-style civility, the foreigner is just as ready to hide behind his foreignness.

The majority of Chinese are much less sensitive. Since China is a society in which most people have no time to indulge in chitchat, they prefer to get straight down to the bare facts: hence questions from stranger to stranger such as 'How much money do you have?'.

Manners

You don't have to mind your Ps and Qs in China. It is not necessary to be polite or thank people in shops or restaurants. Furthermore, there is no such thing as a queue in China.

People rarely say 'thank you' or 'excuse me'. It is far too polite. There are several non-verbal ways of acknowledging gratitude. For example, when someone pours your tea, use your fingers to tap lightly on the table a couple of times.

The Chinese regard 'table manners' as we know them in western cultures as a lot of standing on ceremony. Although knowledge of western dining etiquette is a prized trophy of sophistication among mainlanders, the whole thing is regarded as excruciatingly ritualistic and an awful amount of fuss to stop you from just digging in. Table manners exist, but, Chinese being the people they are, they are functional not flowery and never get in the way of the actual eating. There are only a small number of important things to observe at a Chinese table:

1 Fill your host's teacup or glass continuously. It is important especially if one person is buying that he does not have to pour his own drink.

2 Chinese hosts like to bury the table with food. It is a token of respect for his guests if the host provides more food than they can eat. Thus, refusing is not a good idea (at least at first) neither is polishing off the dishes, as your host will feel compelled to order another mountain.

3 Many people are shocked when their hosts put food into their bowls for them. This is because they are helping you to get good pieces. Chinese know the most succulent slices of any dish (particularly fish and duck) and will be aware that their foreign or more reserved guest does not. Do not be surprised if your less considerate tablemates are practising chopstick kung fu in the scramble for the juicy bits!

4 Try not to separate food knife and fork fashion. Chinese people love to suck on bones till they gleam and will think it odd if you tackle the food in a surgical manner. Trying to separate noodles into mouth-size bundles is also futile, just pick up what you can and slurp the rest.

5 Never pass food from chopsticks to chopsticks since this is how the ashes of the dead are transferred. Also, do not use your chopsticks like harpoons, impaling pieces of food. This is tempting, especially if you are still a beginner, but it looks bad. Your hosts will not be pleased if you leave your chopsticks standing upright in the bowl since this also has associations with the dead.

Competition

Chinese and foreign people have slightly differing notions of competitive behaviour. Chinese people do not consider it wrong to compete with each other in events that are considered primarily social. Take for example, ten-pin bowling or table tennis. These are played at a level of competition that would make many foreigners feel uncomfortable. Western cultures associate competition with a degree of hostility, albeit usually a very refined one. Chinese seem to make this association far less readily (except in the case of international sport which has been ideologically repackaged for political purposes – see last chapter). Consequently, they like to win and do not see their efforts to do so as even slightly unfriendly. This extends into other areas of life and, unfortunately, is particularly relevant for foreigners, with whom Chinese people appear to be obsessed with comparing themselves (see the education section in Chapter 9 for a reason why this may be the case). Several bizarre scenarios develop from this inclination towards competition: joggers may suddenly be joined by people who want to race them and soccer games can take a surreal turn when players start to desert the losing side to join the winning team.

Ridicule (讥笑 Jīxiào)

Another side to Chinese life is the use of nicknames. 'Big Nose', 'Fatty' and every conceivable mockery of an individual's physical makeup is considered fair game. Although these are at the very least not complimentary, they are perfectly acceptable and not considered overly offensive. Why call a person 'Pockmark Chan'? Because his face is pockmarked and his name is 'Chan'. Simple as that.

Chinese people seldom consider the ethical implications of asking someone 'Why are you so fat?' or 'Are you a boy or girl?'. This is a little speculative but the reason may be put down to the Confucian/ Communist passion for conformity, so thoroughly drummed into Chinese society. If someone's appearance is a little unusual, then perhaps the majority feels justified to ask such questions.

Foreigners are the ultimate out-group: this will confront anyone who is not Chinese on a regular basis. The degree of ridicule you should expect to receive depends on the degree to which you differ from the Chinese in appearance. It is, however, important to remember that they do not mean to insult you, even if they are! If you are speaking Chinese, do not be surprised if your efforts are ridiculed and people laugh in your face. I've even seen teachers do this!

Humour and wit (风趣 Fēngqù)

The Chinese are not famed for their humour. What there is of it (and there isn't much) gets very little attention. There is no culture of self-mockery the way there is in Anglo-Saxon societies or Ireland. Telling jokes to be sociable, as people in western countries do, is also not done, maybe because of the risk of losing one's face, should the punch line fall flat. Jokes and humorous anecdotes have never gripped the Chinese imagination and they certainly don't travel well. Take the following, common-format example:

> A tiny man marries a big fat woman and every time the woman wants some attention, the little man tries to hide. After many nights, the woman finally says: 'Come out from under that bed if you are a real man!' To which the man replies: 'No. And when a real man says "no" he means no!'

Slapstick, toilet humour and the play on words seem the most popular form of joke. Generally, the comedians who appear on TV (mostly around New Year, for some reason) get their laughs through a combination of shouting, falling over and hitting each other (à la Three Stooges).

Foreigners and racism

I still don't know whether Chinese people like foreigners or simply pretend to do so to separate them from their money. It is more likely that since most have no dealings with them, they are indifferent. One thing is certain: the Chinese do view their relationships with foreigners very much in 'us-and-them' terms. The concept of in- and out-groups runs deep in Chinese society. As we already discussed, an individual is as good as powerless in a culture that values the group and the opinion of the majority as fact. In recent years the Chinese government has exploited this to maximum political effect. Remember that Chinese people make friends for practical benefits. Be prepared for 'friendly' people sharply to about heel when they discover you don't have what they want (if you don't speak English, for instance).

That China is a single unified nation is a myth, but the propaganda seems to be working, if the experiences of foreigners are anything to go by. Travellers are often shocked by the fact that all the people they meet ask the same questions, such as: 'Where are you from?' 'You can't be English if you're black, can you?' 'How much money do people earn, on average, in your country?' and so on.

Why? Because mainland Chinese are fascinated by people who come from other countries. The reason is stereotyping. It is not unethical or in any way politically incorrect in China to generalise massively, moreover it is reinforced by the government and media. The government recommends that foreigners be charged at least double prices when buying at the same places as Chinese. This might seem sensible enough, given the difference in material wealth between developed and developing countries, but the same applies to Africans or other foreigners who come from less wealthy countries.

Chinese racism does not take the form of direct prejudice, although verbal attacks are to be expected. Chinese racism takes the form of distancing and indirect hostility. Foreigners are thought to know absolutely nothing about Chinese ways, constantly expected to make mistakes and be basically stupid. Not everybody in China thinks this way, but education is still a luxury for most, so the majority can only learn about foreigners from ludicrous books, movies and propaganda.

Uniqueness

Another reason for this fascination in foreigners is the popular belief in Chinese uniqueness. China is unique, only inasmuch as any other country is unique, but propaganda teaches children that they are unique among the unique. The argument is that no other country is comparable in terms of complexity and history and the Chinese people were the first and most civilised of all people. It is important to note here that, traditionally, such ideas were not based on race, the way they are today. In old China, anybody could become Chinese if they made an effort to live in the Chinese way and preserve traditions. Africans, Arabs and Europeans immersed themselves in Chinese life successfully. Concepts of nationhood and race did not exist until the dawn of the 20th century. Before that, Chineseness was culturally defined (after all, even the Qing Dynasty were not Chinese, that is not *Han* Chinese).

Chineseness

Beliefs in 'uniqueness' (a subtle way of saying 'we're better than you') characterise the culture of many countries, but especially those in the Confucian sphere.

It is this sense of uniqueness that stands in the way of effective cross-cultural communication. Chinese love to play the race card. If situations with foreigners become difficult, there exists an infuriating tendency to reduce this to cultural differences. In politics this serves as an extremely convenient way to bypass or stall on sticky matters such as human rights. On a personal level you might be confronted by questions such as: 'Don't you find that you and your [Chinese] wife/husband have many cultural problems?'. The answer to such difficulties is to do as the Chinese themselves do: grin and bear it, then get on with it anyway. Anger or emotional reactions will result in a 'see what I mean?' situation.

Unfortunately, belief in race and the qualities and inadequacies of members of different racial groups is the byproduct of the Chinese brand of cultural awareness. The Chinese media would have people believe that 'racism' is something inflicted Ku Klux Klan style by whites on blacks and since nothing comparable exists in China (they say) racism doesn't exist. Despite this, whites are 'ghost people' and blacks are 'black devils'.

Sadly, it appears that a kind of racial hierarchy is at work in the attitudes of Chinese to foreigners. Whites have acquired (temporarily and recently) top position. Chinese are next and identifiable peoples (Koreans, Mongols etc.) nearby. Beneath this are Arabs and Indians (they are thought of as one and the same). Blacks are at the bottom. Mythology may be to blame here. Fairer skinned people are consistently depicted as good. Evil characters and the gods of hell have darker, even black skins. How you are treated depends on where you are on this scale.

Chinese outside China are beyond the influence of propaganda and are far less likely to exhibit or believe in such nonsense. Nonetheless, distinct preferences for the Chinese group persist. Look at Chinatowns or Chinese student associations for evidence of this. Neither is hostile to foreigners but Chinese togetherness (a sense of cultural unity?) is what brings such things into existence.

GLOSSARY

爱情　**àiqíng**　love
一见鍾情　**yījiàn zhōngqíng**　love at first sight
恋爱　**liàn'ài**　love affair
感情　**gǎnqíng**　feelings, emotion
结婚　**jiéhūn**　marriage
离婚　**líhūn**　divorce
分手　**fēnshǒu**　separation
骄傲　**jiāo'ào**　pride, arrogance
怕　**pà**　fear
华侨　**huáqiáo**　overseas Chinese
外国人　**wàiguórén**　foreigner
老外　**lǎowài**　common (semi-polite) spoken term for foreigners
鬼子　**guǐzi**　devil (offensive term for foreigners)
种族　**zhǒngzú**　race, ethnic group
歧视　**qíshì**　discrimination
种族歧视　**zhǒngzú qíshì**　racial discrimination
心理学　**xīnlǐxué**　psychology
性交　**xìngjiāo**　sexual intercourse
性别特徵　**xìngbié de tèzhēng**　sexuality
子嗣　**zǐsì**　male offspring
断子绝孙　**duànzǐ juésūn**　'May you die without sons and grandsons!' (a term of abuse)

Taking it further

Books

Society

The Chinese: A Portrait, David Bonavia, Penguin Books, 1991.

Chinese Lives: An Oral History of Contemporary China, W.J.F. Jenner and Delia Davin (eds), Penguin Books, 1989.

Beyond The Chinese Face: Insights From Psychology, Michael Harris Bond, Oxford University Press, 1991.

The Psychology of The Chinese People, Michael Harris Bond (ed.), Oxford University Press, 1986.

Sons of the Yellow Emperor: The Story of Overseas Chinese, Lynn Pan, Secker & Warburg, 1990.

The Dragon Syndicates: The Global Phenomenon of the Triads, Martin Booth, Doubleday, 1999.

History

Chinese Civilization and Society: A Sourcebook, Patricia Buckley (ed.), Macmillan, 1988.

The Origin of the Chinese People, John Ross, Pelanduk Publications, 1916.

13 | THE FUTURE

The horizon beckons

China's rapid entry into the world community has made many people nervous. Southeast Asian countries such as Thailand stand to lose most from China's rise to power since their economies are based on similar formulae (low wages, enormous workforces) making it increasingly difficult for them to compete. On paper, it is possible that China could take the position held by Japan as the world's second most powerful economy (behind the USA) by the year 2010 or safely by the year 2020. In reality, however, it is practically impossible for a country the size of China to keep the rate of growth constant.

Problems facing the economy

■ The present system relies heavily on the leadership's assumption that China will stay together the way it has done since 1949. If they succeed in maintaining the unity of the nation, it will be the first time in history that so many have been under the law of a single system.

■ China's government faces the enormous responsibility of feeding one-fifth of the world's population.

■ As the economy improves, so do citizens' expectations in terms of standards of living and social liberalisation entailing human rights issues (not a favourite topic of the government).

■ The disparity between rich and poor continues to grow. Many are poorer than they were before the reforms.

■ There is a growing shortage of experts, desperately needed if the country is to shift from agrarian to industrial society within a few decades.

■ Environmental problems cause health problems among the population. Reluctance to take a decisive approach on tackling them has earned China little respect in the international community.

Ethnic issues

Heavy handedness in the sensitive area of ethnic diversity is not helping the image of the Chinese government. There are strong movements against the rule of Beijing in Tibet but, more importantly, from the coal and mineral rich areas of Xinjiang and Inner Mongolia. In all these places, the elements of opposition to Chinese rule are growing increasingly outspoken and hostile to central government. The far western hinterlands of the country (where the greatest numbers of minority people live) are still dirt poor. To suffocate ethnic solidarity, the Chinese government has a population transfer programme at work. This ensures that Tibetans and Mongolians are significantly outnumbered to ease Chinese control.

Ideological contortions

The government continues to wave the banner of Socialism while swatting away anything that does not bring hard currency into the country. While it appears that the Chinese idea of utopia would be a mega-Singapore, the government faces a huge loss of face if it publicly abandons Communism. As long as people remain free to make money and the government go unchallenged in their rule of the country, this looks like the way things will be for a long time. The influence of successful satellites like Taiwan and Singapore are providing the formula, but making it fit into the language of Socialism is becoming ever more difficult. Fortunately for the government, interest in democracy is heavily outweighed by popular interest in making money, making it highly likely that future governments will prioritise measures to maintain the economic flow. If this turns out to be the case, concentrations of industry and finance will flourish in coastal areas and the interior will become a backyard source of materials, food and workers (this is more or less the situation today too). However, there is no accounting for unpredictability and who knows what changes would come about in the wake of another Tiananmen incident?

Greater China

The mainland, through connections with its more dynamic capitalist children (Hong Kong, Taiwan and Singapore), is set to benefit. Before the reforms, mainland China was the workshop, these places the shop front. The formula worked and is continuing today. As the economy of the mainland grows, so too does the international significance of its supporters. It may be many years before there is a politically unified China at work, but in economic terms Greater China already exists and its influence is definitely expanding.

War

The size of China's war machine worries many countries, but since war is bad for business, it is unlikely that Chinese forces will be committed to confrontations with foreign powers. It is much more probable that they will be used to quell internal uprisings. Military power is relative and China's armed forces dwarf that of her neighbours. This, however, meant very little when the Chinese were decisively defeated by Vietnam in 1979. The only cause for concern is the nuclear arsenal, but given that China is now heavily dependent on its position as a big league player, it is implausible that she would risk losing everything for the sake of war. Nevertheless, Chinese aggression on unification problems (that is, with the 'rebel' government of Taiwan) will involve more North Korea-style intimidation (military exercises, missile tests and so on) but this can be put down to a face-saving tactic.

Society

As living standards improve, the demands of the population will go up. This will necessitate fundamental reforms in public services such as health and education. A better educated populace is likely to press for freedom of speech, travel, religion and eventually democratic changes of some sort. As interaction with foreign powers and, inevitably, individual foreigners becomes more widespread, logically notions of nationhood and race must change. The effects of global awareness are hard to predict but are likely to spark independence movements and generally weaken the influence of nationhood and sovereignty in its current form.

Conclusion

Chinese culture is truly vast. Its greatest adversary, Communism, is, despite the propaganda, well on its way to the graveyard. Throughout history China demonstrated resilience and resourcefulness in times of hardship and culture has always survived. Now only about 1% of China's national treasures are intact the way they were before the 20th century began but there is still reason for optimism. Chinese people have taken their customs with them (good and bad) everywhere they have settled. On the mainland, cultural preservation has become a fad, if only to bring in tourist dollars. For whatever reason, Chinese culture looks set to make a comeback (although thanks largely to foreign interest it never really went away).

China faces many crises: maintaining the growth of the economy, controlling its population, coping with crumbling ideas of identity and playing its part in world concerns such as peace and the environment. Although there will be many mistakes along the way, China will overcome them all.

APPENDIX

Chinese history – a quick reference

Period / dynasty	Dates	Famous for
Xia Dynasty	21st to 16th Century BC	Beginnings of Chinese civilisation
Shang Dynasty	16th to 12th Century BC	China's Bronze Age
Zhou Dynasty	1122 to 256 BC	Confucius
Qin Dynasty	221 to 206 BC	Great Wall and the Qin Emperor
Han Dynasty	206 BC to 220 AD	Progress in science and culture
Tang Dynasty	618 to 907	Buddhism, the arts and poetry
Song Dynasty	960 to 1279	Commerce and cities
Yuan Dynasty	1279 to 1368	Mongol invasion and conquest
Ming Dynasty	1368 to 1644	Porcelain and the emperors' tombs
Qing Dynasty	1644 to 1911	Defeat by foreign (western) powers
Republican Period	1911 to 1949	Sun Yatsen and Chiang Kaishek
People's Republic	1949 to present	Mao Zedong and the CCP
Reform Era	1976 to present	Economic improvement

INDEX

Other related titles

 TEACH YOURSELF

BEGINNER'S CHINESE SCRIPT

Elizabeth Scurfield and Song Lianyi

Do you want to learn the basics of reading and writing Chinese and understand how the script works? Are you planning a trip to China or thinking about learning the language? If so, *Teach Yourself Beginner's Chinese Script* is for you!

In this book, Elizabeth Scurfield and Song Lianyi have written a step-by-step introduction to reading and writing simple Chinese. They guide you through the basic techniques and teach you how to build your skills, with tips and practice suggestions to help you memorise what you are learning and make it enjoyable along the way.

Teach Yourself Beginner's Chinese Script features:

- the origins of the language
- a systematic approach to mastering the script
- lots of 'hands on' exercises and activities
- practical examples from real-life situations

TEACH YOURSELF

BEGINNER'S CHINESE

Elizabeth Scurfield and Song Lianyi

Do you really want to learn Chinese? Do classes terrify you and other coursebooks overwhelm you?
Then *Teach Yourself Beginner's Chinese* is for you!

Elizabeth Scurfield and Song Lianyi have written a friendly introduction to Chinese that's easy right the way through. It's written in two parts: the first teaches you the basic grammar you'll need, with lively dialogues, explanations and vocabulary. In the second you will be introduced to the character systems, and move on to practising what you have learnt in a range of real-life situations. *Beginner's Chinese* is ideal for you because:

- Everything is explained in simple English
- There are hints throughout to make learning Chinese easy
- What you learn is useful right from the start
- Key words are listed at the back of the book
- Basic Chinese characters are introduced in an accessible way

Other related titles

TEACH YOURSELF

CHINESE

Elizabeth Scurfield

Written for complete beginners, this book explains the complexities of spoken and written Modern Standard Chinese (otherwise known as Mandarin). Its logical and enthusiastic approach makes this notoriously difficult language straightforward and easy to learn.

Teach Yourself Chinese has many unique features:

- You can decide whether or not to learn the script. If you don't need it, just followed the *pinyin* transcriptions
- The summary of key grammar allows you to look up difficult points in seconds
- The extensive two-way vocabulary lists mean that this truly is a complete course in one volume

By the end of this course you will be able to take a part in the life and culture of China and Chinese-speaking people everywhere.